Hustlers

Beats,

and

Others

HUSTLERS,

BEATS,

AND

OTHERS

Expanded Edition

Ned Polsky

Distributed by:
Airlife Publishing Ltd
101 Longden Road, Shrewsbury SY3 9EB, England

Learning Resources
Centre

12066737

Printed in the United States of America

10 9 8 7 6 5 4 3 2 1

Library of Congress Cataloging-in-Publication Data
Polsky, Ned.
    Hustlers, beats, and others / Ned Polsky.
        p.   cm.
    Originally published: Garden City, N.Y.: Anchor Books,
[1969]. With new foreword and concluding ch.
    Includes bibliographical references (p.   ) and index.
    ISBN 1-55821-404-6 (paperback)
    1. United States—Social conditions.   2. Deviant
behavior.   3. Subculture—United States.   I. Title.
HN57.P57   1998
302.5'42—dc21   97-43059
                                              CIP

This book is printed on acid-free paper.

For Claudia

Contents

Foreword to the Expanded Edition

This essay collection was originally published in 1967 and was followed by a revised paperback edition in 1969. The expanded edition offered here reprints the 1969 revision, including its Preface, and expands the book by means of this Foreword to begin with and a large additional chapter to end with. That new chapter, "Thirty Years On," deals with changes that have taken place regarding the subjects of the earlier essays, including changes in my own thinking about them.

Here I discuss aspects of my style and stance that surprised or puzzled or provoked, mostly in a positive way but in a couple of cases not, a number of the book's original reviewers and other readers. Some of those aspects are not so unusual now in this age of the "personal essay"—whose rediscovery was pioneered in Leslie Fiedler's 1958 anthology, *The Art of the Essay,* and whose current acceptance is mainly the work of Phillip Lopate—but the following notes on them, inescapably autobiographical, may aid the reader. Knowing what formed the author often helps in understanding his book, not only with fiction or poetry but also with nonfiction (as Darwin scholars have perhaps most notably shown). William Empson is a better guide to all that than such naysayers as the New Critics or the Proust of *Contre Sainte-Beuve.*

Some readers, correctly, found these essays to be discursive or digressive. They are that way almost entirely by intent. (Most of the digressions are kenneled in footnotes, where sleeping readers may let them lie.) That stems largely, I think, from like tendencies in the two most inspiring teachers I ever had, Hans Gerth and Miles Lawrence Hanley (see the following Preface), who in their different ways were concerned not with specialist training but with a liberal education. Gerth was one of Hitler's gifts to America, a refugee product of Germany's humanistic educational tradition. In one course I took from him, History of Social Thought Up to Herbert Spencer, in the penultimate week of the term he realized that he was still on Aristotle, threw up his hands, apologized, devoted a couple of sessions to Machiavelli, and that was it—except that meanwhile we had been given grand lectures on such things as how Napoleon lined up his cannons and on Schubert's four-hand piano music. Similar, but less extreme, was Hanley, who was part of America's old three-named WASP academic elite and had been trained by some of its outstanding members (Charles Hall Grandgent, George Lyman Kittredge, Charles Rockwell Lanman). When I took his graduate seminar on *Beowulf* (admitted as an undergraduate because I had taken the prerequisite course in Anglo-Saxon), we "covered" in class only about 300 of the poem's 3182 lines, but received invaluable discourses on such things as the principles of emendation and on the history of scientific folklore study. Neither Gerth nor Hanley was much concerned to "stick to the point." Both were of course anathema to the sort of student who asks, "Professor, will we be responsible for that on the exam?"

Digression may be interesting or amusing or enlightening in itself, but not sticking to the point is more usefully employed in establishing, at least inferentially, a larger point. And most usefully of all, I think, it is employed in establishing the kind of larger point that involves making connections among numerous items that ordinarily are kept in separate compartments or "fields" of knowledge. What directed me to the virtue of that kind of effort (and to Gerth and Hanley) was Ernst Cassirer's *Essay on Man*, which I happened upon as a young teenager. In what are, of course, far lesser ways, I have tried in each chapter of this book to link up and to make cohere a good number of seemingly heterogeneous and disparate details.

Such an associative and synthesizing bent is not to every reader's taste. It is more likely to appeal if you enjoy such novels as *Finnegans Wake* and *Mulligan's Stew* and *Life A User's Manual*.

It is also more likely to appeal if, as Nabokov and Auden did, you enjoy reading reference books, for a related aspect of my prose that often struck readers is that it is replete with myriad little shards of information (such as about Nabokov and Auden). Relevant to that aspect of my stylistic "formation," as this book's Preface indicates, is that in my early career as a publisher I was endlessly confronted with manuscripts from academe that were loaded with repetitions and other forms of inanity. In reaction I embraced this stylistic principle: Every sentence should convey something that is not conveyed in any other sentence. Even the prose of the nonacademic and otherwise enjoyable essayist Gore Vidal almost always strikes me as repetitious and longwinded, provoking me to this deconstructionist reading of Wittgenstein: When you have nothing more to say, shut up.

That my reaction involved an overreaction is suggested by the fact that some people with excellent literary taste have asked me for prose that is not so crammed with information and interpretation, prose that "breathes" more. I have often tried to oblige them by inserting more filler sentences or phrases, ones that neither offer new material nor advance the argument in other ways, but in revising I almost inevitably strike them out. I seem to be stuck with my compressed style. So be it. At least the reader will get more substantive content for the money than in most other books of comparable length.

My predilection for combining scholarship with polemics, which had to be justified in the Preface written thirty-odd years ago, no longer needs justifying because today it is not only tolerated but widely practiced by professors, even by conservatives who prize not getting too uppity (a.k.a. "civility"). However, I think it is now common for reasons that are harmful to humane learning and the disinterested exercise of intellect. The polemics usually come from ideologues with nonscientific or antiscientific or even anti-intellectual agendas: neo-Marxists, ethnicity freaks, neo-Burkeans, reverse racists, gender benders, cold warriors searching for new enemies, Leo Strauss epigones, Billy Graham crackers, populist multiculturalists or anti-elitists, neo-Jungians, and various road companies of the Paris Follies.

Another aspect of this book's style, though less objected to than formerly, has not become popular. Sometimes in my writing I deliberately abandon "unity of tone" and "consistent level of usage," whenever I feel that in doing so I can best attain exactness of meaning and avoid possible ambiguity. Most of the published guides to expository writing, teachers of such writing, and editors frown on that practice, but I am willing to trade gracefulness for greater precision.

One large substantive aspect of this book puzzled several reviewers and other readers: the way that its essays reflect and depend on an uncommon type of wideness or dual allegiance, that is, my ongoing and intensive involvement in both very "highbrow" and very "lowbrow" worlds. Though you would not imagine it from the pages you have just read, I have, on a conservative estimate, spent at least fifteen thousand hours in poolrooms, most of that time in lower-class poolrooms. My friends include people who did not graduate from high school and who do not read books of any kind. Some, although they have been out of school for many years, do not have a Social Security number. I have also hung around with two people, maybe more, who would not have hesitated to have me murdered if they had thought that I might talk to a grand jury (and I began avoiding such people only after becoming a parent). My double cultural life has also been an intensively double social life, unlike that of, say, the typical intellectual who also follows sports or studies "popular culture."

Almost everyone finds my two worlds incompatible if not antithetical. But somehow I, on first encountering those worlds, instead of saying "either/or" said "both," and for more than half a century I have abided that decision with no strain, without any grinding of gears when shifting from one world to the other. The only real difficulty, which I soon learned to avoid, came when I brought friends from my two worlds together socially, the problem there being the behavior of the highbrows.

Some earlier readers expressed wonder, even skepticism, about how I could possibly find the time for such heavy involvement in both lowbrow culture and highbrow culture. It is largely time gained by a firm rejection of what is in between: middlebrow culture.

To illustrate only one of many such aversions: I have hardly ever bothered with those increasingly numerous middlebrow entertainments, public literary readings, whether of fiction or poetry. They strike me as kitsch. As Geoffrey Grigson noted long ago, poetry readings are for people who are too indifferent or too lazy to read poetry; I'll stick with my personal library, which includes somewhere between six and seven hundred books of poems. Reading a poem is what allows you to experience it fully, for a poem needs to be turned over a bit in the mind's ear, and also its effects often depend significantly on the way that the words look on the page. Full appreciation of a novel also requires immersing yourself in printed words—*audio book* is an oxymoron—which is why William Gaddis won't give public readings. And Charles Lamb was right about the need to *read* Shakespeare.

If drug researchers are correct in saying that the chief factor associated with drug use is propinquity, probably much time has also been saved by the fact that I have never owned a television set. Of course, as a sociologist, I do feel obliged to keep aware of what the general public is consuming, and so at friends' houses or in other venues I have always made it my business to watch television occasionally, for an estimated average of around eight to ten hours per year. That is enough viewing time to find out what is happening on television.

The Preface acknowledges help that I received for the first edition. The 1969 revision was aided by Leon Festinger, James McGrath, Joseph Polsky, Eddie Robin, and

Stanley Schachter. For this enlarged edition, helpful in various ways were Charles Antin, Robert Byrne, Alice Denham, Mark Finkelstein, Pete Harley, Michael Karp, David Kramer, Bill Maloney, David Markson, Claudia Polsky, Chris Stefano, Evelin Sullivan, Esteban Vicente, and especially Sarah White. I am also indebted to New York University's Bobst Library and its Fales Collection, and to the Shadek-Fackenthal Library of Franklin & Marshall College.

During research for this new edition I discovered the only surviving copy of what is either the first or the second English book on billiards. Through the gracious permission of its owner, the Winterthur Library of Winterthur, Delaware, I am able to offer here the first reproduction of the book's title page.

For each edition of this book, the most helpful people of all, of course, were those who were at least part of the time my "research subjects." Most of them cannot or would not wish to be named here.

Preface

This book is about the sociology of deviance. The differences among the chapters are in basic approach to the subject as well as in substantive content: one chapter reports on field research that relied heavily on participant observation, and another reports on field research that did not; a third chapter is a study in historical sociology; a fourth analyzes questions of research method; and the fifth is an exercise in theory.

The chapters cohere not only because of their concern with the sociology of deviance, but because all of them sharply disagree with the accepted views of their respective subjects. I have excluded those writings of mine on deviance that seem, on hindsight, to have differed merely in detail from the work of predecessors. Albrecht Dürer's insistence that the chief task of the artist was to "pour out new things which had never before been in the mind of any other man" has always struck me as the only decent attitude to take toward one's intellectual endeavors. Whether the "new things" in this book are also true or beautiful is for the reader to decide; but at least he will find much that is new, will find that every chapter radically dissents from one or more received opinions.

In another respect I have tried to give the reader more for his money than is usual. That is the result of special circumstance which it may be edifying to relate.

Back when I was publishing scholarly books instead of writing one, I would frequently reject a manuscript by sending the author a letter like the following: "You have things to say that are both new and useful. But all that is new and conceivably useful can easily be said in a 20-page article. I don't see much point in distending it to 300-odd pages." (Actually, I had to hold tight rein on such letters, for had I followed all my inclinations to send them I would have been left with hardly any books to publish.) The realization grew that these manuscripts resulted not merely from the moronic promotion standards of American universities— according to which one book is held automatically to be "worth" several articles—but equally from the scholar's natural addiction to vacuities. I resolved that whatever the defects of any book by myself, it would not have *that* defect, but would be as tightly packed as possible.

The desire to present much material in little space makes for a pinched utilitarian style, laden with footnotes, lacking in simile and metaphor, heavily adjectival, flat-footedly direct, and difficult for readers inclined to skim. I note the fact for literary gents and pass on to consider other aspects of style that might be more annoying to the scholar.

The book's vocabulary comes from several different bags. I don't believe in the alleged natural superiority of a diction that takes care always to stick to one "level of usage" and to preserve "unity of tone." I use whatever words that I think will most neatly convey my exact meaning, whether polysyllabic technical words or lowbrow slang words, fashionable words or unfashionable words, serious words or funny words. It bothers me not a bit that words having very different social statuses cohabit in my prose. A few readers agree, and even find such democracy exhilarating; most readers find it merely jarring.

Many readers of this book will feel that I object to the views of other scholars in terms that are overly fierce. These days the more usual mode in academia, thronged as it is with *arrivistes* aspiring to be gentlemen, is to voice such objections oleaginously. But luckily I cut an eyetooth on that masterpiece of English prose, A. E. Housman's introduction to his edition of Manilius, and so am forever immune to the notion that polemical writing and scholarly writing shouldn't mix. I believe that polemical scholarship improves the quality of intellectual life—sharpens the mind, helps get issues settled faster—by forcing genteel discussion to become genuine debate.

Although we learn from many teachers, there is a very special debt owed to the first great teacher whose acquaintance we make, the man who truly opens our eyes. That debt I owe to the late Miles Lawrence Hanley of the University of Wisconsin—phonetician, historian of the English language, and Chaucerian—who in his practice and precept first showed me the meaning of the life of learning, showed me what genuine scholarship was supposed to be and how to distinguish the real variety from the fake.

Hans Gerth, also of the University of Wisconsin, overcame my humanistic bias that sociology was not worth a serious man's time. From previous contacts with its practitioners, I had concluded that sociology consisted alternately in producing detailed proof of what everyone knew already (platitudes) and producing new knowledge not worth knowing (trivia). Hans Gerth's brilliant lectures convinced me in myriad ways that although this is usually the case, it is not always so—convinced me so fully that I entered the graduate department of sociology at the University of Chicago.

At Chicago I learned much from Herbert Blumer and the late Louis Wirth, among others. My deepest Chicago debt is to a man who gave me the most misery in graduate school, Everett Hughes. I took his course in methods of field research only because it was required, hated it, suffered through it, and did not begin to see its enormous value or apply its lessons until years later. How much my appreciation has grown for Everett Hughes and his work will, I trust, be clear in many of the following pages.

Some material in this book previously appeared in different form in the following periodicals, to which grateful acknowledgment is made: *Dissent, Social Problems,* and *Soundings.*

For providing bibliographical help, I am indebted to

Linda Asher, William Cole, Seymour Hacker, James Williams Hoffman, the late Dr. Julian A. Miller, Charles Westoff, Robert Wheeler, Elias Wilentz, and the staffs of the New York Public Library and the New York Historical Society Library.

My research in England connected with chapters 1 and 2 was greatly aided by the British Museum staff, who assiduously located early books on billiards amidst their tangle of sporting books badly hit by World War II bombings. I am indebted more heavily still to John Harris, Keeper of the Drawings Collections at the Royal Institute of British Architects, for instructing me in procedures of research on English architectural history, for making available to me his personal library of rare early guidebooks to country houses, and for many other kindnesses.

An early draft of chapter 1 was read critically by Robert B. Silvers; Erving Goffman criticized a draft of chapter 2 and, along with John F. Gallagher, gave me similar help on chapter 4. I have gained much from their advice. Howard Becker instigated this book, nagged me until it was done, read the entire manuscript, and made many improvements in it.

NED POLSKY

HUSTLERS, BEATS, AND OTHERS

Of Pool Playing
and
Poolrooms

A STUDY IN
HISTORICAL SOCIOLOGY*

The game of pool, or "pocket billiards" as the men who
make playing equipment or run the fancier poolrooms
would like you to call it, has been undergoing a renaissance. This revival, accidentally touched off by the enormous success of the movie *The Hustler* (late 1961, re-
released 1964), has been kept going via an adroit and
energetic public relations campaign by certain sporting
equipment manufacturers, chiefly Brunswick. The manufacturers are running scared: bowling alleys have been
overbuilt, and equipment makers are faced not only with
declining demand but the prospect of having to repossess
thousands of automatic pinsetters, costing $9,000 each,
which they have financed on long-term notes. Thus the attempt to cash in on *The Hustler* and revive pool and billiards. The campaign just might work, for such a reversal
of fashion is not without precedent in our sports history; an
observer wrote in 1869 that "Popular favor for ten-pins
having about this time—the close of 1858—yielded to the

* Part of this essay was presented at the annual meeting of
the Eastern Sociological Society, New York City, April, 1965,
and appeared in *Soundings* (State University of New York,
Stony Brook), Vol. 2, No. 1, Spring, 1965.

superior attraction of billiards, Mr. Kingsley changed his
alleys into a poolroom devoted to the latter game."[1]

The current upsurge in pool playing is not nearly as im-
pressive as many press releases and planted feature stories
would have one believe. Four decades ago the number of
American poolrooms was four times what it is today, and
on a per capita basis (number of pool and billiard tables
compared with the total population) poolrooms were then
about ten times as popular as they are now after three years
of "revival." But there has undoubtedly been a recent
growth of interest in poolroom games, after more than
three decades of unrelieved decline: witness the installing
of many pool and billiard tables in bowling establishments;
a sharp rise in the sale of private tables to suburban homeowners; pool contests on nationwide television; and most
importantly, the opening of more than 3,000 new poolrooms.[2]

As one whose chief recreation since the age of 13 has
been billiards, I am as much in favor of renewed public
interest in poolrooms as any professional yea-sayer in the
industry. But sociological analysis of the available historical data, reported below, forces me to conclude that
the present revival will soon peter out, and that American
per capita participation in poolroom games will never again
become even a sixth of what it once was.

In this conclusion I am in sorrowful disagreement with
the manufacturers and poolroom owners, who at this improved moment in their fortunes are understandably opti-
mists almost to a man. Recollecting, as they do, the once-
great popularity of poolrooms, they believe that the revival
will not only be maintained but hugely expanded. Moreover,
they are confident that they have hit upon a method to
assure this end.

Being aware of the moral stigma attached to poolrooms, they place faith in publicly and loudly casting out
sin—the method of "deviance disavowal" as the sociologist

---

[1] Cf. Dudley Kavanagh, *The Billiard World* (New York:
Kavanagh & Decker, 1869), p. 27.

[2] For statistics on the number of poolrooms and pool and
billiard tables, see note 44.

has it, or of "upgrading" one's "image" as the adman has it. In the poolroom business this process is known as "cleaning up the game," and currently it revolves about such things as installing carpets and bright lights and pastel colors, curbing obscene language, getting rid of hustlers and hoodlums and alcoholics, and trying to bring women in. On the advice of public relations counsel, the trade has also given outward and visible sign of the inward and spiritual grace by undergoing rebaptism: "poolrooms" have been replaced by "billiard lounges."[3]

Lately the trade has, in addition, made use of public relations men in the latter's role as inventors and purveyors of conscious, deliberate falsehoods.[4] To give but one example: The 1963 world professional pocket billiard (pool) tournament saw the emergence of a new champion, Luther Lassiter, who later won the 1964 tournament as well. Now the central fact of Lassiter's previous occupational life is that he had been for many years, under the monicker of "Wimpy," a genuine pool hustler of the old school—indeed such a good one that many of his hustler colleagues had long acknowledged his supremacy in one form of the grift, the game of nine ball.[5] But the public relations men who now write of Lassiter alternately suppress and blatantly deny this, and their fabrications are conveyed to mass audiences by reporters who conceive of journalism as the rephrasing of press handouts (see, for example, the mindless

[3] In an earlier attempt to reduce stigma, just before the turn of the century, many "poolrooms" and "poolhalls" became "billiard academies." But the effectiveness of this substitute—if any—soon wore off, as often happens with euphemisms. On the "wearing out" of euphemisms, cf. Leonard Bloomfield, *Language* (New York: Henry Holt, 1933), p. 410.

[4] This sort of thing poses ticklish research problems in any study that must, like this one, draw upon mass periodicals for some source material. Over four-fifths of the news items in the modern newspaper, and the large majority of articles in most mass magazines, derive from material supplied by public relations men, publicity men, official press representatives and the like—men whose jobs require them to serve with extraordinary frequency as professional liars.

[5] The following chapter explores what the hustler is and does.

article on pool in the *Saturday Evening Post* of April 18, 1964).

In this access of real and imagined virtue the manufacturers and poolroom owners are proceeding, I think, on a mistaken assumption. They subscribe to the commonly accepted view that the game's popularity waned because of the growing association of poolrooms, in the public mind, with gamblers, loafers, criminals and the like. It seems to me that the historical evidence reveals this explanation to be dead wrong, and that poolrooms instead declined because of certain long-term changes in America's social structure that are, apparently, irreversible.

I

The historical evidence on pool or any other sport is not conveniently "given" and merely awaiting sociological analysis. In this regard the sociologist, concerned with tracing how the history of an American sport is related to such things as social structure and social change, finds himself confronted with two unanticipated research problems.

His first special problem is that America's professional historians have not done what might be deemed their part of the job. Some of their works on various historical periods give, to be sure, once-over-lightly accounts of sports and games popular at different times; and they have written surveys of American sports history as such, the most notable being John Krout's *Annals of American Sport* (1929) and Foster Rhea Dulles' *America Learns to Play* (1940). But except possibly for baseball, the grand total of professional historical writing on any particular American sport does not begin to resemble a reasonably detailed and reliable history of that sport—whether social history or any other kind.

A related problem is that amateurs have rushed in where professionals fear to tread, and have set many traps for the unwary researcher. Much published material that calls itself the history of this or that sport is, in considerable part, nonsense. It may be found in the introductory sections or appendices of instruction manuals on sports, in encyclopedia articles, and in specialized periodicals about sports. The writer of such "history" sometimes is professionally connected with the sport, sometimes is a devoted fan, but in any case is not trained to do historical research. Some of his material is unavoidably important and must be drawn upon, especially if it gives an eyewitness account behind which one can detect no ulterior motive or sloppiness or undue play of the writer's imagination. But even when written out of purest intent, almost invariably this material contains much that is demonstrably wrong.

Quite representative of the genre are the historical discussions in the two latest billiard instruction books.[6] Their accounts of events beyond living memory are uncritically compiled from secondary sources and repeat errors that infest even the best of these sources (such as the *Encyclopaedia Britannica* and Frank Menke's *New Encyclopedia of Sports*). They tell us, for example, that billiards entered America about 1565 when Spaniards brought a form of the game to St. Augustine; but my own research on the American history of billiards has failed to uncover any reference before the late seventeenth century. The notion that the American game began over a century earlier is a myth passed on from one lazy billiard historian to the next; hardly one of them has ever bothered his head about finding a primary source for the alleged fact of sixteenth-century origin, which isn't surprising when you consider that most such "historians" don't know there is such a thing as a distinction between primary and secondary sources.[7]

The real pity in the lunkhead tradition of cobbling together secondary material is that just a little original searching reveals all sorts of useful data never cited by any sports

[6] Cf. the historical sections in Luther Lassiter, *The Modern Guide to Pocket Billiards* (New York: Fleet Publishing Co., 1964), and in Clive Cottingham, Jr., *The Game of Billiards* (Philadelphia: Lippincott & Co., 1965).

[7] An honorable exception, who is not faultless but sees some of the myths for what they are, is the anonymous author of *Modern Billiards* (New York: Brunswick-Balke-Collender Co., 1908), pp. 5–6. His warnings have gone unheeded by later writers on billiard history except Louise Belden, *op. cit. infra,* note 32.

historian, amateur or professional. Let us look at some of these data.

II

As soon as one begins seriously to examine primary sources, the standard explanation for the decline of poolrooms collapses. Material from every historical period reveals one fact overwhelmingly: poolrooms *always* had "middle-class morality" very solidly against them, were *always* highly stigmatized. This opposition to public poolrooms even extended, on occasion, to private playing at home by the ultrarespectable. When President John Quincy Adams installed a billiard table in the White House (with his own money), his opponents in Congress were able to raise a big stink about this acquiring of "gambling furniture" and to use the purchase as campaign material against him in the election of 1828.[8]

Literally hundreds of sources show that from the very beginning in America of public poolrooms (which started out as adjuncts to taverns and roadside inns), and uninterruptedly throughout their history, they were always associated with gambling and various forms of low life, ministers were always denouncing them, police were always finding wanted criminals in them, and parents were always warning their children to stay out of them. Here, for example, is Jerome Keogh, world's pool champion five times between 1897 and 1910, reminiscing about the 1890's:

> Despite the vaunted glamour of the great billiard academies of the gay nineties . . . the fact was that during this period "nice" young men stole surreptitiously through the by-ways of the night to enter them, lest detection should result in the stigma of being "fast." . . . The game struggled against the dictates of society, the raising of eyebrows, and the word "pool" uttered with caustic venom.[9]

[8] Cf. Samuel Flagg Bemis, *John Quincy Adams and the Union* (New York: Alfred A. Knopf, 1956), p. 94.

[9] Quoted in Russell J. Phillips, "Jerome Keogh Opens Palatial Room in Rochester, New York," *Billiards Magazine* (Chicago), June, 1932, pp. 14–15.

Moreover, poolrooms grew steadily in popularity despite the fact that, at times, opposition to them was far more severe than that encountered during the era of their decline. In some parts of the country there were periods when they could not even advertise their existence but had to remain hidden from passing view and draw their customers strictly by word of mouth. When the playwright William Dunlap of New York visited Baltimore in 1806, for example, he wrote home as follows:

> I have seen several counting houses open on sunday with the clarks at work; & Billiard tables publicky notefied by sign boards. From the first I onely infer that less attention is paid to appearances here than to the northward; & from the second that gambling is not in such *general* disrepute.[10]

III

It is true that England exported billiards to America with no stigma attached to it. Billiards entered America as "the gentleman's game." But at home in England, the social context of billiard playing had long been more complex than that oft-quoted phrase reveals. It is instructive to look at this complexity, because it foreshadowed similar developments that began in America soon after billiards arrived.

Much of early English billiard history is obscure, and much of what Englishmen have written about it is absurd—one unfortunate parallel with America being that English professional historians have also left the subject to incompetent amateurs.[11] But the main point of that history for

[10] *Diary of William Dunlap* (New York: New York Historical Society, 1930), Vol. 2, p. 376.

[11] No English billiard historian has even compiled a halfway reliable bibliography of his subject. Some (by no means all) of the most serious bibliographical problems are as follows: (1) The best-known early British book on billiards, E. White's *The Game of Billiards* (London: W. Miller, 1807), seems on internal evidence to be largely an unacknowledged translation of a French manual, but no one has tried to confirm this or even taken account of the internal evidence. (2)

our purposes is clear enough: billiard playing in England involved two separate, equally important traditions.

The first in point of time, and the one exported to America, consisted of "respectable" playing by the upper class, which flourished especially in country houses.[12] It is diffi-

___

English billiard historians unanimously, and American counterparts with one exception, agree that White's is the first English-language book on billiards (see, for example, the *Encyclopaedia Britannica*). They are wrong. (3) The exception is Louise Belden, *op. cit. infra,* note 32, who cites a book by John Dew as *"Treatise on the Game of Billiards* (London, 1799)."* But as a separately issued publication, Dew's treatise seems to be a ghost. I cannot find it in the catalogues of the British Museum, Ashley Library, London Library, Patent Office (London), Edinburgh University Library, Library of Congress, and Bibliothèque Nationale, nor in the National Union Catalogue, nor in Robert Watt's *Bibliotheca Britannica,* nor in the lists of new books in the *Gentleman's Magazine* for 1799 and the *Annual Register* for 1799. (4) But there is another book earlier than White's, cited by no one, in the British Museum. It is an anonymous work ("By an Amateur") of 72 duodecimo pages entitled *Game of Billiards* (London: T. Hurst, 1801). And in it, p. [10], is a reference to playing instructions "laid down by Mr. Dew." (5) A still earlier English book on billiards was almost certainly published in 1772; the "Catalogue of New Publications" in the *Gentleman's Magazine* for that year (Vol. 42, p. 140) has this entry:

> The Odds of the Game of Billiards; accurately calculated by a Gentleman who has studied them many Years. To which are added some observations on the Game, that should be attended by every Player. 12mo. 1s. Bladon.

The book is also listed in *Bibliotheca Britannica.* Apparently no copy of this 1772 volume survives.

The bibliography of British writing on billiards to be found elsewhere than in billiard books (e.g., periodicals, diaries, general books on sports and games) is in still worse shape—but I have no space to deal with this.

[12] Among early guidebooks to country houses that mention billiard rooms are the following: Anon., *Aedes Pembrochianae: Being a New and Critical Account . . . of the Antiquities at Wilton-House* (London: R. Baldwin, 1744), p. 45; J. Seely, *Stowe: A Description of the House and Gardens* (Buckingham: The Author, 1797), pp. 43, 49 (Stowe had two billiard rooms; its two regular billiard tables are listed in the sale catalogue of 1848, and another, miniature, billiard table is listed

cult to determine the dates of country-house billiard rooms because such rooms were often additions, i.e., were converted from rooms initially devoted to other uses, and because the original architectural plans (unlike the ground plans published much later in guidebooks) almost never label the use for each room.[13] But there were some billiard rooms of this sort in the last quarter of the sixteenth century. The inventory of Howard House made in 1588 lists "a billyard bord covered wth a green cloth wth a frame of beache wth fower turned postes," and also "three billyard stickes and 11 balles of yvery"; and in the same year the Earl of Leicester's goods at Wanstead, as listed for probate, included "a billiarde table with the tools appurteyninge."[14] Other country-house billiard rooms which available information indicates are both original and early include those at Burghley House (completed 1589), Bramshill (completed 1612), Knole (completed 1608), Dorton House

in the sale catalogue of 1921); Anon., *A History and Description . . . of Burghley House* (Shrewsbury: J. and W. Eddowes, 1797), p. 126; D. Jacques, *A Visit to Goodwood* (Chichester: The Author, 1822), pp. 48, 52 (Goodwood had two billiard rooms); Anon., *A Description of Hagley, Envil, and the Leasowes* (Birmingham: The Author, n.d. [*ca.* 1765]), p. 136; John Britton, *Graphic Illustrations of Toddington* (London: The Author, 1840), plates [1] and [16] (the latter plate illustrates Toddington's billiard room); John Young, *Catalogue of the Pictures at Leigh Court, Near Bristol* (London: The Proprietor, 1822), p. 27; John Brady, *The Visitor's Guide to Knole . . .* (Sevenoaks: James Payne, 1839), p. 125; William Dean, *An Historical and Descriptive Account of Croome D'Abitot* (Worcester: T. Eaton, 1824), p. 50 (description of the billiard room); Anon., *An Historical and Descriptive Account of Stoke Park in Buckinghamshire* (London: W. Bulmer, 1813), p. [79].

[13] But cf. James Gibbs, *A Book of Architecture containing Designs of Buildings and Ornaments*, 2d ed. (London: W. Innys and R. Manby, 1739), p. xiii and plate XLVIII.

[14] Quoted from "Tables, Billiard," in Ralph Edwards (Ed.), *Dictionary of English Furniture*, 2d ed. (London: Country Life, 1954), pp. 187 ff.; this article is in every respect the best account of early billiard history in England. Note that these 1588 quotations slightly antedate the *O.E.D.*'s first record of the word "billiards" in the English language (1591).

(completed 1626), and Hatfield House (completed 1611).[15]

Although the billiard room was as richly appointed as any other in the country house—with, for example, paintings by such artists as Holbein, Canaletto, and Van Dyck—the table itself was often an object of great interest to visitor and owner alike. Thus John Evelyn, in his seventeenth-century diary, carefully noted the billiard tables in the houses he visited. In 1844 the Duke of Devonshire proudly described his table at Chatsworth as follows:

> The Billiard-table, made by Thurston, full size—which means that there is still a fuller size—is suited to the small-ness of the room. . . . The table, of birds-eye maple, is a chef d'oeuvre of workmanship, and has been pronounced excellent by no less a man than "Jonathan" [a famous player of the time].[16]

Among the prize-winning examples of English craftsmanship at the Great Exhibition of 1851 were two billiard tables (by different manufacturers) with elaborate marquetry and other ornamentation.[17]

[15] Anon., *Guide to Burghley House, Stamford* (Stamford: Doby Brothers, 1933), p. 19; William Cope, *Bramshill: Its History and Architecture* (London: H. J. Infield, n.d. [after 1875]), p. 36; H. Avray Tipping, *English Homes: Late Tudor and Early Stuart, 1558–1649* (London: Country Life, 1929), p. 246; James Hakewell, *An Attempt to Determine the Exact Character of Elizabethan Architecture*, 2d ed. (London: John Weale, 1936), p. [30]; Robert Kerr, *The Gentleman's House*, 3rd ed. (London: John Murray, 1871), plate 9.

[16] Anon. [Duke of Devonshire], *Handbook of Chatsworth and Hardwick* (London: Privately printed, n.d. [1844]), p. 35.

[17] Color lithographs of these tables comprise plate 190 of the exhibition catalogue. Among the more notable English tables preserved is the present one at Burghley House, whose mountings are of oak from the Royal George, sunk at Spithead in 1782. A table from about 1660, now in the Victoria and Albert Museum, is illustrated in Ralph Edwards, *op. cit.* Probably the oldest English table extant is the one at Knole. It is illustrated in Tipping, *op. cit.*, and Edwards, *op. cit.*; its construction is briefly discussed in Margaret Jourdain, *Stuart Furniture at Knole* (London: Country Life, 1952), p. 13. Edwards, following Tipping, dates it around 1690, but I think Jourdain correctly dates the base of it about a century earlier.

By the time of Robert Kerr's *The Gentleman's House; Or, How to Plan English Residences* (first edition, 1864; third edition, 1871), it was taken for granted that any house of reasonable size should have a billiard room, and Kerr devoted a good deal of attention to the matter.[18] So did some of the Victorian manuals on billiards.[19]

From the beginning, billiard tables also were installed in some other meeting places of the upper class. Most important of these, perhaps, were the two billiard tables in the New Assembly Rooms at Bath (built 1769–1771).[20] Some upper-class coffee houses also had billiard tables—starting with Colsini's Chocolate House, which had two billiard tables by 1693, and ending with the Smyrna Coffee House in St James's Street, which advertised itself in 1801 as a place where "Gentlemen meet on purpose to play billiards."[21]

But if billiards could be played in public places frequented by gentlemen, there was little to prevent it being played in public places frequented by the not-so-gentlemanly; and little did prevent it. This newer type of English billiard playing, which represented a "trickling down" of the upper-class pastime, appears to have been already well under way in the seventeenth century, to judge from Charles Cotton's remarks of 1674:

[18] The construction of billiard rooms in English country houses continued well into the present century. For photographs of billiard rooms in houses not already cited, consult the files of *Country Life* and also Charles Latham's *In English Homes* (London: Country Life) as follows: Vol. 1 (1904), pp. 24, 56, 348, 365, 405; Vol. 2 (1907), pp. 166, 359, 431; Vol. 3 (1909), pp. 412, 414.

[19] See especially the lovely architectural elevations for Greek Revival and Tudor billiard annexes attached to mansions, in William Dufton's *Practical Billiards* (London: George Routledge, 1873), plates 2, 3, 4, and 5.

[20] See the floor plan in Mowbray A. Green, *The Eighteenth Century Architecture of Bath* (Bath: George Gregory, 1904), p. 161.

[21] Cf. Bryant Lillywhite, *London Coffee Houses* (London: George Allen and Unwin, 1963), entries numbered 7, 500, 1178, 1223, and 1604.

> The Gentile, cleanly and most ingenious game at Billiards
> . . . is much approved of and played by most Nations in
> *Europe,* especially in *England* there being few Towns of
> note therein which hath not a publick Billiard-table, neither
> are they wanting in many Noble and private Families in
> the Country.[22]

As this second tradition developed, the "respectable"
upper class who played at home or in meeting places restricted to their own kind (Bath, private clubs, etc.) were
immediately concerned to distinguish themselves from it,
and in doing so they conceived it as morally deviant. In
their view, it was bad enough that *hoi aristoi* had occasionally spent too much time and money gambling at billiards amongst themselves (Edmund Spenser's complaint of
1591),[23] but much worse that *hoi polloi* should now become wastrels over it and even (worst of all) sometimes
seduce their weaker-minded betters into joining with them
in a life of dissolute gaming. That is why even as early as
1674 Charles Cotton, for all his remarks about "The Gen-
tile, cleanly and most ingenious game at Billiards," had to
leaven his book with remarks such as these:

> Mistake me not, it is not my intention to make Game-
> sters.
> This restless man (the miserable Gamester) is the
> proper subject of every man's pity. Restless I call him, be-
> cause (such is the itch of play) either winning or losing he
> can never be satisfied, if he wins he thinks to win more,
> if he loses he hopes to recover.
>
> To conclude, let me advise you, if you play (when your
> business will permit) let not a covetous desire of winning
> another's money engage you to the losing of your own.[24]

As billiards spread downward from the upper class, these
kinds of warnings increased in frequency and severity.

[22] Gamester [Charles Cotton], *The compleat Gamester; or,
Instructions how to play at billiards, trucks, bowls and
chess.* . . . (London: Henry Brome, 1674), p. 23.
[23] "With all the thriftless games that may be found. . . .
With dice, with cards, with billiards." *Mother Hubberd's Tale*
(1591).
[24] Charles Cotton, *op. cit.,* pp. [vi], [vii–viii], 3.

There were also occasional efforts to go beyond moral suasion and legally clamp down on public billiard playing by the lower strata, such as this attempt in the Dublin of 1744:

> At the Court of *King's Bench,* in *Ireland,* were convicted 15 of the Billiard Tables, presented by the Grand Jury of *Dublin,* (who had traversed) The Citizens have determin'd to prosecute, in the same Manner, all Billiard Tables that shall be erected for the Future, or those which now remain, if kept open after 9 o'Clock at Night, or knowingly suffer Merchants, Apprentices or Clerks belonging to Gentlemen of any Business, to play in their Houses.[25]

These attempts, whether in England or Ireland, succeeded only rarely and temporarily. But in any case there had developed, in addition to the approved "gentleman's game" played in country houses, public billiard playing by nongentlemen that was heavily stigmatized.

IV

In America as in England, billiards began at the top. It came as a direct importation from the English upper class to the American upper class. For example, one of the earliest genuine references to billiards in America reveals that the Colonial statesman William Byrd of Westover—who was educated in England and called to the bar at the Middle Temple—had a billiard table: in his diary entry for 30 July 1710, Byrd writes, apropos of having laid his wife, "It is to be observed that the flourish was performed on the billiard table."[26] On September 26, 1725, I find the Colonial Governor of New York, George Clinton, writing to Cadwallader Colden that "I . . . gave orders for my Billiard tables to be Set up."[27] By 1768, according to an account written

[25] "Historical Chronicle," *Gentleman's Magazine,* Vol. 14 (1744), p. 337.

[26] Cf. Louis B. Wright and Marion Tinling (Eds.), *Secret Diary of William Byrd of Westover, 1709–1712* (Richmond, Va.: Dietz Press, 1941), p. 207.

[27] Cf. *Letters and Papers of Cadwallader Colden.* Vol. IX: *Additional Letters and Papers, 1749–1775* (New York: New York Historical Society, 1937), p. 122.

in that year, the demand for billiard playing equipment was
already so great that cue sticks manufactured along the
James River in Virginia were being exported all the way to
Boston.[28] (Despite sharply increasing demand over the
next 150 years, this early American industry died out in
Virginia, presumably because of the realization that the
most warp-resistant woods for cue sticks are the extremely
hard varieties of maple which flourish much further
north.[29])

The better-off merchant of the times could avail himself
of such offerings as this one in the New York *Royal Gazette*
of October 24, 1781:

> To be let a new house in an excellent stand for business,
> it has a good cellar, two rooms below, a large billiard room
> above, a bed chamber, a large garret, a back kitchen, and a
> convenient back yard. . . .

And early American newspapers also contain quite a few
advertisements addressed to the upper class along the lines

[28] Cf. *Virginia Gazette*, March 3, 1768, p. 3, col. 1.

[29] Cue sticks are usually 56½ to 57 inches long, the better
ones being take-down models comprising two pieces of equal
length, a butt and a shaft, joined via an inset brass female screw
in the bottom of the shaft and a brass male screw and bushing
in the top of the butt. The relatively thick butt can be made of
any of various heavy woods (e.g., my own is of West African
black ebony) and traditionally has a good deal of marquetry
using inlays of ivory, colored woods, and mother-of-pearl. But
the shaft, since it tapers to a width of only 12½ to 13½ milli-
meters throughout the last several inches of its length, must,
if it is to resist warping, be an unadorned piece of very hard
maple, turned so that the grain runs straight down the shaft,
from stock that has been thoroughly kiln-dried. To produce
maple shafts that are all of first quality—a criterion ignored by
the newer stickmakers—one must also take care to use only the
heartwood near the center of the log (for which last information I am indebted to the best of the old cue-stick craftsmen,
octogenarian Herman Rambow of Chicago).
Although the best kind of maple for cue sticks does not
grow in England, an English variety of ash is virtually as warp-
resistant. Consequently most English cue sticks are made of
ash. (For this information I am indebted to the London
billiard firm of Burroughes and Watts, Ltd.)

of this one from the *Minerva & Mercantile Advertiser* of February 12, 1795:

> William King, Ivory and Wood Turner, Informs the citizens . . . that he has commenced the turning business. . . . Billiard balls made at the shortest notice . . .

Upper-class billiard playing long survived the Colonial era. For instance, the education typically given a scion of wealth in the mid-nineteenth century was described accurately, albeit sarcastically, by Charles Nordhoff in 1868 as follows:

> J. Augustus . . . was of course in due time sent to college, where he acquired the proper proficiency in Greek, Latin, and Mathematics, slang, billiards, and brandy smashes.[30]

In fact, the British tradition of upper-class participation in billiards has in America had a continuous, if latterly rather modest, history.[31] A good many illustrious Americans have played billiards. And today the members of the Billiard Room Proprietors Association, Billiard Players Association, and the Billiard Congress of America tirelessly cite such personages in the hope that this will improve their "image." But their hope is misplaced, for they thoroughly misunderstand the relation of billiards to upper-class life.

In the first place, genteel upper-class billiard playing in America, as in England, was insulated from the rest of society, and its rise and fall have followed a dynamic of their own. What professional players and poolroom owners

[30] Charles Nordhoff, "Maud Elbert's Love Match," in his *Cape Cod and All Along the Shore: Stories* (New York: Harper and Brothers, 1868), p. 217.

[31] See especially the house organs and archives of upper-class men's clubs with billiard rooms. The first national amateur billiard tournament was organized by the Racquet and Tennis Club of New York in 1887. A good account of the billiard enthusiasts in nineteenth-century clubland is A. L. Ranney, M.D., "A Historical Sketch of Amateur Billiards," in *Amateur Billiard Championship of America (Class A)—Souvenir of the First Tournament Given Under the Auspices of the Amateur Athletic Union of the United States* (New York: Knickerbocker Athletic Club, 1899), pp. 7–24.

conveniently ignore is that "the gentleman's game," to the
extent that gentlemen really played it, throughout its history
has had precious little to do with public poolrooms, but instead has been restricted to the billiard rooms of private
men's clubs and private homes.[32] And the upper class
knows what this means even if the professionals don't. The
point of the remark falsely attributed to Herbert Spencer,
"To play a good game of billiards is the sign of a well-
rounded education, but to play too good a game of billiards
is the sign of a mis-spent youth," is precisely the point made
in that *locus classicus* for the ideology of the "gentleman,"
Lord Chesterfield's letters to his son, when Chesterfield
warns his son against becoming too good a flute player: the
upper class must uphold the distinction between the amateur
and the professional, and the true gentleman takes care
that he cannot possibly be mistaken for a professional or
vice versa.

This moral has never been lost on the American billiard-
playing elite, and the traditional attempts of professional
pool and billiard players to identify themselves with such
circles, e.g., by wearing tuxedos when appearing in professional tournaments, are merely pathetic. To be sure, a
Luther Lassiter or a Willie Mosconi may be invited to give
an exhibition before the assembled members of a men's
club—a comedown from the days when Willie Hoppe gave

[32] For one of the more interesting examples in the American
private home, see the photograph of the billiard room designed
about 1900 by Louis Tiffany for his country estate, The Briars,
Long Island, in Robert Koch, *Louis C. Tiffany: Rebel in Glass*
(New York: Crown Publishers, 1964), p. 183. See also C. V.
Boyd, "Billiard Room of a Country House," *Suburban Life*,
Vol. 18 (January 1914), pp. 10–12.

The earliest surviving billiard table of American manufac-
ture, made in Maryland between 1790 and 1810, is in the Winterthur Museum. A picture of it, and background information,
are in Louise C. Belden, "Billiards in America Before 1830,"
Antiques, Vol. 87, No. 1 (January 1965), pp. 99–101. Miss
Belden's is easily the best writing on its subject heretofore published, but is more restricted than its title indicates: it deals
exclusively with upper-class billiard history, and in a limited
way (e.g., using none of the pre-1830 material from the upper
class that I have quoted).

command performances for presidents and royalty, but still something. And if the professional should need money in his later years he may even end his days in their permanent employ (for example, the old balk-line billiard champion Jake Schaefer, Jr., has for some time run the billiard room of the Cleveland Athletic Club). But it is all part of the relation of master to hired performer. Even Willie Hoppe, who was a real stuffed shirt and tried his damnedest to dissociate himself from the poolroom subculture (he didn't even smoke or drink), for all his wealth and gentlemanly yearnings and polite manners never quite made it in the upper class as an equal.

In the past, major poolrooms did indeed manage to attract some upper-class patrons, not only *nouveaux riches* businessmen but occasional scions of old wealthy families as well. However, such people were a different breed from the gentlemen who played at the Union League or at home over cigars and sherry, and in fact constituted the most disreputable segment of the upper class. One of the latent functions of the American poolroom, like the racetrack in many of its phases, was as a place where the "sporting" fringe of the upper class—the hedonists and hellraisers given to heavy drinking and gambling and whoring—could get together with the "sporting element" of the lower class and lower-middle class to the exclusion of those who subscribed to "middle-class morality."[33] Poolrooms were major

[33] For example, see the further remarks of Keogh in Russell Phillips, *op. cit.*, p. 15. Public billiard rooms in England of course had a similar function; cf. Edward Russell Mardon, *Billiards: Game 500 Up. Played at Brighton, on the 18th of January, 1844. A Description of the Above Game, with Diagrams Shewing the Position of the Balls for the Last Nine Breaks* (Brighton: W. Leppard, n.d. [1844]), pp. 4, 102–103.

Many criminologists believe that if we had accurate statistics on victim crime (including a proper accounting of white-collar crime), we would find a sharply bi-modal distribution of such crime by social class, with the least of it in the middle class. See especially Walter Reckless, *The Crime Problem*, 2nd ed. (New York: Appleton-Century-Crofts, 1955), pp. 28–30. My point about the latent functions of poolrooms and racetracks is that the same pattern also seems true of the "vices," that is, non-victim crime and legal but morally stigmatized behavior.

gathering places for the sporting fraternity and served them
in various ways; for instance, in the early 1920's, Jack
Doyle's Billiard Academy was the place where the daily
"line" (more or less official bookmakers' odds) was determined for every sports event in New York City.[34]

V

What used to be called "sporting life," the orientation of
leisure around a set of hedonistic and deviant concerns, has
in America not died out or even diminished. Rather, it has
retained many of its old institutional forms (bookies and
racetracks, orgies and stag shows, after-hours liquor-cum-
gambling joints, cocaine, bars where prostitutes are permitted or encouraged to operate, floating crap and card
games), while sloughing off some others (poolrooms,
whorehouses, opium, burlesque houses) and developing
some new ones (call-girl organizations operating through
model agencies and escort services, marihuana, the gambling centers of Lake Tahoe and Las Vegas, free-lance
call girls operating via telephone-answering services, phe-
nomenally increased gambling at golf). It remains to be
explained why poolrooms got lost in the shuffle.

One answer sometimes given, and at first glance an appealing one, has to do not with the poolroom's latent functions but its manifest functions: a place where one plays or
watches pool and billiards. It is occasionally said that pool
and billiards were killed by other sports, especially the rise
of mass participation in bowling and mass spectatorship for
professional football.

It has been claimed apropos of the first that, relative
to bowling, pool and billiards are too hard to learn well.
The argument goes that thousands of regular bowlers can
work up to an average of 180 or better, but that getting to
the point in pool where you can average nearly 10 balls an
inning and occasionally run more than 50, or to the point
in three-cushion billiards where you can average nearly

[34] For this information on Doyle's Academy I am indebted
to my father, Joseph Polsky.

1 an inning and occasionally run more than 7, is a very much more difficult matter.

There are some genuine grains of truth at the bottom of this argument. Outstanding pool or billiard play requires thousands of hours of practice, and, to boot, early entry, as much as outstanding piano playing does. I have never met or heard of a really first-class pool or billiard player who was not playing regularly by his early teens. An additional fact supporting this position, though it seems never to have been adduced, is that many of the greatest pool and billiard players, probably the majority, started training well before their teens because they were sons of poolroom owners (e.g., Ralph Greenleaf, Willie Hoppe, Babe Cranfield, Jay Bozeman, Willie Mosconi, Welker Cochran) and in one case the son of a professional player (Jake Schaefer, Jr.). But this entire line of argument really doesn't hold up, for it assumes that true enjoyment of the game depends on attaining to the level of the top one-fifth of 1 per cent of players. The fact is that millions of Americans have greatly enjoyed playing pool regularly even though they have never come close to running 50 balls—have enjoyed it just as much as, say, the millions of golfers who have never broken 80 have enjoyed playing golf. And as we saw earlier, in the 1850's billiards in fact superseded bowling in popularity; there seems to be no reason intrinsic to these games themselves why such a reversal couldn't happen again.

The second point of view sees a shift in spectator sports interests as perhaps the chief villain in the piece. For example, Willie Mosconi has recalled that, in Chicago in the early 1930's, it was common for him to draw 1500 spectators to a Saturday night pool exhibition while the Chicago Bears would draw 1200 the next day.[35] It is undeniably true that from about 1930 on poolrooms steadily declined while, during the Depression era, spectator interest in football, basketball, etc., began slowly to rise; and it is also true that as the Depression eased, most Depression-hurt sports made recoveries but pool and billiards declined very

[35] Cf. Mosconi as quoted in the New York *Post,* December 18, 1961, p. 62.

much more. However, there is no evidence of a real cause-and-effect relationship here. Pool and billiards have always had plenty of competition for spectators (and players) from any number of other sports and games, and did quite well nonetheless.

Similarly, it is illogical to blame the decline of poolrooms on the spread of radios, automobiles, and the movies.[36] There is no evidence whatsoever that their negative effect on poolroom attendance was any greater than that provided by the many popular diversions which existed in the palmy days of the poolroom (such as the home phonograph and player piano, vaudeville and the legitimate theatre, public dance halls and ballrooms, taverns, racetracks, and so on).

And if mass spectatorship for sports has any relevance as such, then the post-1945 role of television in fantastically increasing that spectatorship should, if anything, have helped pool and billiards even more than most other sports. For a pool or billiard game is ideal for TV: it is not as spread out and hard to follow on television as football or baseball, and when the camera looks down on the table from a reasonably steep angle (as it usually does), the home viewer gets a truer picture of the game than even the front-row spectators do. Yet television did nothing to revive pool and billiards; such games did not become TV fare until mid-1963, after the revival was well under way.

Finally, one should note that although the current poolroom revival is already exhibiting danger signs (more on this below), the sale of small-sized pool tables to homeowners is still sharply increasing. The ups and downs of poolrooms, as we shall see, have had not so much to do with pool as with poolrooms.

VI

As we have observed, the various alleged "causes" for the decay of the American poolroom have had a minor

[36] As, for example, Robert Coughlan does in his "Pool: Its Players and Its Sharks," *Life*, Vol. 31, No. 15 (October 8, 1951), p. 166.

role at best. The genuine prime cause seems never to have been mentioned: poolrooms were the exact center and veritable stronghold of a special kind of subculture that has become increasingly rare and unimportant in America—the heterosexual but all-male subculture, which required that certain gathering places (clubs, barber shops, taverns) serve as sacrosanct refuges from women. The poolroom was not just one of these places: it was *the* one, the keystone.

The once-great attraction of pool and billiards, both for spectators and players, was in large part factitious; it had not so much to do with the games themselves as with the poolroom's latent function as the greatest and most determinedly all-male institution in American social life. The poolroom got so thoroughly bound up with this function that it could not readily adapt itself to changed conditions; when the subculture died, the poolroom nearly died with it.

To see the true dimensions of this historical drift, one must realize that the old poolroom depended not merely, or even primarily, on the equivalent of today's audience of unmarried teenagers combined with husbands out for a weekly "night with the boys" or playing at lunchtime, but on people who spent far more time than these in the poolroom: adult men who were heterosexual but nevertheless committed to remaining unmarried. Moreover, the ideology of this bachelor subculture spilled over to married life itself; that is, married men spent more nights "out with the boys" than they do today, which of course further helped poolroom attendance. (Both the "pure" and the "married" subcultural types linger in the nation's historical consciousness, or nostalgia, via highly anachronistic comic-strip characters; Moon Mullins pre-eminently represents the first type, while the second is notably represented by Mutt and by Major Hoople.)[37]

As everyone appears to know thanks to Kinsey, if an

[37] Married pool players given to frequent nights "out with the boys" are most fully delineated in Clare Briggs' cartoon feature, *Kelly Pool,* which appeared regularly in the sports section of the New York *Tribune* from 1912 to 1917. (For recollecting and calling my attention to these cartoons I am indebted to my father, Joseph Polsky.)

American male over the age of 35 has never been married there is a strong chance that he is actively and primarily homosexual.[38] But what everyone seems to forget is that this is a major change in the odds and represents a recent shift in America's sexual history. For various reasons connected with our country's economic development and its historic patterns of immigration, not too long ago the heterosexual confirmed bachelor was a common American social type. For example, the bachelor "uncle"—sometimes a real uncle, sometimes an honorary one, but in any event a bachelor—was a fixture in hundreds of thousands of American families. He may not have been very active sexually, but his sexual activity, such as it was, was rarely homosexual. (I am talking about overt behavior only; what existed in repressed form may be another story.) His sexual needs were met throughout his life partly by masturbation and partly or mainly by regular recourse to professional whores. Today American men use whores pre-maritally, extra-maritally, and post-maritally, but hardly ever any more as a way of maintaining lifelong bachelorhood.[39]

Curiously, American historians seem never to have assayed, indeed to be oblivious of, the swiftly growing role of a confirmed-bachelor subculture in the social history of nineteenth-century America. Yet the evidence is plain enough.

For one thing, a number of American institutions whose

[38] Among unmarried American males 35 or older with at least a ninth-grade education, about 42 per cent have at least as much homosexual experience per year as heterosexual experience; among those with less than a ninth-grade education, about 28 per cent have at least as much homosexual experience per year as heterosexual experience. Cf. Alfred Kinsey, Wardell Pomeroy, and Clyde Martin, *Sexual Behavior in the Human Male* (Philadelphia: W. B. Saunders Co., 1948), p. 644, fig. 164.

[39] In this connection note the Kinsey data, which reveal that although the percentage of males born after 1900 who visited prostitutes was not significantly different from the percentage among males born earlier, the frequency with which they made such visits had been reduced to about half what it was in the pre-1900 generation. Cf. Alfred Kinsey, Wardell Pomeroy, Clyde Martin, and Paul Gebhard, *Sexual Behavior in the Human Female* (Philadelphia: W. B. Saunders Co., 1953), p. 300.

palmy days were in the later nineteenth or early twentieth century immediately reveal themselves, once their histories are examined, as having drawn sustenance from that subculture and often, indeed, having been part and parcel of it—not only the poolroom, but institutions as various as the I.W.W., lodges and other fraternal organizations, red-light districts, middle-class and upper-class men's clubs, boarding houses, tramp and hobo life. Secondly, there increasingly emerged, in the lowbrow and middlebrow literature of the times, much that gave bachelors a consciousness of kind and gave ideological expression to permanent bachelorhood (as in the *Police Gazette*, whose formerly vital role in our popular culture is hard to appreciate now). Thirdly, the most sophisticated compilation of historical statistics on American marriage—the work of Paul Jacobson—reveals the early American rate of permanent bachelorhood to have been a steadily rising one that peaked during the lifetimes of the men born around 1865–1870 (i.e., men just entering their adulthood in the late 1880's and early 1890's). Jacobson's cohort analyses of bachelors and spinsters (single whites aged 15 and over) from successive decades of the late eighteenth century through the nineteenth century show that

> there was a gradual decrease in the proportion ultimately marrying among persons born in successive periods up to the years immediately after the Civil War, and thereafter a gradual increase.

Jacobson notes further that

> the marriage rate for bachelors and spinsters has generally moved upward during this century. Among single men, for example, the average annual marriage rate rose from 64 per 1,000 in the 1900's to 69 in the 1920's. Although the rate dropped sharply during the depression of the 1930's, it soared upward in the next decade to the unusually high level of 92 per 1,000.
>
> Another indication of the increased propensity to marry is afforded by the extent to which the single population has been depleted. Among males aged 15 and over (including those in the armed forces overseas) the proportion single

declined from 42 percent in 1890 . . . to less than 25 per cent in 1950.[40]

Not only were there more lifelong bachelors earlier, but there were more "bachelor years" for men who eventually married (the average age at marriage was greater).

VII

Toward the middle of the nineteenth century, hard upon the great waves of Irish and German immigration, the American poolroom began to emerge as the major physical locus of the rising bachelor subculture. One witness to the start of the boom wrote as follows in 1850:

> The rapidity with which Billiard rooms have increased in this and other cities of the Union, is extraordinary. Within the writer's memory, the number of rooms in New York, did not exceed seven or eight, and perhaps not more than sixteen tables in all; now, there are from fifty to sixty rooms, with a number of tables, varying from one to sixteen each, and amounting, on the whole, to something over four hundred.[41]

The periodical of the time most concerned with "popular culture," *Frank Leslie's Illustrated Newspaper,* in January 1859 began a regular column on billiards. April of the same year saw the first thing approximating a national championship contest, the Phelan-Seereiter match in De-

[40] Paul Jacobson, *American Marriage and Divorce* (New York: Rinehart, 1959), p. 35. For additional details, see especially Tables 7 and 8, pp. 34–35. The paragraphs above assess fully neither the heterosexual bachelor subculture nor its former place in American life, but attempt merely to indicate that such assessment is a desideratum in American historiography.

[41] Michael Phelan, *Billiards Without a Master* (New York: D. D. Winant, 1850), p. 122. This, the first American book on billiards, went into several editions. Phelan also issued the first American billiard periodical, *Billiard Cue,* from 1856 to 1874; it was a monthly of four folio pages. Cf. Frank Luther Mott, *A History of American Magazines 1850–1865* (Cambridge, Mass.: Harvard University Press, 1938), p. 203.

troit.[42] The popularity that the sport had already gained is indicated by the fact that this match, the first professional billiard event for which admission was charged, was a sellout at the high admission price of $5, was played for the enormous prize of $15,000 (surely over $100,000 in today's currency), and was altogether one of the most gripping events on the American "sporting imagination" of the nineteenth century. *The New York Times'* coverage of the match—this when the whole newspaper was only eight to twelve pages—appears in several columns over three separate issues. In 1865 the periodical *Round Table* took note of "the mania for playing billiards which has developed itself in this country in the last five or six years."[43]

The swift increase noted at mid-century was a mere beginning. The pace of poolroom growth accelerated throughout the second half of the nineteenth century and well into the twentieth. By the mid-1920's America had over 42,000 poolrooms (over 4,000 in New York City alone), many with more than 50 tables each and even a few with 100 tables each.[44] Detroit Recreation, a poolroom in De-

[42] The names of the contestants are significant. In keeping with ethnic shifts in American immigration, most of the early non-WASP billiard professionals are of Irish origin (Phelan, Daly, Kavanagh, Gallagher, Keogh, McKenna, *et al.*) or of German origin (Seereiter, Schaefer, Kieckhefer, Reiselt, Hoppe, *et al.*), with Italians and Jews becoming prominent in the picture only after the turn of the century.

The heavy extent to which German-Americans were involved in billiards has been overlooked by billiard historians, probably because the first American billiard books were written by Irishmen, but there is much evidence apart from the names of early professionals. For example, in the middle of the nineteenth century a number of the German beer gardens along the Bowery in New York City had billiard tables. Cf. Matthew Hale Smith, *Sunshine and Shadow in New York* (Hartford, Conn.: J. B. Burr, 1869), p. 216. For an amusing sidelight on German-American billiard playing, cf. Max Weber, "The Protestant Sects and the Spirit of Capitalism," in H. H. Gerth and C. Wright Mills, eds., *From Max Weber: Essays in Sociology* (New York: Galaxy Books, Oxford University Press, 1958), pp. 310–311.

[43] Quoted in Mott, *op. cit.*, p. 203.

[44] Statistics on the number of poolrooms, put out from time to time by such organizations as the Billiard Congress of Amer-

troit that claimed to be the world's largest, had 125 tables.
In the 1920's, Ralph Greenleaf, the greatest pool champion
in the history of the game, played the Palace Theatre at a
salary of $2,000 per week. And note what happened to
one of the instruction manuals, *Daly's Billiard Book,* which
was published in 1913: in its first ten years, it achieved a
larger sale than any other book devoted to a physical sport
or game that had ever been published.[45]

The timing of all this is significant beyond the fact of
bachelorhood *per se.* It is not accidental that poolrooms
began rapidly to increase in number and size as the American frontier rapidly receded, for one function of the frontier was as a male escape-hatch from effete and "feminized"
urban civilization.[46] As towns and cities spread ever west-
ward and as they more and more "settled down," the poolroom blossomed as a kind of behind-the-lines or inner
frontier, the new no-woman's land, catering to internal
refugees from the world of female-imposed gentility, cater-

ica, National Billiard Council, and Billiard Room Proprietors
Association of America, vary considerably. The consensus
seems to be that in 1964 there were 11,000 poolrooms, up
more than 3,000 from 1960. Estimates of the peak number of
poolrooms in the 1920's vary between 40,000 and 45,000, with
42,000 the most frequently used figure. Estimates of the peak
number of poolrooms in New York City in the 1920's range
from 4,000 to 5,000; according to reporter Robert Deasy
(*World Telegram & Sun,* June 24, 1963), in 1961 New York
City had only 257 licensed poolrooms with a total of 2,177 tables
and in 1962 (after the revival had begun) had 291 poolrooms
with 2,504 tables. According to Dixie Dean Harris (*Pageant,*
August, 1964, p. 114), Detroit had a thousand poolrooms in
the 1920's but only 156 poolrooms in 1964. Robert Coughlan
(*op. cit.,* p. 166) estimates that the number of pool and billiard
tables in use had declined from over 500,000 in the 1920's to
only one-fifth that number in 1951. Although these and other
published statistics permit of no exact agreement, the enormous
magnitude of the decline from the 1920's is clear enough in all
of them.

[45] Cf. Maurice Daly, *Daly's Billiard Book,* 6th ed. (Chicago:
A. C. McClurg & Co., 1923), p. [viii].

[46] Awareness of this role of the frontier runs through much
of early American literature; cf. Leslie Fiedler, *Love and
Death in the American Novel* (New York: Criterion Books,
1960), *passim.*

ing to men who wanted to be able to curse and spit tobacco, fight freely, dress sloppily, gamble heavily, get roar-
ing drunk, whore around.

Nor is it accidental that Mark Twain, the American author we most associate with chafing at his entrapment in
the respectability of urban civilization and with nostalgic
longing for woman-free frontier days, should of all American authors be the one most truly to fall in love with billiard playing and poolroom life.[47] Nor is it accidental
that the poolroom and the heterosexual bachelor disappear
simultaneously from the American landscape (which is
why not the Depression, but the easing of the Depression
was the real death-knell of the poolroom). Nor is it accidental that the most regular and devoted of today's poolroom spectators, the old men who come day after day and
use the poolroom as a poor man's club, consist overwhelmingly of old-style bachelors and once-bitten-twice-shy
widowers. Nor, finally, is it accidental that the most regular and devoted of today's poolroom players, the pool and
billiard hustlers who virtually live in the poolroom and
build their very careers around poolroom life, comprise
one of the last American occupational groups in which
the majority of adults are non-homosexual bachelors.

VIII

As Friedrich Nietzsche first observed, an institution when
deprived of its major function does not *eo ipso* go out
of business, but often survives and prospers by taking on

[47] Cf. William Dean Howells, "My Memories of Mark
Twain," *Harper's Monthly Magazine*, Vol. 121 (July 1910),
pp. 170–71; Albert Bigelow Paine, *Mark Twain: A Biography*
(New York: Harper and Brothers, 1912), Vol. 2, pp. 613–14,
and Vol. 3, pp. 1324–32, 1366–70; Willie Hoppe, *Thirty Years
of Billiards* (New York: G. P. Putnam's, 1925), pp. 109–
114, 117. According to Hoppe, Twain attended every big billiard
match in New York for years. From Paine's account, especially
pp. 613–14, it appears that Twain used his own billiard playing
as a means of getting together with male cronies to the exclusion of his wife and daughter.

new functions.[48] Modern sociology, with its studies of the
changing role of the family, the church, the settlement
house, etc., has abundantly confirmed Nietzsche's insight.
Might not the poolroom in this way flourish once more—
by redefining itself as a place "for the family" and catering to women as well as men, as indeed most new-look
poolrooms are trying to do? In theory, yes; in practice, no.
An institution that tries to change its function sometimes
fails, and this appears to be the poolroom's fate. Of course,
poolrooms will not cease to exist, and their number may
even increase a bit over the next few years, but there are
several reasons why "cleaning up the game" and changing
its "image" so as to attract women will never restore to
poolrooms anything remotely like the degree of popularity
they once had.

Bringing women in—with the attendant paraphernalia of
free instruction for them, special women's tournaments,
the curbing of obscenity and other loutish male behavior
so that women will feel comfortable, etc.—has been tried
several times before.[49] Each time it has had a modicum
of initial success and then died. This is only to be expected.

Granted three notable exceptions—the billiard player
May Kaarlus around the turn of the century, the pool
player Ruth McGinnis in the 1930's, and the billiard player
Masako Katsura today—poolroom games pose near-
insuperable problems for women. First, male-female differences in the structure of the arm affect development of a
good stroke, making it very difficult for a woman to become good at these games relative to other games (just
as a woman can, if she is athletically adept, become a good
bowler or underhand softball pitcher but can never learn
to throw a ball overhand very well). Secondly, many shots
require leaning way over the table or even putting one leg
up on the table, involving a display of legs (if a skirt is

[48] Cf. Section XII of " 'Guilt,' 'Bad Conscience,' and the
Like," *Genealogy of Morals*.
[49] For example, see *Billiards Magazine* (June, 1932), pp.
6–9. See also "Swank Pool Hall Attracts Women of Spring-
field, Ill.," *Life*, Vol. 23 (November 17, 1947), pp. 71–72; the
poolroom described in this article later went out of business.

worn) or buttocks (if slacks are worn) that most women find quite embarrassing. Thirdly and most importantly, there are the kind of teenage boys and men who hang around poolrooms. No poolroom proprietor can completely curb their profanity, leering, attempts to pick up the women. Nor can he really get rid of them, for the simple reason that they represent the great bulk of his business.

That last point is crucial. For nearly all the women who play, it is a passing fad, something that lately *Mademoiselle* and *Vogue* and even *Saturday Evening Post* have told them is "in" but that is forgotten when the next new kick comes along. For the reasons just stated, women almost never stick with poolroom games; they soon tend to visit the poolroom infrequently or drop out completely, whereas the men are far more likely to be or become regular players.[50] And the new-style poolrooms hopeful of catering to women are quickly finding this out. Once the initial novelty has worn off, the proprietor finds that his trade consists

[50] Private (non-poolroom) playing by the upper class, which I have not tried to discuss in detail in this study, shows a different pattern of female participation. Although women were of course excluded from playing at men's clubs, the attitude toward their playing at home varied at different times and places; sometimes the home billiard room was an exclusively male preserve, but usually women were also allowed to play, and often did so. Thus Robert Kerr advised that the home billiard room should "be situated not exactly amongst the Dwelling-rooms, but still in close connection with them, for the access of the ladies" (Kerr, *op. cit.*, 3rd ed., p. 120). Women playing billiards at home are shown in many British and American engravings of the eighteenth and nineteenth centuries, e.g., in Rowlandson's "The Billiard Table" (1820) from his *Dr. Syntax* series. This tradition of upper-class female billiard playing has few exemplars today, the most notable being the Queen Mother of England.

On the other hand, since *The Hustler* America has witnessed a spectacular rise in playing at home by the upper-middle class (as evidenced by the continuing boom in sales of small-sized tables to homeowners). Thus, despite the shaky prospects of today's poolrooms, pool *playing* might yet become almost as popular as it once was—but as a home activity rather than a public one. New York's most experienced billiard table mechanic, Robert Cappelli, informs me that today over three-fourths of his installation jobs are for tables in suburban homes.

mostly of teenage boys, especially the school dropouts, and
secondarily the old-style "sporting" types among the adult
males. They play so much oftener and longer than women
or teenage girls that he can't afford to kick them out.

Many of the new poolrooms are doing good business,
notably those in postwar population centers that never had
poolrooms before. The revival has indeed found enough
of a market to support such places. But already the cream
has been skimmed off this market. Already a number of
poolrooms that opened with the fanciest of intentions now
must rely on clientele who are anything but fancy; for example, one suburban poolroom that two years ago received
acres of publicity about its "respectability" is now a center
of narcotics distribution. Already, in every section of the
country, the rate at which new poolrooms are opening is
going down. Already many of the snazzy new poolrooms
are in financial trouble, falling behind in their payments
to the equipment manufacturers. Already, as some fall so
far behind that their creditors will no longer carry them,
the bankruptcy rate is rising sharply. And that's with only
about a fourth as many poolrooms as America had when
its population was little over half what it is now. The hey-
day of the poolroom is over.

The
Hustler*

Such a man spends all his life playing every day for small
stakes. Give him every morning the money that he may
gain during the day, on condition that he does not play—
you will make him unhappy. It will perhaps be said that
what he seeks is the amusement of play, not gain. Let him
play then for nothing; he will lose interest and be wearied.

BLAISE PASCAL

They talk about me not being on the legitimate. Why, lady,
nobody's on the legit when it comes down to cases; you
know that.

AL CAPONE[1]

The poolroom hustler makes his living by betting against
his opponents in different types of pool or billiard games,
and as part of the playing and betting process he engages
in various deceitful practices. The terms "hustler" for such
a person and "hustling" for his occupation have been in
poolroom argot for decades, antedating their application
to prostitutes. Usually the hustler plays with his own
money, but often he makes use of a "backer." In the latter

---

* Approximately the first third of this chapter appeared, in
slightly different form, in *Social Problems*, Vol. 12, No. 1
(Summer, 1964), pp. 3–15.

[1] The Pascal quotation is from *Pensées*, V. Al Capone's remark is quoted in Paul Sann, *The Lawless Decade* (New York:
Crown Publishers, 1957), p. 214.

event the standard arrangement is that the backer, in return for assuming all risk of loss, receives half of the hustler's winnings.

The hustler's offense in the eyes of many is not that he
breaks misdemeanor laws against gambling (perhaps most
Americans have done so at one time or another), but that
he does so daily. Also—and again as a necessary and regular part of his daily work—he violates American norms concerning (a) what is morally correct behavior toward one's
fellow man and (b) what is a proper and fitting occupation. For one or another of these related reasons the hustler
is stigmatized by respectable outsiders. The most knowledgeable of such outsiders see the hustler not merely as
a gambler but as one who violates an ethic of fair dealing;
they regard him as a criminal or quasi-criminal not because he gambles but because he systematically "victimizes"
people. Somewhat less knowledgeable outsiders put down
the hustler simply because gambling is his trade. Still less
knowledgeable outsiders (perhaps the majority) regard hustlers as persons who, whatever they may actually do, certainly do not hold down visibly respectable jobs; therefore
this group also stigmatizes hustlers—"poolroom bums" is
the classic phrase—and believes that society would be better
off without them. Hustling, to the degree that it is known
to the larger society at all, is classed with that large group
of social problems composed of morally deviant occupations.

However, in what follows I try to present hustlers and
hustling on their own terms. The material below avoids
a "social problems" focus; to some extent, I deliberately
reverse that focus. Insofar as I treat of social problems,
they are not the problems posed by the hustler but for him;
not the difficulties he creates for others, but the difficulties
that others create for him as he pursues his career.

This approach "from within" has partly dictated the
organization of my materials. Some sections below are
built around conceptual categories derived less from sociologists than from hustlers, in the hope that this may
help the reader to see hustling more nearly as hustlers see
it. The disadvantage for the scientifically-minded reader

is that the underlying sociological framework may be obscured. Therefore I wish to point out that this framework is basically that of Everett Hughes's approach to occupational sociology.

I try mainly to answer three types of questions: (*a*) *The work situation.* How is the hustler's work structured? What skills are required of him? With whom does he interact on the job? What does he want from them, and how does he try to get it? How do they make it easy or hard for him? (*b*) *Careers.* Who becomes a hustler? How? What job risks or contingencies does the hustler face? When and how? What is the nature of colleagueship in hustling? What are the measures of success and failure in the career? In what ways does aging affect the hustler's job skills or ability to handle other career problems? What leads to retirement? (*c*) *The external world.* What is the place of the hustler's work situation and career in the larger society? What changes in the structure of that society affect his work situation or career?

Previous Research

A bibliographic check reveals no decent research on poolroom hustling, sociological or otherwise. Apart from an occasional work of fiction in which hustling figures, there are merely a few impressionistic accounts in newspapers and popular magazines. With a couple of exceptions, each article is based on interviews with only one or two hustlers. No article analyzes hustling on any but the most superficial level or provides a well-rounded description. The fullest survey of the subject not only omits much that is vital, but contains numerous errors of fact and interpretation.[2]

[2] Jack Olsen, "The Pool Hustlers," *Sports Illustrated,* Vol. 14 (March 20, 1961), pp. 71–77. Jack Richardson's "The Noblest Hustlers," [*Esquire,* Vol. IX (September, 1963), pp. 94, 96, 98] contains a few worthwhile observations, but it is sketchy, ill-balanced, and suffers much from editorial garbling, all of which makes it both confusing and misleading for the uninitiated. One article conveys quite well the lifestyle of a

The desirability of a study of hustling first struck me upon hearing comments by people who saw the movie *The Hustler* (late 1961, re-released spring 1964). Audience members who are not poolroom habitués regard the movie as an accurate portrait of the contemporary hustling "scene." The movie does indeed truly depict some social characteristics of pool and billiard hustlers and some basic techniques of hustling. But it neglects others of crucial importance. Moreover, the movie scarcely begins to take proper account of the social structure within which hustling techniques are used and which strongly affects their use. *The Hustler* is a reasonably good but highly selective reflection of the poolroom hustling scene as it existed not later than the mid-1930's. And as a guide to today's hustling scene—the terms on which it presents itself and on which the audience takes it—the movie is quite misleading.

Method and Sample

My study of poolroom hustling extended over eight months in 1962 and 1963. It proceeded by a combination of: (a) direct observation of hustlers as they hustled; (b) informal talks, sometimes hours long, with hustlers; (c) participant observation—as hustler's opponent, as hustler's backer, and as hustler. Since methods (b) and (c)

---

particular hustler: Dale Shaw, "Anatomy of a Pool Hustler," *Saga: The Magazine for Men*, Vol. 23 (November, 1961), pp. 52–55, 91–93. Useful historical data are in Edward John Vogeler's "The Passing of the Pool Shark," *American Mercury*, Vol. 8 (November, 1939), pp. 346–51. For hustling as viewed within the context of the history of pool in America, see Robert Coughlan's "Pool: Its Players and Its Sharks," *Life*, Vol. 31 (October 8, 1951), pp. 159 ff.; although Coughlan's account of the game's history contains errors and his specific consideration of hustling is brief (p. 166), the latter is accurate.

Among novels that deal with hustling, Walter Tevis's *The Hustler* (New York: Harper, 1959) has the most external documentary detail; but Don Carpenter's *Hard Rain Falling* (New York: Harcourt, Brace & World, 1963) is much superior in its exploration of a hustler's character, as well as more satisfying stylistically.

drew heavily on my personal involvement with the poolroom world, indeed are inseparable from it, I summarize
aspects of that involvement below.

Billiard playing is my chief recreation. I have frequented
poolrooms for over 20 years, and at one poolroom game,
three-cushion billiards, am considered a far better than
average player. In recent years I have played an average
of more than six hours per week in various New York
poolrooms, and played as much in the poolrooms of Chicago for most of the eight years I lived there. In the course
of traveling I have played occasionally in the major rooms
of other cities, such as the poolrooms on Market Street in
San Francisco, West 25th Street in Cleveland, West Lex-
ington in Baltimore, and the room on 4th and Main in
Los Angeles.

My social background is different from that of the
overwhelming majority of adult poolroom players. The
latter are of lower-class origin. As with many American
sports (e.g., baseball), pool and billiards are played by
teenagers from all classes but only the players of lower-
class background tend to continue far into adulthood. (And
as far as poolroom games are concerned, even at the teenage level the lower class contributes a disproportionately
large share of players.) But such differences—the fact that
I went to college, do highbrow work, etc.—create no problems of acceptance. In most good-sized poolrooms the
adult regulars usually include a few people like myself
who are in the poolroom world but not of it. They are
there because they like to play, and are readily accepted
because they like to play.

The poolroom I play in most regularly is the principal
"action room" in New York and perhaps in the country,
the room in which heavy betting on games occurs most
often; sometimes, particularly after 1:00 A.M., the hustlers
in the room well outnumber the non-hustlers. Frequently
I play hustlers for money (nearly always on a handicap
basis) and occasionally I hustle some non-hustlers, undertaking the latter activity primarily to recoup losses on the
former. I have been a backer for two hustlers.

I know six hustlers well, and during the eight months

of the study I talked or played with over 50 more. All are
now usually based in New York, except for two in Chicago,
two in Cleveland, one in Philadelphia, one itinerant hustler whose home base is Boston and another whose home
base is in North Carolina. However, the hustlers based in
New York are of diverse regional origins; almost a third
grew up and started their hustling careers in other states.

It is not possible to demonstrate the representativeness
of this sample because the universe (all U.S. pool and
billiard hustlers) is not known exactly. But the hustlers I
asked about the number of real hustlers in America, i.e.,
the number of people whose exclusive or primary occupation is hustling, generally agree that today the number
is quite small. In response to my queries about the total
number of poolroom hustlers, one hustler said "thousands"
and another said "there must be a thousand," but the next
highest estimate was "maybe 400" and somewhat lesser
estimates were made by nineteen hustlers. Moreover, the
three hustlers making the highest estimates have rarely
been out of New York, whereas over half the others either
come from other parts of the country or have made several
road trips. It seems safe to assume that the sample is at
least representative of big-city hustlers. Also, it is probable
that it includes the majority of part-time hustlers in New
York, and certain that it includes a good majority of the
full-time hustlers in New York.

Poolroom Betting: The Structure of "Action"

Hustling involves betting against one's opponent, by definition. But the converse is not true. The majority of poolroom contests on which opponents bet do not involve any
element of hustling. In order to understand how hustling
enters the picture, one must first establish a perspective
that encompasses all betting on poolroom games, hustled
or not.

In pool or billiard games, the betting relationship has
three possible modes: (1) player bets against player; (2)
player against spectator; (3) spectator against spectator.

In most contests only the first mode occurs, but combinations of the first and second are frequent, and slightly less so are combinations of the first and third. Combinations of all three are uncommon, but do occur when there is more "ready action" offered to the players by the spectators than the players can or wish to absorb. I have never seen the second mode occur alone, nor a combination of second and third. I have seen the third mode occur alone only twice—at professional tournaments. The betting relationship, then, involves the mode player-vs.-player, whatever additional modes there may be.

If two mediocre players are betting, say, upward of $15 per game, and at another table two excellent players are playing for only a token amount, the first table will invariably draw many more people around it. The great majority of spectators, whether or not they bet much and whatever their own degree of playing skill, are attracted more by the size of the action than the quality of the performance. (A visiting Danish billiardist tells me this is not so in Europe, and also that betting on poolroom games is far less frequent there than in America.)

There is an old American poolroom tradition that players should make some kind of bet with each other, if only a small one. This tradition remains strong in every public poolroom I know. (It is weak in the pool or billiard rooms of private men's clubs and YMCAs, weaker still in student unions, and virtually nonexistent in faculty clubs.) When one player says to another, "Let's just play sociable," as often as not he means that they should play for only a dollar or two, and at the very least means that they should play "for the time" (the loser paying the check). It is only some of the newer and least skilled players who refuse to bet at all (who want to "split the time"), and nearly always they rapidly become socialized to the betting tradition by a carrot-and-stick process—the stick being that it is often hard to get a game otherwise, the carrot that better players are always willing to give poorer ones a handicap (a "spot"). Most of the regular players will not even play for the check only, but insist on a little money changing hands "just to make the game interesting."[3] The player who claims that just playing the game is interesting enough in itself is regarded as something of a freak.

Few serious bettors, hustlers excepted, care for big action; but nearly all, including hustlers, want fast action. Although they may not want to bet much per game, they want the cash to change hands fairly quickly. Consequently, in an action room the standard games are redesigned for this purpose. Some are simply shortened: players gambling at snooker will remove all the red balls but one; or three-cushion billiard players will play games of 15, 20, or 25 points instead of the usual 30, 40, or 50. In straight pool (pocket billiards), where the standard game is 125 or 150 points, good players are usually reluctant to play a much shorter game because scoring is so easy—any really good player can occasionally run more than 50 balls—that shortening the game makes it too much a matter of chance. Therefore, in an action room one finds most of the pool players playing some variant of the game that not only requires high skill but also minimizes chance, and that therefore can be short (taking only 5 to 20 minutes per game). Today the chief of these variants are "nine ball" and "one pocket" (also called "pocket apiece"), although there are several others, such as "eight ball," "bank pool," and "rotation."

Every poolroom has at least one "No Gambling" sign on display, but no poolroom enforces it. The sign is merely a formal gesture for the eyes of the law (and in some cities required by law). It is enforced only in that the proprietor sometimes may ask players to keep payoffs out of sight—not to toss the money on the table after the game—if the room is currently "heaty," e.g., if an arrest has recently been made there. Police are hardly ever concerned to stop the gambling on poolroom games, and everyone knows it. (But police sometimes check to see that the minimum age law is observed, so proprietors will often ask youths for identification.) Betting is so taken for granted that in

---

[3] This attitude has of course existed among some regular players elsewhere. For example, see chapter 1 of Alexander Pushkin's novella *The Captain's Daughter* (1836).

most poolrooms the proprietor—the very man who displays a "No Gambling" sign over his desk—will on request hold the players' stake money.

However, in no poolroom does the house take a cut of the action; the proprietor gets no fee for permitting gambling or holding stake money, and wouldn't dream of asking for one. His payment from bettors is simply that they comprise most of his custom in equipment rental. And hustlers, as he and they well know, count in this regard far beyond their numbers, for they play much oftener and longer than other customers; indeed, they virtually live in the poolroom.

The only non-bettor whose payment is somewhat related to the size of the action is the rack boy (if one is used), the person who racks up the balls for the players after each frame. The bigger the action, the larger the tip he can expect, and if one player comes out very much ahead he tips the rack boy lavishly. The rack boy's position is thus analogous to that of the golf caddie, except that a rack boy is used in only about half of hustler-vs.-hustler contests and in but a tiny fraction of other contests. Sometimes he is an employee (sweeper, etc.) of the poolroom, but more often he is a spectator performing as rack boy on an *ad hoc* basis.

Non-hustled Poolroom Gambling

Hustling is *not* involved when the games played for money are any of the following:

(a) *Non-hustler vs. non-hustler.* A "sociable" game in which the bet is a token one. The only betting is player vs. player.

(b) *Non-hustler vs. non-hustler.* A game for significantly more than a token amount. The players play even-up if they are fairly equal. If they are aware of a significant difference in skill levels, the weaker player is given an appropriate handicap. Usually the betting is just between players; rarely, one or both players will bet spectators; spectators do not bet each other.

(c) *Hustler vs. non-hustler.* The players are aware of
the difference in skills, and this is properly taken into account via an appropriate spot. Usually the betting is only
player vs. player, though sometimes spectators bet players
or each other. The hustler tries to avoid this type of game,
and agrees to it only when he has nothing better to do.

(d) *Hustler vs. hustler.* Each player knows the other's
mettle, if only by reputation ("Minnesota Fats" vs. "Fast
Eddy" in *The Hustler,* for example). The hustler, contrary to the impression given by the movie, does *not* prefer
this type of game (though he does prefer it to the foregoing
type) and does *not* regard it as hustling. But he plays it
often because he often can't get the kind of game he wants
(a true "hustle") and this alternative does offer him excitement—not only the greatest challenge to his playing
skill, but the most action. The average bet between two
hustlers is much higher than in any other type of poolroom
contest.[4] And betting modes 2 and 3 (player vs. spectator,
spectator vs. spectator) occur much more often.

Be that as it may, the hustler much prefers to hustle,
which means to be in a game set up so as to be pretty
much a sure thing for him, a game that "you're not allowed to lose" as the hustler puts it. In order to achieve
this, to truly hustle, he engages in deception. The centrality
of deception in pool or billiard hustling is perhaps best indicated by the fact that the poolroom hustler's argot origi-
nated that widespread American slang dictum, "never give
a sucker an even break."[5]

[4] When two high-rolling hustlers agree to play each other
there is often a real race among poorer spectators to offer
rack-boy services because, as previously noted, if one is engaged for such a session he can expect a good tip. I witnessed
one six-hour session between hustlers in which the winning
hustler came out $800 ahead and tipped the rack boy $50.

[5] Its pool-hustler origin is noted by Vogeler, *op. cit.,* p. 347.
It is recorded in none of the slang sourcebooks (Mencken,
Mathews, Berrey and Van den Bark, *et al.*) except Harold
Wentworth and Stuart Berg Flexner, *Dictionary of American
Slang* (New York: T. Y. Crowell, 1960), p. 527. Wentworth
and Flexner do not attempt to account for the phrase's origin.
They claim that it dates to around 1835, but this seems impos-

The Hustler's Methods of Deception

The structure of a gambling game determines what methods of deception, if any, may be used in it. In many games (dice, cards, etc.) one can deceive one's opponent by various techniques of cheating. Pool and billiard games are so structured that this method is virtually impossible. (Once in a great while, against a particularly unalert opponent, one can surreptitiously add a point or two to one's score—but such opportunity is rare, usually involves risk of discovery that is judged to be too great, and seldom means the difference between winning and losing anyway; so no player counts on it.) One's every move and play is completely visible, easily watched by one's opponent and by spectators; nor is it possible to achieve anything via previous tampering with the equipment.

However, one structural feature of pool or billiards readily lends itself to deceit: on each shot, the difference between success and failure is a matter of a small fraction of an inch. In pool or billiards it is peculiarly easy, even for the average player, to miss one's shot deliberately and still look good (unlike, say, nearly all card games, where if one does not play one's cards correctly this is soon apparent). On all shots except the easiest ones, it is impossible to tell if a player is deliberately not trying his best.

sibly early. The only source they cite is its use as the title of a 1941 W. C. Fields movie.

Actually, Fields used the phrase earlier in his *Poppy* (1936), where it is his exit line and the last line of the movie. Fields's partiality to "never give a sucker an even break" is thoroughly in keeping with Vogeler's account of the origin of the phrase: Fields was the son of a Philadelphia poolroom owner, spent much of his boyhood in his father's poolroom, was an excellent player, and built his funniest vaudeville act around his pool-playing skill (at the act's climax he sank fifteen balls with one shot). Cf. Douglas Gilbert, *American Vaudeville* (New York: Whittlesey House, 1940), pp. 273–74.

Another of Fields's pool-playing vaudeville skits became the core of his first movie, a one-reeler of 1915 entitled *Pool Sharks.* Cf. Donald Deschner, *The Films of W. C. Fields* (New York: Citadel, 1966), p. 35.

The hustler exploits this fact so as to deceive his opponent as to his (the hustler's) true level of skill (true "speed"). It is so easily exploited that, when playing good opponents, usually the better hustlers even disdain it, pocket nearly every shot they have (intentionally miss only some very difficult shots), and rely chiefly on related but subtler techniques of failure beyond the remotest suspicion of most players. For example, such a hustler may strike his cue ball hard and with too much spin ("english"), so that the spin is transferred to the object ball and the object ball goes into the pocket but jumps out again; or he may scratch (losing a point and his turn), either by "accidentally" caroming his cue ball into a pocket or by hitting his cue ball hard and with too much top-spin so that it jumps off the table; or, most commonly, he pockets his shot but, by striking his cue ball just a wee bit too hard or too softly or with too much or too little english, he leaves himself "safe" (ends up with his cue ball out of position, so that he hasn't another shot). In such wise the hustler feigns less competence than he has.

Hustling, then, involves not merely the ability to play well, but the use of a kind of "short con." Sometimes the hustler doesn't need to employ any con to get his opponent to the table, sometimes he does; but he always employs it in attempting to keep his opponent there.

The best hustler is not necessarily the best player among the hustlers. He has to be a very good player, true, but beyond a certain point his playing ability is not nearly so important as his skill at various kinds of conning. Also, he has to possess personality traits that make him "rocklike," able to exploit fully his various skills—playing, conning, others—in the face of assorted pressures and temptations not to exploit them fully.

The Hustler's Cardinal Rule

As the foregoing indicates, the hustler's cardinal rule is: *don't show your real speed.* Of course, an exception is permitted if by some miracle the hustler finds himself hustled, finds himself in a game with someone he thought would be easy but who turns out to be tough. But this is not supposed to happen, and it rarely does. For one thing, hustlers generally know each other, or of each other, and their respective skill levels. Secondly, any pool or billiard game is overwhelmingly a game of skill rather than luck—even in the chanciest type of poolroom game the element of skill counts for much more than in any card game whatsoever—and this means it is possible to rate the skill levels of various players (to "handicap" them) along small gradations with a high degree of accuracy. For example, if one has seen the three-cushion billiard players X and Y play various people over a period of time, it is possible to arrive at the judgment "On a 30-point game, X is two or three points better than Y" and to be dead right about it in at least eight out of ten contests between them.

The corollaries of the hustler's chief rule are: (a) The hustler must restrain himself from making many of the extremely difficult shots. Such restraint is not easy, because the thrill of making a fancy shot that brings applause from the audience is hard to resist. But the hustler must resist, or else it would make less believable his misses on more ordinary shots. (b) He must play so that the games he wins are won by only a small margin. (c) He must let his opponent win an occasional game.

It may be thought that once a hustler has engaged an opponent, a bet has been agreed upon and the stake money put up, and the game has started, the hustler might safely let out all the stops. This would be terribly short-sighted.

In the first place, as noted earlier, the typical non-hustler bets only a small amount on the game. The hustler's only hope of making real money, therefore, is to extend the first game into a series of games, entice his opponent into doubling up when he is behind, etc. If the hustler does this well, the opponent will hang on for a long time, may even come back after the first session to play him on another day, turn into a real "fish" (the poolroom term for an inferior opponent who doesn't catch on that he's outclassed, and keeps coming back for more). And when the opponent starts demanding a spot, as sooner or later he will, the hustler can offer him his (the hustler's) average winning margin, or even a little better, and still have a safe game.

Secondly, there are spectators to take into account. Some of them will bet the hustler if he offers the non-hustler a seemingly fair spot. More importantly, some of them are potential opponents. Nearly all poolroom spectators are also players. The hustler doesn't want to look too good to spectators either.

He knows that as he beats various opponents his reputation will rise, and that increasingly he'll have to offer spots to people, but he wants to keep his reputation as low as possible as long as possible with as many people as possible. He also knows that he has to play superbly on occasion—that he will play fellow hustlers when there's no other action around, and that then he must show more skill—but he wants to keep these occasions few. (It helps considerably, by the way, that because hustler-vs.-hustler games occur when hustlers give up hope of finding other action, these games usually take place after midnight when there aren't so many non-hustler potential victims around to watch.)

The sooner everyone in the poolroom knows the hustler's true speed, the sooner he exhausts the real hustling possibilities among the room's regular players. Such a situation constitutes one of the career crises that every hustler has to face. (For reasons which will become apparent below, he now has to face it earlier in his career than hustlers formerly did.) When it occurs, either he must move on to a poolroom where he's less known or, if he stays in the room, he has to take games he shouldn't take or else restrict his pickings to strangers who wander in.

Job-Related Skills and Traits

Although the hallmarks of the good hustler are playing skill and the temperamental ability to consistently look poorer than he is, there are other skills and traits that aid him in hustling. Some are related to deceiving his opponent, some not.

Chief of these is argumentative skill in arranging the terms of the match, the ability to "make a game." The prospective opponent, if he has seen the hustler play, may when approached claim that the hustler is too good for him or ask for too high a spot, i.e., one that is fair or even better. The hustler, like the salesman, is supposed to be familiar with standard objections and with "propositions" for overcoming them.

Another side of the ability to make a game reveals itself when the prospective opponent simply can't be argued out of demanding a spot that is unfair to the hustler, or can be convinced to play only if the hustler offers such a spot. At that point the hustler should of course refuse to play. There is often a temptation to do otherwise, not only because the hustler is proud of his skill but because action is his lifeblood (which is why he plays other hustlers when he can't find a hustle), and there may be no other action around. He must resist the temptation. In the good hustler's view, no matter how badly you want action, it is better not to play at all than to play when you are disadvantaged; otherwise you are just hustling yourself. (But the hustler often will, albeit with much argument and the greatest reluctance, agree to give a fair spot if that's the only way he can get action.)

The hustler, when faced, as he very often is, with an opponent who knows him as such, of course finds that his ability to make a game assumes greater importance than his ability to feign lack of skill. In such situations, indeed, his game-making ability is just as important as his actual playing ability.

On the other hand, the hustler must have "heart" (courage). The *sine qua non* is that he is a good "money player," can play his best when heavy action is riding on the game (as many non-hustlers can't). Also, he is not supposed to let a bad break or distractions in the audience upset him. (He may pretend to get rattled on such occasions, but that's just part of his con.) Nor should the quality of his game deteriorate when, whether by miscalculation on his part or otherwise, he finds himself much further behind than he would like to be. Finally, if it is necessary to get action, he should not be afraid to tackle an opponent whom he knows to be just about as good as he is.

A trait often working for the hustler is stamina. As a result of thousands of hours of play, all the right muscles are toughened up. He is used to playing many hours at a time, certainly much more used to it than the non-hustler is. This is valuable because sometimes, if the hustler works it right, he can make his opponent forget about quitting for such a "silly" reason as being tired, can extend their session through the night and into the next day. In such sessions it is most often in the last couple of hours, when the betting per game is usually highest, that the hustler makes his biggest killing.

Additional short-con techniques are sometimes used. One hustler, for example, entices opponents by the ancient device of pretending to be sloppy-drunk. Other techniques show more imagination. For example, a hustler preparing for a road trip mentioned to me that before leaving town he was going to buy a soldier's uniform: "I walk into a strange room in uniform and I've got it made. Everybody likes to grab a soldier."

One of the most noted hustlers of recent years, Luther "Wimpy" Lassiter, reports that in his own forays he has sometimes worn a wedding band and flashed a wallet (because the typical hustler is unmarried and, like dedicated gamblers generally and lower-class gamblers especially, carries his money loose in his pocket).

Finally, the hustler—the superior hustler at any rate—has enough flexibility and good sense to break the "rules" when the occasion demands it, will modify standard techniques when he encounters non-standard situations. An example: Once I entered a poolroom just as a hustler I know, X, was finishing a game with non-hustler Y. X beat Y soundly, by a higher margin than a hustler should beat anyone, and at that for only $3. Y went to the bathroom, whereupon I admonished X, "What's the matter with you? You know you're not allowed to win that big." X replied:

Yeah, sure, but you see that motherfucking S over there?

[nodding discreetly in the direction of one of the spectators]. Well, about an hour ago when I came in he and Y were talking, and when S saw me he whispered something to Y. So I had a hunch he was giving him the wire [tipping him off] that I was pretty good. And then in his middle game it looked like Y was stalling a little [missing deliberately] to see what I would do, so then I was sure he got the wire on me. I had to beat him big so he'll think he knows my top speed. But naturally I didn't beat him as big as I *could* beat him. Now he'll come back cryin' for a spot and bigger action, and I'll nail him.

And he did nail him.[6]

The Art of Dumping

As we saw, the structure of a pool or billiard game makes it virtually impossible for the hustler to cheat his opponent. By "stalling" (deliberately missing some shots, leaving himself out of position, etc.) and by "lemoning" or "lemonading" an occasional game in the session (winning in a deliberately sloppy and seemingly lucky manner, or deliberately losing the game), the hustler keeps his opponent on the hook and entices him into heavier action, but such deception falls short of outright cheating. However, in examining betting we saw that there is considerable variation in the interpersonal superstructure of the game, i.e., that there are several types of betting relationships between and among players and spectators. One of these varieties does lead to outright cheating by the hustler—not cheating his opponent, but cheating some spectators.

When two hustlers play each other, not only is the bet-

[6] This sort of situation is unusual. One part of the poolroom code, adhered to by nearly all regular players, holds that a player is supposed to watch out for himself in the matches he gets into, find out for himself whom he can and cannot beat. Ordinarily one does not warn a player about who is superior or who the hustlers are, unless one is a close friend of that player. (And even if one is a friend, the code demands that such a warning be given only before any match is in prospect; that is, once a player has started to "make a game" with another, third parties are supposed to stay out.)

ting between players relatively heavy, but the betting of
spectators against players is also, typically, at its height.
Therefore, two hustlers sometimes will agree before their
session that if, on any game, there is a good disparity between the amounts of action that each gets from spectators,
the player with the most to gain from side bets with spectators will win the game and the players will later share
the profits. The amount that spectators bet each other is of
course irrelevant to such calculations, and in such circumstances the amount that the players bet each other automatically becomes a phony bet, strictly for deluding the
spectators.

For example, one such game I know of went as follows:
Hustler A played hustler B for $70. A's side bets with
spectators totaled $100 and B's side bets with spectators
totaled $380. Therefore A deliberately lost to B, paying
him $70 and paying $100 to spectators, with B collecting
$70 from A and $380 from spectators. Later, in private,
B gave A $310 (the $70 that A had "lost" to B, the $100
that A had paid to the audience, plus $140 or one-half
the overall amount won from the audience). Each player
thus made $140 on the deal.

Sometimes the hustlers will set up the audience for such
disparity in side betting, via previous games in the session.
An example: Hustler X played hustler Y for $20 per game.
By pre-arrangement, both players refused to make side
bets with spectators on the first three games and player Y
deliberately lost the first three games. At the end of the
third game Y became enraged, claiming that bad breaks
had beat him, that X was just lucky, etc.; he raised his
bet with X to $50 and also offered to bet spectators. Natu-
rally, he got lots of action from spectators—and just as naturally he won the fourth game.

More commonly, however, such setting up does not occur. Rather, the hustlers will agree before their session that
they will play each other in earnest and the bets between
them will be real, but that if there is a disparity in side
betting with spectators on a given game and one player
gives the other a prearranged signal (gives him "the of-

fice," as the hustler's argot has it), the player with the most side action will win.

In the hustler's argot, the above type of deliberate losing is called "dumping." It is always distinguished from "lemoning" (where deliberate losing is strictly a means of conning one's opponent). Though all hustlers use the verb "to dump" in referring to a game that the hustler deliberately loses for the purpose of cheating spectators, hustlers vary in the object they attach to the verb. Some hustlers would say that the hustler who lost "dumped the game," others that he "dumped to" his opponent, and others that he (or both players in collaboration) "dumped the bettors." Some hustlers on occasion prefer a nominal use: "the game was a dump."

Because dumping involves outright cheating and could lead to serious, in fact violent, reprisals if discovered, it is the aspect of hustling that hustlers are most evasive about. No hustler likes to own up to dumping, even in talk with other hustlers. One learns about dumping indirectly, via hustlers' comments on other hustlers, and only rarely via a hustler's direct admission that he has engaged in it. It is my impression that such reticence is always pragmatic rather than moral, i.e., that no hustler has strong compunctions about dumping and that every long-time hustler has dumped at least on occasion.

Although dumping is a possibility whenever two hustlers playing each other make unequal amounts of side bets with spectators, it actually occurs in only a minority of such situations.[7] For dumping is risky even when it is not literally discovered; sometimes the spectators' suspicions are aroused even though nothing can be proven, and hustlers can't afford to have this happen often, because it would kill their chances of side betting.

In this regard there are two kinds of spectator-bettors that the hustler distinguishes and takes account of: First, there are the ignorant majority of spectators who don't know about dumping; the hustler doesn't want talk, much

[7] Under certain special circumstances, dumping can also occur when there are no bets with spectators or such bets are approximately equal on both sides; see below.

less actual knowledge, of dumping to reach their ears. Second—and equally important to the hustler because, though they are in the minority, they bet more—there are some knowledgeable spectators (including other hustlers) who know about dumping but *also* know that it occurs in only a minority of hustler-vs.-hustler contests and therefore will often risk a bet. That is to say, just as some horse players assume that at certain tracks there probably will be one race per day that is fixed (one race "for the boys") and are willing to discount this because it's only one race out of nine or ten, similarly there are poolroom spectators who will bet on one hustler against another because they know that dumping occurs but seldom. (Among the knowledgeable spectators there are also, of course, some cautious types who refuse to make such bets because of a possible dump, even though they know the odds are against it.)

In sum, the fact that spectators will bet players in hustler-vs.-hustler games not only permits dumping but at the same time restrains its extent. Hustlers must severely limit their dumping, both to prevent it becoming known to the ignorant and, just as importantly, to prevent knowledgeable spectators from feeling that hustlers *generally* dump when they play each other. No hustler wants to get a reputation as a dumper; therefore he cautiously picks his spots. As a result, dumping provides only a small portion of his true hustling income, i.e., his "sure-thing" income. The great bulk of such income derives from his games with non-hustler opponents.

The Hustler and His Backer

The hustler frequently uses a backer, who pays the losses if the hustler loses and receives 50 per cent of any winnings. A backer hardly ever assumes any managerial function. All he does is put up the hustler's stake money in return for a half share in the profits.

Once in a very great while, a hustler will work out a standing agreement for backing, that is, have someone agree to back him regularly. There is no time limit specified for such an arrangement; the deal lasts only as long as both parties consent to it.

But almost always the hustler has no standing agreement with a backer. Rather, he looks for backing on an *ad hoc* basis as the occasion for backing arises. The "occasion" is not that the hustler decides, in the abstract, to play on someone else's risk capital; it is a specific match with a particular opponent, whose handicap terms (if any) the hustler has already arranged or knows he can get. Indeed, even a topnotch hustler rarely can get backing without being able to tell the backer who the prospective opponent is and what the terms of the game are; the hustler has to convince the backer that the particular deal is a good one.

After tentatively arranging a game with his opponent, the hustler asks one of his acquaintances in the room to back him, and if he can't find backing in the room he phones a potential backer to hurry on down with some cash. Sometimes the hustler enters the poolroom with his backer in tow.

The backer specifies the maximum amount per game that he is willing to invest, but makes no guarantee about a total investment. That is, if the hustler starts to lose, the backer can pull out after any game. And if the hustler starts winning, he cannot then bet only his "own" money and dispense with the backer; the backer is in for 50 per cent of the profit made on the entire session.

Under what conditions does the hustler seek a backer? The obvious answer is that when the hustler is broke or nearly broke (as he very often is), he looks for backing, and when he has his own money to invest he plays with that. This is indeed how the average hustler operates. The superior hustler, however, figures more angles. As one of the most intelligent hustlers explained to me:

> If you've got lockup action [a game impossible to lose] and you're broke or maybe you need a bigger stake, you should first try like hell to *borrow* the dough. It's crazy to cut somebody in on action like that unless you have to. The other big thing—what some of these jerks don't understand —is that when you have a real tough game you should

always look for a backer, even if you've got the dough.
You should take out insurance.

The backer, then, should not assume he is being approached for backing because the hustler can raise stake
money no other way (though this is usually the case), but
has to consider the possibility that it's because the hustler
has a very difficult game he wants to "insure."

Also, the backer must consider the possibility that he
may be dumped by the hustler: If the hustler is playing a
colleague, they may have agreed that one of them will win
the good majority of games and that they will later split the
profits. (When both hustlers making such an agreement
are using backers, the decision as to which hustler will lose
is more or less arbitrary. If one hustler is using a backer
and the other is not, it is of course the former who agrees
to lose.) Or, if the hustler is playing a non-hustler with
whom no such collusion is possible, he may deliberately
lose on the backer's money until the backer quits, and
then, after the backer has left the room or on some other
occasion, the hustler, playing with his own money, will
slaughter the opponent he has set up on the backer's money.

All in all, it takes as much sophistication to be a good
backer as to be a good hustler.

The Hustler as Con Man

As several parts of this study illustrate in detail, hustling
demands a continuous and complicated concern with how
one is seen by others. Attention to this matter is an in-
eluctably pervasive requirement of the hustler's trade, and
is beset with risks and contradictions. The hustler has not
only the concerns that one ordinarily has about being es-
teemed for one's skills, but develops, in addition to and
partly in conflict with such concerns, a complex set of
special needs or desires about how others should evaluate
him, reactions to their evaluations, and behaviors designed
to manipulate such evaluating.

The hustler is a certain kind of con man. And conning,
by definition, involves extraordinary manipulation of other

people's impressions of reality and especially of one's self, creating "false impressions."[8] If one compares the hustler with the more usual sorts of con men described by David Maurer in *The Big Con,* part of the hustler's specialness is seen to lie in this: the structural contexts within which he operates—the game, the setting of the game within the pool-room, the setting of the poolroom within the larger social structure—are not only more predetermined but more constraining. Structures do not "work for" the poolroom hustler to anywhere near the extent that they often do for other con men, and hence he must involve himself in more personal ways with active, continuous conning.

The point is not simply that the hustler can't find an ideal structural context, but that much less than the ordinary con man is he able to bend a structure toward the ideal or create one *ab ovo* (come up with an analogue of the con man's "store"). That is, the hustler is far less able to be a "producer" or "director" of ideal social "scenes." To a much greater extent he must work in poor settings, and to a correspondingly greater extent he must depend on being a continuously self-aware "actor."[9] (In this connection,

[8] Of course, conning is only a matter of degree, in that all of us are concerned in many ways to manipulate others' impressions of us, and so one can, if one wishes, take the view that every man is at bottom a con man. This form of "disenchantment of the world" is central to Herman Melville's *The Confidence-Man* (one of the bitterest novels in all of American literature) and to the sociological writings of Erving Goffman. Its principal corollary is the view expressed by hustlers, by other career criminals, and by Thorstein Veblen, that all businessmen are thieves.

[9] The kinds of structural problems faced today by the pool or billiard hustler are by no means all endemic; some are the result of recent social change (see pp. 67–70 below). On the other hand, such change has not created structural problems for all types of hustling. Today the golf hustler, for example, finds that with precious little "acting" he can (a) get heavy action from non-hustlers, (b) lose the majority of the eighteen holes and still clean up, and at the same time (c) not be suspected as a hustler. The structure of the game of golf itself, the peculiar structurally predetermined variations in the betting relationship as one makes the round of the course ("presses," etc.), and the present setting of the game within the larger so-

note the ease with which many passages of this essay could be restated in dramaturgical or Goffmaniacal terms.)

There is another significant respect in which the hustler's conning differs structurally from the work of ordinary con men. The latter's work, according to Maurer, falls into one or the other of two structurally distinct types of con games: the short con, in which the mark is played for the money he happens to be carrying, or else the big con, in which an essential feature is that the mark is "put on the send" to withdraw much larger sums from his bank. (Some con men also on occasion "throw the send into" a short-con game, but this is unusual.) There is no analogous distinction made by pool hustlers in theory or practice. Virtually every hustle is in Maurer's sense a short con, i.e., the sucker is simply taken for the cash he has on him at the time, or as much of it as he will allow himself to lose.

There are two situations in which the hustler's conning involves his victim going on the send, but they are accidental and rare; the hustler doesn't expect them, though he is of course pleased when one or the other of them happens: (a) As we have noted, the ideal kind of sucker is the "fish" who doesn't realize he can never win and makes himself available on other days for return matches, much like the sort of mark whom con men call an "addict." In order to reinforce any propensity his victim might have for being or becoming a fish, the hustler tries to win the last game of a match by only a small margin even though he *knows* it is the last game, i.e., knows that after he beats the sucker the latter will quit because he is cleaned out or unwilling to risk the small amount he may have left. On very rare occasion, to the hustler's surprise and delight, when the sucker is thus cleaned out he may not end the match but instead become a sort of instant fish (my term, not used by hustlers): he may have the hustler wait while he (the sucker) runs out to get more cash and comes back with same. (b) As a result of having watched the hustler stall with some other opponent (or in solitary practice), the sucker may decide that before he challenges the hustler, or

_____

ciety—all these combine to create a situation that is tailor-made for hustling. But that is another story.

accepts the hustler's challenge, he should go get more of a bankroll so he can make bigger bets.

Although in both of the above situations the victim goes on the send as a result of the hustler's actions, such actions are not, strictly speaking, calculated to achieve that result. The sucker essentially puts himself on the send.

The hustler, in any case, needs to be continually concerned about evaluation of him by other persons. But the nature and degree of his concern vary with the particular kind of "others" that these persons represent. The victim or prospective victim, the hustler's orientation toward whom we have discussed at several points, is only one kind of other. Obviously the hustler must take cognizance of at least two additional types of significant others: outsiders and colleagues. Let us look at how he relates to them.

Outsiders

By "outsiders" I do not mean those poolroom players and spectators who aren't hustlers (most such people most of the time are considered by the hustler to be prospective victims), but rather the public at large whose interests lie outside the poolroom world entirely. As far as the hustler is concerned, the central fact about such people is that they are not potential sources of income for him.

Another relevant fact about such people was noted at the beginning of this essay: nearly all of them, insofar as they have any knowledge or opinion about hustling at all, stigmatize the hustler and his trade. But this fact—and here hustlers differ in a major way from other socially deviant groups—is not at all important in hustler thinking. The fact that hustlers are put down by society at large is extraordinarily rare as a topic of hustlers' conversation or consciousness. Nor, despite the fact that hustlers come from a subculture whose values differ from those on the basis of which they are stigmatized, do they bother to develop a definite counter-ideology about why outsiders should themselves be put down. In this respect hustlers seem to be unlike, say, most drug users, homosexuals, bohemians and jazz musicians, and unlike the great majority of career criminals.

To be sure, the hustler is aware that outsiders in general stigmatize him. But he is aware of it less often, and less strongly, than other people are aware of their negative status in the larger society—for he comes in contact with it far less. The homosexual may elicit negative reactions in a variety of "straight" work situations and other public situations unless he is successful in disguising his homosexuality (and even then he hears a lot of putdowns of "queers"); the Negro, even if he elects to live in the heart of his ghetto and remain as "black" as possible, is raised on white mass media and at the least cannot help internalizing white ideals of physical attractiveness (on this see Chapter 4); the typical criminal cannot pick up a newspaper or look at TV without being faced with the fact that the public rejects him and his kind. The hustler's lifespace and lifeways, however, cut him off much more fully from outsiders' negative judgments. Unlike Negroes, he is segregated not only from his "betters" but from their opinions of him. There are three reasons for this.

(1) My statement earlier that hustlers "virtually live in the poolroom" was meant literally. About four-fifths of the hustlers are unmarried. Moreover, almost every unmarried hustler resides by himself in one small furnished room or hotel room, hardly conducive to developing a "home life." His real psychological home is the job site, the poolroom. This is where he spends almost all his waking hours. This is not only where he works but where he loafs, plays, and as often as not eats—and also where he sleeps when he can't make room rent. In fine, it is his leisure-place as much as his work-place.

The typical hustler has very few interests outside the poolroom and reads nothing except (sporadically) the racing page of the newspaper. Even his few outside interests are intermittent: watching sports events on TV once or twice a week, occasionally making a pickup in a bar and getting laid, once in a while seeing a movie, going to the track several times a year, now and then playing cards—that's the sum total of non-poolroom life for most hustlers.

(2) When the hustler does temporarily take a non-hustling job, it tends to be one that takes him out of the

poolroom not at all or hardly at all, or else provides only fleeting, fragmented contacts with the non-poolroom world.

(3) The hustler seldom runs into non-hustler players who put him down. First of all, most non-hustler poolroom habitués not only accept the poolroom tradition that all players should bet, but tend in varying degrees to accept the "sporting life" ethic accompanying it (especially the notion that if a player overmatches himself that's his own problem), and their attitudes toward hustlers range from ignorance or indifference to tolerance to sympathy to outright admiration. Certainly such attitudes (except for ignorance) are true of nearly all those non-hustlers who play regularly in "action rooms."

As for the players who strongly object to hustlers: whether they play regularly or infrequently, they seldom are in the action rooms where hustlers hang out but prefer the sedater poolrooms (or, if upper class, prefer to play in private clubs). Also, more often than not such players are so unperceptive of all but the crudest hustling that they can't tell a hustler when they see one. Many a player who believes he has never played a hustler has in fact been hustled by several.

Of course, the hustler doesn't proclaim his trade to the outside world, for typically he has neither a masochistic urge to be put down nor the reactive hostility to majority opinion that one finds in the flamboyant homosexual or "professional Negro" or "professional Jew" and the like. On the other hand, he isn't much concerned with hiding his trade from outsiders so long as openness would not adversely affect his income. He actually runs into putdowns so seldom and his world is so self-contained that the majority's negative opinion neither significantly affects his life-chances nor bruises his psyche.

In other words, though the hustler cares about what the outside world thinks of his role, he cares about it much less than other deviants do. Outsiders as a class may comprise a significant other for the hustler, but they are not a genuine "reference group" for him: he has not even the most latent of aspirations to membership in their world, and thus is not about to change his behavior to accord with their moral

standards. As a result he is likely to practice a peculiar
kind of inconsistency about revealing his occupation to
outsiders—an inconsistency that has the mark not of "conflict" or "ambivalence" but rather of genuine flexibility and
free choice, i.e., choice based on rational calculation of
what, in any given situation with outsiders, might be most
to his advantage.

An example of this flexibility or rational inconsistency in
the presence of outsiders may be seen by comparing two
samples from the behavior of the man known among hustlers as Wimpy, America's foremost nine-ball hustler, and
known to larger circles as a professional player under his
real name, Luther Lassiter (on the relation between hustling and professional playing, see below). In April, 1963,
he won the World Professional Pocket Billiard Tournament. One day during the tournament—after he had won a
game that made it almost certain he would be the next
champion—a few spectators, including myself, were talking
with him when a reporter from the Associated Press came
up and started interviewing him. The reporter asked,
among other things, how Mr. Lassiter made his living—and
did he make it playing pool? Wimpy smiled and said no;
he said that he lived with his mother, that he had a rich
brother who helped him out, and that it just seemed that
the good Lord looked after him. Yet only a few weeks later
he appeared on a nationwide TV program called *To Tell
the Truth,* in which the panelists were to guess which one
of three persons, including Lassiter, was a pool hustler,
and in which his occupation was revealed. In the first situation, there was nothing to be gained from revealing his
occupation to the reporter, and possibly negative consequences for the "image" of pocket billiards—which both
the players and the sponsors of the tournament were concerned to improve.[10] In the second situation, there was a

[10] Apropos of the public relations or "image-making" aspect
of this tournament: members of its sponsoring group, the
Billiard Room Proprietors Association of America, admitted to
me that because of their desire not to jeopardize the game's
comeback attempt (this was the first world tournament held in
several years), they had not invited two players who doubtless

nice fee for him in going on TV to own up publicly to his trade.

Colleagueship

Colleagueship among hustlers is partly typical of colleagueship in occupations generally, and partly not. One way in which it is untypical has to do with entry to and expulsion from the occupation.

In most kinds of work, the colleague group can debar someone from entry, either by formal means (e.g., deny him job training, or a license, or tools, or union membership) or by informal means (e.g., ostracize him socially, refuse to work with him, deny him the recommendations needed to get work). But entry to hustling does not involve elements that can be effectively controlled by colleagues. There are no formal entrance criteria such as examinations or licenses or diplomas. And job training (the development of playing and conning ability) is publicly available to anyone, as are the tools of the trade (playing equipment), a workplace (the poolroom), and the market for one's skill (suckers). In most of his job activities, and in all that are truly essential, each hustler is basically an individual entrepreneur. For this reason also, the colleague group cannot really "expel" anyone from hustling.

It is true enough that to enjoy colleagueship means first of all to be recognized and accepted as a colleague by others. But it does not always follow that to be denied colleagueship is to be denied work. It may make the work situation tougher, but by no means impossible. Thus, if a hustler is denied acceptance by other hustlers, it can rule out dumping and other forms of cooperation between him and them, but it has no discernible effect on his main job activity, which is to lure suckers into games with him.

were superior to at least one of the ten contestants invited. The two uninvited players might have damaged the "image" that the tournament was trying to convey: one of them had recently been in jail on a felony charge, and the other was noted for, among other things, his refusal to wear a tie and the unrelieved profanity of his speech.

In any case, outright rejection of a hustler by his colleagues, by refusal to cooperate or associate with him, is actually quite rare. It is invoked only on those whose personalities can cause associates plenty of grief. An example: after this study was under way for three months I began avoiding games with one of the hustlers I had until then played billiards with—this on the advice of other hustlers, who warned me that my playing companion was both armed and unpredictably short-tempered.

A colleague group creates *esprit de corps,* a feeling of "we-ness." It also creates awareness that although colleagues are equals, some colleagues are more equal than others; that is, it creates an intra-occupational stratification system, mostly along the dimension of prestige. I mention these together because in the hustling world the two are peculiarly intertwined: Non-rigged games between hustlers —ever more frequent these days, for reasons to be indicated later—constitute on the one hand intense, focused interaction between friendly colleagues, in the context of an audience consisting largely or exclusively of other colleagues, and thus such games contribute much to group identity feelings. But on the other hand, they are also serious, fierce competitions, whose results provide colleagues with their chief basis for rating a hustler's playing skill, which rating is in turn a major ingredient of his general prestige rank. Thus the *esprit de corps* of the hustling world and its internal stratification system are to some degree functions of each other. That noted, we can now look at each separately.

At the bottom of the prestige hierarchy are those few players with so little skill that, even though they hustle, colleagues question their right to be regarded as hustlers at all. Thus, of one hustler it was contemptuously remarked:

> He calls himself a hustler but he always dogs it for the cash. I guess his old lady supports him.

And of another:

> I've hardly never seen him take down the cash. That movie turned him on to thinking he was a hustler, but he ain't.

> You could give him 12 on 30 [points in three-cushion
> billiards] and still have a lock. He should get a job.

At the top of the hierarchy are, of course, the players
of outstanding skill. Although most hustlers can play any
poolroom game well—and in addition many can, if need
be, offer a sucker the handicap of shooting with the hand
other than the one they normally use—they tend to specialize in one game or another. A hustler's standing among
colleagues is based on this functional specialization, and
he may be rated highly in one game but not in another (or
not even thought of in connection with the other). Thus
Wimpy, though he can play any pool game superbly, is
known chiefly as the outstanding nine-ball hustler, Eddy
Taylor (the Knoxville Bear) is rated best at bank pool,
and so on. Some hustlers are noted for their ability to make
a difficult shot with great frequency and to win bets thereby;
e.g., Don Willis is admired especially for his consistency in
making "wing shots" (in which you shoot at an object ball
that is moving rapidly down the table away from you, and
pocket it in a far corner).

There is by no means unanimity about who is the best in
each specialty. Usually there are two or three candidates
for that rating among the hustlers. For example, there is
disagreement about who is the most adept specialist in the
"I'll play you one-handed" routine; Lusitay has hustler par-
tisans who claim he is best and so does Miami. And one
can always get a good argument going among hustlers by
asking who is the best one-pocket specialist, Ronnie Allen
or Jersey Red or Marv Henderson.

Although hustlers specialize, most of them will, as noted
above, play a game that's not their specialty if it is the only
game the sucker will play. So if a hustler is a specialist in
versatility, as it were, this also can confer status. It is in
fact the basis of the extraordinary prestige that Boston
Shorty enjoys among his colleagues. Hustlers do not rate
him at the top in any specialty (except for a few who say
he is probably the best at three-cushion billiards), but they
are quick to point out that he is near the top in almost
every specialty. By unanimous agreement, Boston Shorty

is our country's best "all around" hustler. His great prestige
derives not so much from his excellence at the whole gamut
of pool games (a few other hustlers are probably his equals
here), but from the fact that he is, at the same time, the
best or nearly best hustler at three-cushion billiards. Hardly
any hustlers shuttle between pocket and three-cushion
games to the extent that Shorty does, and none with such
success as he; the reason is that although basic skills (such
as how to hold a cue stick, or how to aim) are readily trans-
ferable, some advanced skills are not and, more importantly, actually interfere with each other.[11] That is why
virtually all regular players, hustlers included, tend over
time to concentrate entirely or almost entirely on either
pool or three-cushion billiards.

It is assumed that every hustler knows how to "make a
game," and this aspect of his work influences prestige rank
among colleagues only if he is especially inept at it:

> X has got the heart and he's got the stroke. But he'll never
> be a good hustler, 'cause he's always giving away too many
> points. He's part sucker, that's what he is.

Another aspect of maladroitness in making a game was
put down by Brooklyn Johnny, with whom I was watching
a game in which hustler Y managed to eke out a win over

---

[11] This is especially true of one's stroke: developing a perfect stroke at pool makes it almost impossible simultaneously
to have a perfect stroke at three-cushion billiards, and vice
versa. (An exact parallel exists in the playing of keyboard in-
struments, where the touch someone develops in becoming an
outstanding pianist precludes his being an outstanding harpsi-
chordist, and vice versa.) In the entire history of pool and
three-cushion billiards only two professional players, Alfredo
De Oro and Johnny Layton, ever managed to win championships at both (and Layton was able to win these only at widely
separated points in his career).

Studies of transferability of motor skills—the main ones are
summarized in Woodward and Schlosberg's *Experimental Psychology*—have to a slight extent dealt with negative transfer
effects. But the type of situation discussed above, in which
attaining the highest level at one motor skill inhibits a similar
level of performance at a closely related motor skill, seems
not to have been studied at all.

a very tough non-hustler. I said something about hustler Y's great playing, and Johnny replied:

> But it's dumb. Look at the takedown [amount of cash] he got for it. It's dumb to make a game where you have to show the room your top speed for only $5.

Without exception, hustlers contend that "heart" (courage or toughness) is as essential to hustling as playing ability is. We saw earlier that they view it as basic to the job. The point here is that hustlers, in their preoccupation with it, often use judgments about "heart" to confer or withhold prestige. Some examples of such judgments that hustlers have made to me are these (each applies to a different hustler):

> You can't bet on A because you don't know how he's going to stand up for more than $20. No heart.

> Take B over there, thinks he's such a hotshot. But you'll never see him put up his own dough. He's got no heart, that's why. He's gotta have backing even when the game is a lock. B wouldn't play on his own dough unless the sucker had one foot in the grave, the other on a banana peel, and both arms in a cast.

> C don't have the heart for it. He only does okay when he gets out in front early.

> Weenie Beanie's got real heart. He's no locksman. A real strong gambler.

> I tell you one thing about Boston Shorty, the real great thing, is that the guy kisses icewater. He don't frighten out. One time I seen a game where some dude runs over 100 balls on him, and Shorty comes right back with 89 and out. It takes plenty heart to do that.

The *esprit de corps* of a colleague group, especially if it is a deviant group, tends to be strengthened by a well-developed hostility toward outsiders. But as we saw earlier, hustlers, for special reasons, do not have an elaborate ideology or strong feelings about this. They do, of course, sometimes speak contemptuously of outsiders; but in developing solidary feelings they rely much more on emphasizing the joys of hustling, talking of its virtues (such as autonomy and heart), rating each other, discussing its technology, telling tales of its heroes and villains, and so on. When a hustler says of hustling that "it beats working," his emphasis is not on putting down the workaday world; his primary meaning is, rather, a positive one—that hustling is infinitely more pleasurable than any other job he could find.

The fact that the hustler's work-place is to so great an extent also his leisure-place not only lessens his need for putting down the outside world, but at the same time increases those collegial interactions which foster *esprit de corps* by other means. One of those means, as should be obvious by now, is the use of an elaborate argot; I have placed my analysis of hustlers' argot in an appendix to this chapter, for reasons explained there.

Colleagueship involves an obligation to cooperate and rewards for doing so. Cooperation among hustlers takes several forms: (1) The main one, already discussed, is the cooperative swindle known as "dumping." (2) Often a hustler will tell a colleague about a fault he has noticed in the latter's game, although there appears to be no clearly defined collegial obligation to do this. (3) A clearly defined obligation, the strongest element in the hustlers' colleague code, has to do with regulating the competition for opponents: when a hustler has started to make a game (be it with a sucker or another hustler), any hustler who is a third party is not supposed to cut in with a better offer or otherwise queer the pitch; as previously noted, this sanction is observed not only by hustlers but by regular poolroom players generally. (4) When a hustler from out of town is cleaned out by some local hustler, the latter is obligated to give the former, on request, "get-out-of-town money." And whatever the winner's personal feelings about the loser, he doesn't fail to honor the request, so severe would be the castigation from his colleagues otherwise. (5) When a hustler is preparing for a road trip to towns he doesn't know, or hasn't visited in a long time, colleagues who have recently been to those places provide him with information on where the action is, who the best players are, what kind of cons they go for, and what their skill levels are. Conversely, when he returns from the road he fills in his colleagues with any new information he has gleaned on these matters.

More than a word needs to be said about the relationships between hustlers and professional players. The hustler and the professional have quite distinct occupational roles if we view them as ideal types, but empirically there is some overlap, especially today, and it leads to collegial relations between them that are extensive, complex, ambiguous and ambivalent.

The professional's income, years ago when professionalism paid well, derived mainly from tournament prizes, exhibition fees, endorsements of billiard products or representation of billiard supply firms, and teaching fees. Today, except for two or three top professionals, income from such sources is negligible. It is doubtful if even the current titleholder makes as much as $15,000 from them. (Compare this with Hoppe's 1925 estimate that the title was worth as much as $50,000 per year to whoever held it.) Professionals gain their income mostly from other occupations, especially managing a poolroom or owning a piece of one. One of these "other" occupations is hustling, and it appears that even in the earlier period many professionals also hustled on occasion. But it also appears that, except for a few professionals, they have done so infrequently. The great majority of professionals have often made big bets with opponents and spectators, but in situations where their skill levels were known to all concerned, i.e., not true hustling situations. In sum: many, possibly most, professionals have hustled—but seldom; and possibly a majority, certainly a large minority, of professionals either have never hustled at all or hustled only in early youth.

The very large majority of hustlers, on the other hand, have never tried to become professionals: They have stayed out of tournaments—in order, of course, to stay out of the limelight. At least, that's the reason most hustlers give. An additional reason, which they don't give, is that not many hustlers have been good enough to hold their own with the top professionals. However, if a hustler feels that his skill is already so well known that he has nothing much to lose by appearing in professional tournaments, and also feels that maybe he could win all the marbles, he will "go professional." And with the decline of potential income from hustling (see below), such feelings are becoming more common and the percentage of players in professional tournaments who have long hustling backgrounds has been going up rapidly—so that now, perhaps, the majority of professionals have such backgrounds.

Of course, if a hustler appears often in tournaments he severely reduces his chances of true hustling. And should he attain professional stardom, he effectively takes himself out of hustling altogether, whether he wants to or not. For example, as a result of his 1963 and later tournament victories, plus the numerous paid public exhibitions he was able to give after 1963 (including several on television), Wimpy cannot really be a hustler any more—regardless of what his current desire or self-conception may be. Today there is scarcely a poolroom in America, and certainly none with significant action, where he would not be recognized as soon as he walked in the door. He can still play for big bets (and does), but only with top players and, at that, by giving them tremendous handicaps.

All of the above-mentioned blurring and criss-crossing of occupational lines has led to some uneasy relations between the professionals and the hustlers. (1) A good number of professionals who were never hustlers have been against hustlers because the latter give the game a bad "image." There were many such "respectable" professionals in the old days (Hoppe is as good an example as any) and there are still some today (e.g., Irving Crane). On the other hand, even these professionals have a grudging respect for the skill of top hustlers and recognize that they are, after all, in the same sort of trade and have the same love of the game. (2) Most of the professionals who hustled a bit in their earliest days, or who have combined professional play with occasional hustling for a significant part of their careers, or who were basically hustlers before turning professional, don't put down hustlers at all, hang around with them, and in general find their company more congenial than the company of "respectable" professionals. But at the same time they are concerned to improve their chances of income from professional play, and agree with the equipment manufacturers and poolroom owners that the best way of doing so lies in improving the game's public "image"; as a result, they will sometimes be publicly and calculatedly evasive about their hustling backgrounds. (3) A few (very few) players who formerly hustled not only have gone professional but, upon doing well at it, have gone respectable. As one would expect, they become more royalist than the king. For example, Willie Mosconi has been given to making contemptuous remarks in public about "hustlers" such as Wimpy—this despite the fact that Mosconi was himself quite a hustler in his youth. Needless to say, Mosconi's present contempt for hustlers is returned by them.

An Occupation in Decline

Outsiders who saw *The Hustler* gathered that a good pool or billiard hustler can make big money or an excellent living by exercising his skills. In this matter as in some others, the movie falsified by offering past history as if it were the present. The days when the poolroom hustler could readily find non-hustlers willing to play for high stakes are long gone, and probably gone forever. Structural changes in American sporting life over the past thirty years have had disastrous consequences for the hustler (as for the professional player).

The major datum is, of course, the radical decline of American interest in pool or billiards. In the entire history of the United States, no other sport of nationwide appeal seems ever to have had such a proportionate drop in its popularity.[12] As we have seen in Chapter 1, the chief as-

[12] Along with negative consequences for the hustler from decreased participation in pool or billiard playing, there has come disaster for the professional player in the form of decreased spectator interest. Today the final match of a professional tournament is lucky to draw 300–500 people, and the champion is lucky to draw 75 people to an exhibition. But it was not always thus. When Willie Hoppe played George Slosson for the championship in 1906, there were over 4,000 paying spectators (Cf. Hoppe, *Thirty Years of Billiards* [New

pect of this decline is that today, even after the recent
"revival," the number of American poolrooms is only about
a fourth what it was in the 1920's. From talks with old-
timers, I gather that the decline in action rooms has been
proportionately even greater. For the hustler this means,
among other things, that it is much harder to stay unknown.
There are so few action rooms remaining that he cannot
space his visits to them far enough apart to avoid damag-
ing his reputation, i.e., to avoid getting too good a reputation. And, in addition, there are simply many less players
and therefore many less bettors.

As if this were not enough, there has been a devastating
shift (devastating for the hustler) in the ideology of the
regular players who remain or enter the poolroom. They
still adhere to the tradition that players should bet, but
they bet far smaller amounts, absolutely as well as relatively, than they did thirty years ago. The decline of the
game's hold on the American sporting imagination has
meant that, even among the regular players, it is no longer
considered the skill game on which to plunge. The big
betting by non-hustlers on their playing skill has shifted to
other sports. There are now many golf hustlers living high
—several make upward of $25,000 a year—for they find
plenty of cocky amateurs willing to stand heavy action.
(Joe Louis is one such amateur. Part of the reason he went
broke is that the golf hustlers took him so often.) And
some bowling hustlers do fairly well. But the pool or billiard
hustler cannot make out. It is doubtful if today there are
more than half a dozen poolroom hustlers who make even
$7000 per year by their hustling.

Today, when the poolroom hustler plays a sucker, as
often as not the action is "sociable," two or three dollars
per game; the average (mean) action is perhaps $5. $10
or $15 is considered quite good action. $20 and up is uncommon, and games for as much as "half a yard" ($50)
or more are downright rare. And, it must always be re-
membered, the hustler often has to go a good while between

York: Putnam, 1925], p. 103). And high spectator interest
continued into the 1930's; see Mosconi's remark noted in
Chapter 1, p. 19.

games that are true hustles for him. If he makes $90–$100 per week hustling, he's doing much better than average. True, almost any hustler will on the proper occasion tell of a big score he made off a sucker—say, $600 in one session. But if you pin him down as to how many times in the past few years he's made a score like that, it rarely turns out to be more than three or four times.

Games for $50 and more certainly do take place, on occasion, when hustlers play each other. (I have witnessed one series of games between two hustlers for $1,000 per game, and at least a dozen such series for $300–$800 per game.) But even here, really heavy action is uncommon; in hustler-vs.-hustler contests, the mean action is perhaps $15 or $20 per game. And in any case, though hustlers get a great kick out of the relatively big action when they play each other, they know that basically they are just taking in each other's washing.

There are certain peaks of these cannibalistic hustler-vs.-hustler contests: (a) Since 1961 there has been an annual tournament for hustlers in Johnston City, Illinois (pop. 3,900), with cash prizes but much more bet on the side between the players. It is sponsored by the Jansco brothers of that city, whose increased motel and bar business during the tournament makes up for the prize money they offer.[13] (b) When professional tournaments are held, hustlers from various cities come together as spectators and consequently adjourn to the local action room late at night for games with each other. (c) When word spreads that a poolroom

[13] A good description of this scene is Tom Fox's "Hustler's Holiday in the Lion's Den," *Sports Illustrated*, Vol. 15 (December 4, 1961), pp. 53–56, 59–61; a grossly inadequate one is "Battle of the Hottest Sticks," *Sports Illustrated*, Vol. 18, No. 8 (February 25, 1963), pp. 32–37. Students of mass communications may be interested to know that in connection with the 1963 tournament a typical bit of TV fakery took place. Games between Luther Lassiter (Wimpy) and Eddy Taylor (The Knoxville Bear) were videotaped and later broadcast, on December 22, 1963, as a CBS *Sports Spectacular*. Although the tournament was for hustlers, CBS did everything possible to create the impression that it was not: the screen title was simply "World Pocket Billiard Championship," and the word "hustler" was never mentioned on the program.

has come up with a new local player willing to stand big action, hustlers flock to the room—and more often than not end up playing each other. For example, in 1962, New York City hustlers got the wire that a sucker in Lodi, New Jersey, would gamble heavily, and they began traveling across the river to seek him out; of a weekend night there would often be eight or ten hustlers in Lodi, with only the one non-hustler willing to provide decent action, so naturally many hustler-vs.-hustler games developed to pass the time.

But neither the bigger action involved in hustler-vs.-hustler contests, nor their frequency, nor their great fascination, should lead us to blink the crucial fact that they constitute occupational cannibalism. No hustler seriously expects to make a living from playing other hustlers. He wants to find opponents whom he can truly hustle, and in this connection his never-ending problem is, Where's the big action?

A room where suckers play for decent money is so rare these days that when one does turn up, it is likely to be ruined through over-exploitation. An example: In 1962 a new poolroom opened in one of Cleveland's fancier suburbs, and the area's wealthy high school students began playing each other for sizeable stakes even though most of them scarcely knew how to hold a cue stick. Word got out and the hustlers descended—first the local hustlers from Cleveland's West 25th Street, and soon hustlers from all over the country. At its peak several hustlers were each pulling out as much as $400 per week from the room. But they tore it down; there were just too many hustlers taking too much money from too many kids, and mounting pressure from parents and police forced the room to close.

The professional three-cushion billiard player, Arthur Rubin, recently summed up the general situation as follows:

> In the old days when the hustler got too well known in his home town he just went on the road for a while. He did fine. Every town in America had its local champion willing to play for high stakes; and if the champion didn't have money himself, he always had plenty of backers willing to put it up. Today, the hustlers are more and more reduced

to playing each other. And when that happens, that's not hustling—that's gambling.

The poolroom hustler, then, is a highly skilled man whose skills no longer find a lucrative outlet. His occupation, once quite rewarding financially, now can support very few people, and these barely. Why does the hustler hang on? How? What does he do if he can't? How did he come to be a hustler anyhow?

Hanging On, Career Contingencies, and Retirement

The question, Why does the hustler hang on?, is somewhat misleading as applied to most hustlers. It implies that because hustling once was lucrative and now is not, today's hustler once had something valuable—a good living at his trade—that he now tries to "hang onto" after it has gone. But in my sample of *ca.* 59 hustlers (give or take a couple), 40 to 45 of them are under 50 years old and over half are under 40 years old. Now, if the good majority of hustlers are under 50, this means that they never had much to hang onto. The majority of today's hustlers entered hustling after its decline. The question to ask about them is, Why in the world did they become hustlers in the first place—and if they initially had false notions about its lucrativeness, why didn't they quit when they saw the reality (which indeed nearly all do see)? But let us look at the older group first.

The hustlers over 50 years old, who are truly "hanging on," are generally nostalgic, full of stories about famous matches and high stakes in the old days. It is only to be expected, I think, that a number of people who entered hustling when it was still big-time, or at least were in poolrooms when it was big-time, just won't give up hustling. What really needs explaining, it seems to me, is why so few such people are on today's hustling scene.

By all surmises, including their own, the active U.S. hustlers between 50 and 70 can comprise at the very most 5 per cent of living persons in this age group who once were

hustlers. There must be hundreds of living ex-hustlers over
50 who loved the game, i.e., the whole lifestyle involved in
the game, just as much as the old hustlers who haven't
quit. If one can assume what strikes me as two reasonable
assumptions, that "love of the game" is no greater in the
younger generation than in the older and that hustlers over
50 can draw sustenance from memories of the big-time
that the young hustlers cannot, it remains to be explained
why more old-timers are not still hustling.

The reader familiar with sports in general will know an
obvious answer: if the good young hustler has trouble making ends meet, the old-timer's income from hustling must
be worse yet—simply because, as we know from a variety
of sports, one's skill level declines rapidly after reaching
one's forties. But the obvious answer won't do. Pool and
billiards are peculiar, nay unique, in that one can play at
or very near one's top game well into old age—usually even
to compensating fully for the hand tremors that often ac-
company old age. Of course, the older man doesn't have
the stamina he once had, can't engage in all-night sessions
very often. But otherwise, unless and until his sight becomes uncorrectable even with bifocals, he has no skill
problem.

True, when the hustler's eyes no longer can be helped a
great deal with glasses, he has had it. The ex-hustler Tugboat Whaley (so called because part of his con was pretending to be a tugboat captain) reports as follows:

> I'm 65. I haven't played for big stakes in 10 years. This
> game isn't like baseball—your legs don't give out, your eyes
> do. You don't lose your stroke. Your eyes go bad, you can't
> see the edge of the ball.[14]

However, it must be emphasized that the eyes of most hustlers are correctable or almost entirely correctable with
glasses far into old age, and that consequently most hustlers
can keep playing well.

An index of this peculiarity about the game is that the
record time-span over which a player in any sport or game
was still winning world championships is held by billiards:

[14] Quoted from Tom Fox, *op. cit.*, p. 59.

Willie Hoppe won his first world championship in 1906
and his last in 1952, forty-six years later (whereupon he retired, at the age of 65). It is true that Hoppe's skill level
may have been unique.[15] But he was by no means unique
in the number of years he was able to play his best. Nor
can it be said that this is due to the particular varieties of
the game that he played (balk-line and three-cushion billiards). For example, in the professional pocket billiard
(pool) championship tournaments held between 1963 and
1965, there were four competitors over 55 years old out of
a combined field of 23 different players in the three tournaments; i.e., four players over 55 were ranked among the
best 23 players in the world—and one of these four was 69
years old. And I have played several opponents who,
though not of championship calibre, were still superb
players well past the age of 70.

Nor is there a decline in the old hustler's temperamental
ability to feign less playing skill than he has, or in his ability
to "make a game" or his other conning skills. Furthermore, his age does not make him suspect as someone
whose accumulated knowledge and experience might prove
too strong. On the contrary, the older hustler finds that
once in a while his age, as such, helps him to hustle: sometimes an ignorant sucker will assume that a decrepit-
looking old man couldn't possibly play a decent game any
more, and finds out the hard way.

For some hustlers, as they get older, over-indulgence in
alcohol becomes a severe problem. It has wrecked the

[15] And maybe not. Some old-timers claim that whenever
Johnny Layton was even halfway sober (seldom), he beat
Hoppe.

In recent three-cushion tournaments the current world chàm-
pion, Raymond Ceulemans of Belgium, has surpassed Hoppe's
tournament scoring average—but this does not necessarily indicate his basic skill level is greater. Averages today are generally higher than they used to be. Three-cushion billiards has
been made somewhat easier by changes in equipment, changes
in rules, and, above all, an increase in knowledge. Over the
past quarter century knowledge about how to play three-cushion
billiards has increased particularly with regard to "position
play" (in which you play not only to make your shot but so
as to leave the balls in good position for a succeeding shot).

careers both of hustlers and of professionals (e.g., to mention only the most famous among the dead, Ralph Greenleaf). However, alcoholism seems no more frequent among hustlers than in most other segments of our society.

Rather, the scarcity of old hustlers is explained by an aspect of the hustler's way of life today that is particularly hard to take in old age: today the periods in any hustler's career when he goes completely broke are more frequent and of longer duration. A young man may not be too shaken by the fact that once in a great while he can't even pay room rent in a fleabag hotel and has to grab his sleep in the poolroom for two or three days, or that he may get down to just one change of clothes, for he knows that one decent hustle—bound to come along in a couple of days if he keeps sharp eyes out—will get him started again. But an older man finds himself looking for more security than that, finds himself less adaptable to the more frequent and more severe downturns that are a contingency of the hustling career today.

In addition, an indeterminate number of hustlers give up the poolroom life because they eventually get married and find, when they do, that this poses another great occupational problem. That is one reason why the great majority of career hustlers are career bachelors. Marriage is of course a contingency that can adversely affect careers in many occupations, as in, say, the case of the aspiring organization man whose spouse is not a proper organization wife; but in hustling, much more frequently and intensely than in most occupations, marriage precipitates a genuine career crisis.

Perhaps because bachelor ideology had so recently played a prominent part in his thinking, when the hustler does get married he is notably less successful than, say, a jazz musician, in finding a woman to put up with his irregular working hours. Whatever the cause may be, it appears that most women who marry hustlers can't or won't readily —or even unreadily—adjust to the erratic hours that hustling entails, or that are entailed when one wishes to watch or engage in games between hustlers (which, for reasons already indicated, take place mostly between the hours of

1:00 and 6:00 A.M.). Instances of such difficulties are frequently told in the hustling world, being cited most often, of course, by the bachelor majority as reason enough for their continued bachelorhood. Apart from erratic hours as such, the small and unpredictably fluctuating nature of the hustler's income poses an equally severe marriage-vs.-career problem, one that only a few hustlers have been able to ease by finding wives who will work steadily while they (the husbands) continue hustling.

Some hustlers solve this career crisis by eventually walking out on the wife; others solve it by eventually walking out on the poolroom. The latter solution appears to be more frequent, though how much more so I do not have enough data to say.

It is reasonable to speculate—though again I have no data—that some decades ago a hustler's marriage did not pose such a critical problem for him. In the old days hustlers had much more opportunity for good action with suckers in daytime and early evening hours (as opposed to today's frequently fruitless hunt during such hours), far lesser need to play each other, and consequently both greater choice of working hours and greater dependability of income.

The twin factors discussed above—crises posed by financial insecurity in old age and by marriage—strongly suggest that today's young hustlers, as they get older, will also show a very high dropout rate.

Hustlers who retire when young sometimes return to the poolroom for visits, to see friends or watch contests. But the older hustlers who drop out, and the young retired hustlers as they get older, tend to abandon the poolroom world entirely. Among the many old men who hang around or work in poolrooms, there are few former hustlers.

Perhaps the best known of such former hustlers is Carl Zingale, now 70, whose monicker in the poolroom world is Cue Ball Kelly (an illustration, incidentally, that it is not always safe to infer someone's ethnic origin from his ethnic monicker). He was hustling by the age of 10:

> I was what you might call on the hustle. The dough wasn't

too bad for a kid and I figured that I could make more money this way than I could in school. There were many days that I would win three or four games and come home with my pockets jingling. . . . After a few years I suddenly realized that I wasn't the greatest pool player around. So I decided to start picking up some money by refereeing and booking games [professional games]. I've refereed for every top player in the past 40 years and I've also handled bookings for them.

Although Kelly has made a fair living from professional tournaments by alternately refereeing and entertaining the audience with trick shots, the business really isn't big enough to support more than one such person in this manner (and even Kelly has had rough going at times). Retired hustlers who want to stay around the game have to take ordinary jobs in the poolroom. If they are lucky, they end up with ownership or part ownership of a poolroom, but rarely are they that lucky. For the most part they face only ill-paid and dead-end poolroom jobs (desk man, sweeper) and as a result tend to drift out of the poolroom to other jobs that, although also unskilled, pay a bit better.

Recruitment and Induction

Hustlers arise in all regions of the country, and in small cities as well as big ones. (But the decline in action rooms forces the small-town hustlers to move to one or another of America's big cities, and also means that road trips to small towns are far rarer than they were thirty years ago.) The only significant factor common to their backgrounds appears to be that of social class.

At least four-fifths of the hustlers in my sample are of lower-class origin, and those who are not come, by anybody's definition, from the lower reaches of the middle class. One index: with a solitary exception, none of the hustlers attended college (not even those who could have done so on the GI Bill), and probably over half of them, certainly well over a third, did not finish high school. Hustlers' origins are also, by and large, in keeping with ethnic succession in the lower class.[16] For example, most of the Jewish hustlers are over 55; and Puerto Rican hustlers, virtually unknown until ten or fifteen years ago, now are much in evidence among the younger hustlers (one is often reputed to be the best one-handed player in the country).

Hustlers are social deviants, in the sense that they gamble for a living and, in the process, violate societal norms of "respectable" work and of fair dealing (and do worse things, as will emerge presently). However, psychopathology as such has nothing to do with either the origin or maintenance of their hustling. Many a psychiatrically oriented observer might indeed find that hustlers as a group seem to show more mental disorder than people he knows in general, but this would be merely to say that his "in general" includes little acquaintance with the lower class, where, as several researchers have amply demonstrated, the burden of mental illness in our society mainly falls. As a matter of fact, hustlers as a group may well be psychologically healthier than those members of the lower class whose teens were spent in more respectable places than poolrooms; this would not be out of keeping with the data, reported by the Gluecks and others, which indicate that in lower-class neighborhoods of high delinquency the non-delinquents have higher neuroticism rates than the delinquents.

The causes relevant to hustling are not psychopathological but subcultural. In the context of American lower-class subcultures, hustlers are not nearly so "deviant" as they appear to the middle- or upper-class outsider. For one thing, in lower-class areas pool playing is a much commoner pastime and the poolroom is more frequently a neighborhood institution.

Secondly, the "social norms" that the hustler transgresses carry less weight in the lower class than elsewhere, and

[16] This holds as well for the origins of professional players; see Chapter 1, note 42. See also Dudley Kavanagh's prideful observation in 1869: "Ireland, the mother of the majority of billiard professionals. . . ." (Kavanagh, *The Billiard World* [N. Y.: Kavanagh & Decker, 1869], p. 45).

correspondingly the hustler is stigmatized less. After all, in lower-class subcultures the successful neighborhood racketeer or political thief is frequently admired, and hustlers *qua* hustlers are less violative of basic social norms than such people. Nor does the fact that hustling isn't a "steady job" carry in the lower class the stigma that it does elsewhere.

Thirdly, and crucially: hustling, notably unlike most American occupations, represents a career line that is almost completely open to members of the lower class, an occupation where social origin bars one neither from entry nor advancement.

I say "almost" completely open because there is some discrimination against Negroes—not, however, by white hustlers, but by white poolroom owners. Even so, racial integration in the poolroom has been significantly in advance of that in the world outside it. Two examples: (a) Negroes were an accepted part of the Times Square poolroom scene by the early 1940's, in the days when their patronage of Times Square movies was discouraged and they simply couldn't get served by most restaurants in the area. (b) When I visited Cleveland in 1963, its public places were still so segregated that even in the action poolrooms on West 25th Street, the owners would pull the "club members only" routine to keep Negroes out. But the white hustlers objected strongly to this practice, and, moreover, would frequently travel to the Negro section for matches with the better Negro players (hustlers or otherwise). At the main Negro action room, on 105th and Massey, it was expected that white players would drop in, and quite okay for them to do so.[17] This relative lack of anti-Negro dis-

[17] During the course of this study Howard Becker interviewed for me a San Francisco hustler, Harry the Russian, who indicated that in recent years the decline of pool hustling has made it more difficult for a white hustler to move in Negro neighborhoods without being rousted by police. The Russian says that when he went into the Fillmore (the Negro section of San Francisco) in the old days, the police knew he was there to hustle pool and let him alone, but now they assume he is there to score for drugs or girls, stop him, and make him explain his presence.

crimination by white hustlers is part of a larger phenomenon: the social bonds uniting members of any deviant subculture tend to override race prejudice in large degree,
and thus nearly every such subculture is more racially
integrated than is "respectable" society.[18]

Hustling, then, is fully open to lower-class whites, and
more open to lower-class Negroes than are most jobs. Except for the discrimination faced by Negroes, success depends entirely on individual skills. And, still more importantly, it depends on the kind of skills that a lower-class
youth has a good chance to acquire—unlike, say, the skills
whose acquisition depends on parental encouragement of
reading.

In hustling, nepotism or knowing people who are "well
connected" counts for naught; the manly virtue of self-
reliance counts for plenty. Hustling distributes its rewards
strictly on the basis of individual talent and hard work, thus
fulfilling two cardinal tenets of the Horatio Alger "myth"
(as distinguished from the reality of the Alger novels themselves, where, as the late Richard Wohl noted, fortuitous
events always play a key role in success).[19]

---

[18] America's most racially integrated deviant subculture is
probably the homosexual. For example, the homosexuals' annual "drag ball," held on Halloween in several cities, is one of
our country's chief interracial events. And the Negro community knows it; e.g., at the Chicago drag ball I attended in 1955,
the guest of honor was America's second most powerful Negro
political leader, U.S. Congressman William Dawson. (It perhaps needs explaining that Halloween has a latent function as
a sort of homosexual national holiday because at that time
transvestites can go forth in women's clothing ["drag"] without fear of arrest. Mardi Gras has a similar function for homosexuals.)

It is also obvious that among homosexual couples who live
together and define themselves as "married" to each other, the
interracial "marriage" rate is far higher than in the heterosexual world. A hypothesis I hope to test is that these interracial homosexual couples, much more often than interracial
heterosexual couples, settle in neighborhoods that had previously
been entirely white, and thus play an important pioneering
role in opening up such neighborhoods to Negroes generally.

[19] Cf. R. Richard Wohl, "The 'Rags to Riches Story': An
Episode of Secular Idealism," in Reinhard Bendix and Sey-

All in all, for a number of lower-class youths, hustling as a possible ladder of social ascent seems very real. As Boston Shorty put it to me: "If I hadn't got interested in pool when I was a kid, I might have ended up a bum or in jail."

The induction process in hustling has remained unchanged over the decades; it is the same for today's newcomer as it was for the old-timer. The difference is only that far fewer youths enter the career these days because of the decreased chances to earn good money from it. But some continue to enter; in our larger cities, each year the hustling scene reveals a few new young faces.

In general the process goes like this: Hustlers, even those who finished high school, played truant from school often, and in so doing found themselves in poolrooms much more frequently than either their classmates or their fellow-truants. Since the development of pool or billiard skill is, at least in the first several years of play, largely a matter of the number of hours one practices, they quickly developed superiority over their age-mates and were able to earn some fair change thereby. Naturally they wanted to keep a good thing going, and in the process many dropped out of school entirely, while nearly all passed up job experience and training; almost without thinking about it they became hustlers, as much by drift as by decision. The only significant exception to this general line of development is that some hustlers, now in their forties, had an extra reason for spending much of their youth in poolrooms, namely, their teens were Depression years when there were no jobs around.

Because in hustling there is neither a formal entrance requirement nor formal recognition of entry (no examination, license, *rite de passage,* union membership, etc.) and, especially, because the poolroom tradition that all players should bet makes it nearly impossible to recall (or even to distinguish at the time) any hustling analogue of one's "first real job," the transition from non-hustler to hustler status is smooth and almost imperceptible to the person

---

mour Martin Lipset, eds., *Class, Status and Power* (Glencoe, Illinois: The Free Press, 1953), pp. 388–95.

involved. The transition never seems to involve a conscious decision to *become* a hustler, but rather a recognition that one already *is* a hustler, and is good at it. Here is a typical response to my queries about entry:

> How I got to be a hustler? Well it wasn't any special deal, you know. When I was a kid around 14 I was shootin' pool for money like the other kids, only I got to be the best, and after a while you can't get a game if you let on how good you are. And pretty soon I was beating lots older guys, 'cause right away I come up with a real good stroke, you know. And me with my baby face, they didn't know what was happenin' until I took down the cash. I was better at hustlin' pool than anything else, so I figured I would keep on doin' it.

And here is an account by the man sometimes regarded as America's best one-pocket hustler, Jersey Red:

> I thank them, every one of them down there in the New YMCA. That's where I got my start. I hustled for Cokes and change, and if they had some that folded and some nerve, I would unfold it for them. I started in there when I was 13 and when I was 14 I got my stroke. I got my stroke and learned to count [pocket the balls]. I beat every kid in the Y and then I started lookin' around. I just kept looking.[20]

Although the hustler's career decision—if one can call it that—may come late, acquisition of the playing skills requisite to hustling must start early. Every first-rate pool or billiard player, hustler or not, began playing regularly no later than his early teens.[21]

Once embarked in the hustling life, hustlers prefer to stay in it: it's exciting, it has a tradition and ideology that can make them feel heroic, it's fun (the game is enjoyable as such), it's not routine, and so on. The point is that these characteristics of the occupation, appealing as they might be to, say, the readers of this book, are still more appealing to lower-class youths. The hustling career partakes deeply, often passionately, of every one of the orientations that

[20] Quoted from Dale Shaw, *op. cit.*, p. 91.
[21] See Chapter 1, p. 19.

Walter Miller finds to be distinctive "focal concerns" of
American lower-class subcultures: trouble (with the law),
smartness (in the sense of being able to con and of being
no one's dupe), excitement, fate, toughness ("heart"), and
autonomy.[22]

The existence of such orientations in hustling has tremendous positive consequences both for the entry of lower-
class youths and for their continuing with the career in the
face of frequent financial adversity. And on top of all that,
"love of the game" is an important element in the makeup
of most hustlers—the same kind of "hangup" on a game,
as such, that one finds in chess bums, tennis bums, *et al.*
(and that is the main basis of my relationship with hustlers). Thus, although numerous problems confront the
hustler, "alienation" from his work is emphatically not one
of them. It is small wonder that when asked why he stays
in the occupation, many a hustler replies: "It beats
working."

However, despite the fact that the typical hustler supports only himself and pays no income tax,[23] it is frequently hard to make ends meet, and sometimes impossible.
The rate of failure is high, and the hustler knows it. For
example, when a hustler *un*intentionally misses a shot,
sometimes he will curse himself with the exclamation "Get
a job!," whereby he recognizes, if only ironically, that he
is in a very tough racket where only the best survive and
he may not make it.

Some hustlers do indeed give up when still young. It is

[22] Cf. Walter Miller, "Lower Class Culture as a Generating
Milieu of Gang Delinquency," *Journal of Social Issues,* Vol.
XIV (1958), pp. 5–19.

[23] The extent to which hustlers live beyond the ken of our
society's record-keeping bureaucracies is truly remarkable. Most
hustlers, for example, are not counted in the U. S. Census, and
many of them—probably the majority—do not even have Social Security numbers. In a recent pool tournament held at a
Las Vegas hotel, three hustlers finishing in the money had
difficulty collecting their prizes because the management insisted
on paying by check, for which purpose it needed Social Security numbers, and these three had no such numbers to give.
(The problem was eventually solved.)

not uncommon for a young hustler who hasn't been in the
poolroom for a while to say, when he finally does show up
to see his friends and is queried about his absence, "I'm
retired." But most hustlers, once they have entered the
career, stick it out tenaciously for a number of years. The
action (in all senses) provides too many pleasures for them
to worry that much about being broke.

But sooner or later even the best and most determined
hustler finds that if he is to keep hustling he must, at least
on occasion, obtain other sources of income. That is, he
finds that if he is not to retire, then he must moonlight. In
many cases, when hustlers are moonlighting, the major
share of their income derives from the latter source. Sometimes the hustler gets to depend on, or actually to like, his
moonlighting job, and moonlights permanently to all intents
and purposes.

Moonlighting

The purpose of moonlighting is not merely to provide
more income but to provide it in a way that allows you to
keep your primary job, the one you prefer. The job the
hustler takes, therefore, is one that allows him to hustle.
Such jobs fall into two types:

(1) *Poolroom-based.* The hustler may take a job as a
desk clerk, general handyman, lunch-counter man, etc., in
the poolroom. More often, he will engage in some illegal
activity that either can be headquartered in the poolroom
or, because its "working hours" are short and sporadic,
permits him to hang around the poolroom most of the time.
His lower-class origin, his lack of legitimate job training,
the availability of contacts in the poolroom for criminal
jobs, the ethic of hustling life—all these facilitate taking
criminal jobs when moonlighting.

He may moonlight at being a booster, or fence, or drug
pusher, or loan shark, or numbers runner, or forger, or
burglar, or bookie, etc. Several hustlers in my sample are
also skilled card cheats ("mechanics," in the argot). Three
hustlers are also pimps, have women who "hustle" in the

POOL HUSTLER: Wanted by FBI

ALIASES: John Bemis, Henry Milton Bradley, Patrick Bradley, John Frank Fitzpatrick, Charles C. Garrett, Melvin C. Horton, William L. Johnson, Lee Frank Rae, W. L. Wells and others

BACKGROUND AND METHOD OF OPERATION

Bradley allegedly has passed worthless checks at retail stores, gas stations, hotels and motels throughout the United States. Bradley frequently used the name John F. Fitzpatrick and traveled mainly by automobile. He is known in pool halls as a "pool hustler." He has been convicted of interstate transportation of stolen property, forgery and attempting to commit a felony. BRADLEY REPORTEDLY CARRIES A .38 CALIBER REVOLVER IN WAISTBAND OF HIS TROUSERS. CONSIDER ARMED AND DANGEROUS.

DESCRIPTION

Age: 50, born June 16, 1915, Washington, D.C.

Height: 6' to 6'1"

Weight: 305 to 320 pounds

Build: Large

Hair: Brown, graying

Eyes: Blue

Complexion: Ruddy

Race: White

Nationality: American

FBI No.: 4,111,234

F.P.C.: 19 L 13 R 101 15
      M 1 R 100

Occupations: Billiard parlor employee, guard, laborer, insurance agent, private investigator, salesman

Scars and Marks: Scar over left eye, scar left knee

Federal warrants were issued March 4, 1965, and May 28, 1965, at Roanoke, Virginia, and Greensboro, North Carolina, respectively, charging Bradley with causing fraudulent checks to be transported in interstate commerce (Title 18, U. S. Code, Section 2314).

PLEASE FURNISH ANY INFORMATION WHICH MAY ASSIST IN LOCATING THIS INDIVIDUAL TO THE NEAREST DIVISION OF THE FBI AS LISTED ON THE BACK OF THIS NOTICE.

usual sense. (One has rather high poolroom status because his girl always gets at least $50 per trick.) At least three members of the sample, perhaps more, are "heavy men" in their moonlighting roles, i.e., their moonlighting involves the use or potential use of armed violence.

Among hustlers who have moonlighted at crimes that society defines as more serious than hustling itself, the frequency of participation varies all the way from the hustler who has undertaken such activity only once or twice to the hustler who undertakes it more or less continuously. My point is that over half the hustlers have, apparently, undertaken such moonlighting at least once.

But the point as far as the hustler is concerned is that such a job allows him to hustle. In either kind of poolroom-based job, legal or illegal, the hustler is on hand to grab whatever pool-playing action might present itself.

(2) Not poolroom-based. A job based in the poolroom is of course preferable to any other kind of moonlighting; it allows the hustler to stay in the poolroom all or nearly all the time. But if the hustler wanting to moonlight can't get such a job, he tries to make sure that the job he takes at least permits him to drop into the poolroom often. It can't be an office or factory or retailing job, for these would tie him down to another location. It has to let him move around the city, and have somewhat flexible hours if possible, so that he can spend at least some time checking on the action in poolrooms. Among such jobs: window washer, outside salesman, cab driver.

A few (very few) hustlers have become wealthy from outside activities. One made oil investments that paid off; another is associated with racketeers and in a lucrative vending machine business; another is a major bookmaker; another owns restaurants; another has made a fortune cheating at cards; and another has, at this writing, six prostitutes working for him. But poolroom hustling remains their true love. For example, the hustler grown rich from vending machines spends two days a week looking after his business and five days a week in poolrooms. It is entirely possible that a few hustlers who somehow struck it rich from moonlighting may have thereupon retired from hustling, but I have never heard of such. There are, of course, a number of people who retired from hustling and then did well in the other occupations they entered, for example, the baseball pitcher Bo Belinsky.[24]

The Occasional Hustler

So far, except for noting that professional players have hustled, I have considered only the hustling done by hustlers, that is, persons whose primary occupational identification is with pool or billiard hustling and who engage in it as a full-time career whenever they are not forced to moonlight. There are, however, a number of casual laborers in the field.

Over 99 per cent of the more-or-less regular adult poolroom players are not hustlers. Only a small minority of them are even good enough to hustle. But a minority of this minority, such as myself, do hustle on occasion, e.g., "stall" and "lemon" so as to keep opponents playing and betting. However, their primary occupational identification lies elsewhere. I am rather untypical of such persons not only because of my middle-class background, but because most of them have jobs that allow them much more time in the poolroom—are traveling salesmen, professional criminals, holders of political sinecures, etc. The late jazz pianist Jelly Roll Morton was an occasional hustler of this kind.[25]

However, virtually none of these persons is as skilled as the typical hustler. They hustle very little, not merely because they wish to do so less often than the hustler but because they must be more cautious than he in picking

[24] On Belinsky's hustling background see, for example, Walter Lee Jackson, "Bo Belinsky: Baseball's 'Beau'," *Modern Man,* Vol. 12, No. 11 (May, 1963), pp. 36–38, 51.

[25] In his talking and singing autobiography, recorded at the Library of Congress in 1938, Morton has left some fascinating recollections of his pool hustling in the years 1900–1908. Listen to the Jelly Roll Morton Library of Congress recordings, as follows: volume 5, *Georgia Skin Game,* Riverside RLP 9005 (side 1, "Aaron Harris" bands 1 and 2); volume 9, *Jack the Bear,* Riverside RLP 9009 (side 1, "Jack the Bear" bands 1, 2, and 3; side 2, "Alabama Bound" bands 3 and 4).

opponents. They account for only a tiny fraction of all hustled games, perhaps 1 per cent.

Secondly, of the many players who are high school students not yet entered into society's occupational structure, some hustle. A few of the best will eventually become hustlers by trade, though most will not. They hustle their age-mates primarily, as few are skilled enough to beat the more experienced players. They account, I would guess, for perhaps 2 or 3 per cent of all hustled games.

A third group, however, accounts for quite a significant percentage of hustled games, at a guess about 15 per cent.[26] This group consists of people who are no longer students but who have no occupational identity whatever. When indicating how he makes his living, such a person may say that he "scuffles," or that he "gets by" by doing "a little of this and a little of that." His varied activities are more often than not illegal. Often he may say that he "hustles," but he means this in the generalized slang sense that he undertakes any short-term activity for a fast buck. Pool-playing skill is merely one element of his armamentarium. He may be hustling at pool one night, in a crooked dice game the next, hustling his own ass in a gay bar the next, and so on. It is my impression—though the sample is too small to permit sure generalization—that this group shows a greater incidence of mental disorder than other poolroom groups and also that Negroes are heavily over-represented in it.[27]

[26] N.B. that all the remarks above about "percentages" of hustled games are strictly guesses, though informed guesses.

[27] A valuable autobiography of one such "hustler" or "scuffler," transcribed from tape-recorded interviews, is Henry Williamson's *Hustler* (New York: Doubleday, 1965). Its accounts of pool hustling are at pp. 73, 93 ff., and 156 ff. Williamson's vocational drifting (or versatility) is entirely criminal and concentrates on felonies, chiefly armed robbery. Pool hustling, as it merely breaks misdemeanor laws against gambling, constitutes his nearest approach to a legitimate occupation. For the life history of another such "hustler," see Edwin Lemert, *Social Pathology* (New York: McGraw-Hill, 1951), pp. 332–37.

The Hustler in History

Although the techniques of deception that can be used
in a gambling game are modified by the game's social context, these techniques flow fundamentally, as we noted at
the beginning, from the inner structure of the game itself.
Thus we might reasonably suspect analogues of the modern
hustler's techniques to have been used in the earliest forms
of billiard games.

But it doesn't help much to state, as a *terminus a quo* for
hustling, the date when something like billiards first was
played, because nobody has demonstrated what that date
might be. Billiard historians have indeed proposed several
dates and places for the origin of the game; however, as
indicated in Chapter 1, such historians are hopelessly incompetent. (Many of them, for example, state that billiards
was known in ancient Egypt, the "evidence" being that
Shakespeare has Cleopatra say "Let's to billiards.") Until
research on the subject that I have under way is completed
—if my hunch is right, it will demonstrate that billiards
began in fifteenth-century France—we had best skip this
matter and turn from the origin of billiards to the question
of what the historical record might have to say, if anything,
about billiard players' conscious use of hustling techniques
as such. And it does say something.

The earliest evidence of hustling I have found so far (let
me reiterate that my research is not completed) reveals
that not only hustling techniques, but the poolroom hustler
as a distinct occupational type, had arisen in Europe by the
time of the Industrial Revolution. The basic strategies and
tactics of present-day hustling were adumbrated by the
workers of *ancien regime* France.

To be sure, there were differences because the structure
of billiard games and the superstructure of betting relationships differed somewhat from today's practice. But by the
1770's, in the poolrooms of Paris, there had developed
clear-cut equivalents of today's stalling, lemoning, and
dumping. There had also emerged the professional gambler

who lived off his bets on hustlers, the prototype of today's backer, and indeed his was more often a full-time occupational role than that of the hustler.

In addition, the subtle art of "making a game" was highly developed, the principal difference being that in pre-revolutionary Paris, non-playing bettors participated fully in arranging the handicap terms of a match. And the eighteenth-century hustler had a remarkably modern bag of ancillary short-con routines, e.g., he too would pretend to be upset by an unlucky break and to be badly thrown off his game thereby.[28]

A number of modern hustlers, like some other regular players, have so great a love of the game that for all their lack of formal education they show much genuine interest in and knowledge of billiard history. Not only are they more historically minded than other deviant groups, not only has much material written by billiard historians—true and un-true—filtered down to them, but they have preserved a good bit of billiard history and playing technique by means of a long oral tradition. For example, it was from a hustler that I first learned exactly how the structure of the game played by Phelan and Seereiter in 1859 differed from to-day's game.[29] Or, to give an example from playing tech-nique, many refinements and extensions of the mathemati-cal systems for calculating three-cushion billiard shots have never been published, but have been simply passed on orally from one generation of players—including hustlers—to the next.[30] So it did not seem to me fantastic on the face of it

[28] I take all this material on Parisian hustling in the 1770's from the eyewitness account of Restif de la Bretonne; see his *Les Nuits de Paris* (Paris: Hachette, 1960), as follows: "Les Billards: Acteurs," pp. 116–19; "Suite du Billard: Le Prête-Nom," pp. 119–22; "Suite du Billard: La Revanche," pp. 124–26; "Suite: Le Coup de Grace," pp. 127–30.

[29] On the significance of this game, see Chapter 1.

[30] The fullest published information on mathematical systems for three-cushion billiards can be found in Willie Hoppe, *Billiards as It Should be Played* (Chicago: Reilly and Lee, 1941) pp. 64 ff. But full as it may be, it is only a small part of what the best older students of the subject know, use in their playing, and pass on orally to younger players.

to wonder if modern American hustlers knew anything of their European predecessors. I found that a few hustlers and also some non-hustlers did indeed have knowledge, or folklore, about hustlers who were active before they were born, but that this material extended neither beyond the 1890's nor beyond America.

That the oral tradition, strong though it is, knows nothing of American hustlers earlier than the 1890's doesn't rule out the possibility that there were such hustlers. But it led me to think that in comparing modern American hustling with early European predecessors, I was probably seeing "history" where none existed, that what really was involved was not cultural diffusion but independent invention. Such facts as I have been able to gather support this latter interpretation.

Before one can talk of cultural diffusion one must demonstrate cultural contact. For example, it would be absurd to suggest that the syncopation in Negro jazz derives from syncopation's prior appearance in Beethoven's Ninth Symphony (absurd because the slaves didn't go to Beethoven concerts), but sensible to suggest that it derives from the syncopation in West African music (sensible because the slaves did come from West Africa). Now, billiards did not come to America from the sort of poolrooms and persons described by Restif de la Bretonne, nor from similar milieux in England. All the evidence we have indicates that it diffused from the British tradition of upper-class private playing (see Chapter 1). Public tables made their appearance in America very soon afterward, but that was a native development rather than an importation, i.e., private playing by the American upper class quickly "trickled down" to become public playing by the middle and lower classes, at first on tables in taverns and inns, later in poolrooms as such.

Moreover, if we consider Michael Phelan's 1850 comment about the number of public tables in earlier days (p. 24), it is obvious that there wouldn't have been much point for American hustlers to have existed before, say, 1825, because there wouldn't have been anything like the "opportunity structure" that existed in the Paris of Restif.

And the *New York Times* correspondent in Detroit in 1859, reporting on preparations for the Phelan-Seereiter match, wrote that in addition to the good players who had come from all over the country to see the contest, there were also in town "a great many black-legs, sharpers, and the like, and probably some pickpockets," but significantly didn't mention hustlers (neither "black-leg" nor "sharper" had that meaning in America).[31]

The lack of hustlers in 1859 wasn't due to any lack of poolrooms or players; there were plenty of both by then. But one key element of the opportunity structure was still missing: heavy action. The poolroom tradition that all players should bet on themselves—not merely on those battling it out for a championship—was just getting started. In 1850, Michael Phelan correctly noted that billiards was

> sometimes desecrated to purposes of gambling . . . . yet, as a general thing, playing for money is prohibited in the Billiard Rooms and Saloons of this country; in truth, it is a very unusual circumstance to hear, that money is wagered on Billiards at present.[32]

And in 1869 Dudley Kavanagh could still write, with absolute honesty and only slightly less accuracy, that

> Betting on billiards is not common in this country between the players engaged. In England a game is scarcely thought to be worth playing unless for a stake, however small. This is also the custom in Continental Europe. The very little betting which is done here (besides large bets on professional matches) is for the expense of the game and the accompanying refreshments.[33]

But note that Kavanagh says there were "large bets on professional matches." Since that would mark the true beginning in America of the requisite opportunity structure, it is where one would expect to find the first recorded instance of American hustling—and where one does find it:

[31] *New York Times,* April 14, 1859, *Supplement,* [p. 2], col. 3.

[32] Michael Phelan, *Billiards Without a Master* (New York: D. D. Winant, 1850), p. 7.

[33] Dudley Kavanagh, *op. cit.,* p. 67.

the early professionals Carme and Rudolphe, in a match played on November 18, 1868, acted in collusion to dump the bettors.[34] American hustling was started by the professional players themselves.

As more and more of the ordinary players began betting on their own matches in addition to the professionals' matches, hustling arose as an occupation distinct from professional play. For example, one player's recollection (published in 1914) of billiards in South Michigan during the period 1860 to 1890, describes the emergence of hustlers "along near the end of this period," and tells how rumors of a fine young player in Plainville, Michigan, "attracted the attention of what today would be called the 'sharks' in Chicago, Detroit, and other cities."[35] It would seem that the earliest date for American hustlers preserved in today's oral tradition is not far off the mark after all.

By about 1890, then, through an independent line of development, American poolrooms had become what their French and English predecessors had long been: full-fledged action rooms, with suckers ready to plunge on their own skill and hustlers ready to take them. The words of wisdom for players in E. White's British billiard book of 1807 (which, as I indicated, is probably swiped from a French book), by the 1890's applied to America also:

> No billiard room of any notoriety is free from men who are gamesters by profession, and who are constantly in waiting to catch the ignorant and unsuspecting, who occasionally drop in, from motives either of curiosity or amusement; and by constant practice they acquire a degree of dexterity, that enables them to obtain an easy advantage over the generality of their opponents. Their grand object is to conceal their skill from their adversary, and to accommodate their play to his, in such a manner, as to appear to obtain the conquest more in consequence of good fortune than good play. In order to effect this, they . . . chiefly depend upon those strokes, the intent of which are

34 *Ibid.*, p. 32.
35 George Hersch, "Billiards in South Michigan from 1860 to 1890 (Second Installment)," *Billiards Magazine,* Vol. 1, No. 11 (February, 1914), pp. 17–19.

apparent only to those who are intimately acquainted with
the minutiae of the game. They generally suffer their ad-
versary to gain some few games . . . but in the end, it is
well for him indeed, if he escape being fleeced of all the
ready money he may happen to have about him.[36]

That's what the hustler did, and does.

Conclusions

Throughout this study I have used a special orientation
toward the material, an orientation not generally found in
other studies of people who make their living from illegal
work.[37] If, nevertheless, I have managed to make sociological sense out of the data, then it follows that the special
orientation provides the most significant lesson of this study
for the future of criminological research. The lesson is this:
criminologists stand to lose little and gain much in the way
of sociological understanding if, when studying people dedicated to an illegal occupation, they will overcome their
fascination with the "illegal" part long enough to focus
on the "occupation" part. After all, any theory of illegal
occupations can be but a special case, albeit an important
one, of general occupational theory.

Criminologists, following the lead of the late Edwin
Sutherland, recognize that one hallmark of the career
criminal—be he engaged in major crime or, like the hustler
most of the time, in violating generally unenforced criminal
law—is that the illegal activity in question constitutes his

[36] E. White, *A Practical Treatise on the Game of Billiards*
(London: W. Miller, 1807), p. 2.

[37] I know of only one other study of an illegal occupation
that has an orientation similar to mine: James Bryan's "Apprenticeships in Prostitution," *Social Problems*, Vol. 12, No. 3
(Winter, 1965), pp. 287–97. Howard Becker's *Outsiders* (New
York: Free Press of Glencoe, 1963), although it does not deal
with illegal work, is the pioneering application of this framework to the sociology of deviance; Becker employs it to analyze
avocational lawbreakers (marihuana users) and people whose
work is legal but who are nevertheless stigmatized (jazz
musicians).

regular job.[38] Yet their researches seem thoroughly un-
tenanted by what occupational sociologists have learned
about how to look at someone's regular job. An example:
one of the best recent criminological studies of a specific
type of career criminal is Roebuck and Cadwalleder's research on Negro armed robbers.[39] But for all its useful
findings—and there are plenty—the study is also a story of
missed research opportunities because it proceeds with
blissful inattention to what sociology has had mainly to say
about one's "career" and its relation to other matters.

What is especially surprising about criminology's neglect
of these occupational aspects as such, is that people dedicated to an illegal occupation actually *tell* the criminologist
these aspects are central in their thinking and, moreover,
under the right conditions can be observed to behave in
accord with their statements on the matter. Thus one would
think that the criminologist, even if he had read little or no
occupational theory, would become inescapably aware of
its possible relevance just as soon as he began seriously
to study a career-oriented deviant. (This is in fact how I
first became aware of its possible relevance—although not,
as it happened, out of acquaintance with hustlers but out
of acquaintance with a burglar.)

But the criminologist doesn't reach such awareness because he doesn't appreciate the career deviant's statements
indicating the centrality of occupational concerns. (For
example, when a professional criminal describes himself
as being "like a businessman" or "just in a different line
of business," the criminologist takes this to be merely a
rationalization. It is a rationalization all right, but it is by
no means merely that, and often it is not even primarily
that.) The reason the criminologist doesn't appreciate such
statements is that he doesn't confirm them from his own
observation. And the reason he doesn't confirm them from

[38] See, for example, Marshall Clinard, *Sociology of Deviant
Behavior*, rev. ed. (New York: Holt, Rinehart & Winston,
1963), pp. 210–11.

[39] Cf. Julian Roebuck and Mervyn Cadwalleder, "The Negro
Armed Robber as a Criminal Type," *Pacific Sociological Review*, Vol. 4 (Spring, 1961), pp. 21–26.

his own observation is that he doesn't study the deviant under proper conditions. As for what the proper conditions are and why the criminologist doesn't avail himself of them—that is the subject of the next chapter.

As to the possible gain for criminology in the orientation I suggest, consider, for example, one theoretical implication of what the hustler often does when he needs additional sources of income. It suggests the possibility that many of the data criminologists refer to by rubrics such as "the occasional criminal" or "occasional crime" would be more sharply conceptualized and better understood under the heading "crime as moonlighting." This is for two reasons. First, as soon as we think of crime in this way, it becomes clearer that much serious crime (e.g., bank robbery) is undertaken by people who are neither "mentally ill" nor "white-collar criminals" nor oriented to serious crime as a career nor even oriented to milder crime as a career (unlike the hustler), but who are employed in and identify with perfectly legitimate lower-class jobs, get way behind in their bills, and see temporary or "one shot" criminal activity as a way to get solvent without giving up their regular jobs. It would also become clearer that the same often holds true for milder crimes, e.g., non-victim crimes such as prostitution, which is frequently undertaken in a moonlighting way by typists, salesgirls, and the like. (Moonlighters in prostitution are so frequent that the professionals have even developed argot terms for them; they are called "weekenders" by the professional prostitutes in Las Vegas and "party girls" by the professionals in New York.)

Second, a major precondition of moonlighting, according to Wilensky, is the existence of "occupations and industries on flexible work schedules which provide opportunity for part-time help,"[40] and more recent analysis by labor economists confirms the point: "The industries in which 'moonlighters' found their second jobs were typi-

[40] Cf. Harold Wilensky, "The Moonlighter: A Product of Relative Deprivation," *Industrial Relations,* Vol. 3, No. 1 (October, 1963), pp. 106 ff.

cally those providing opportunities for part-time work."[41] Most crime fits these descriptions perfectly. Indeed, one of the most genuinely appealing things about crime to career criminals and part-timers alike—though one would hardly gather this from the criminology texts—is that for most crimes the working hours are both short and flexible.

Criminological research informed by the orientation I suggest would also, of course, turn up material both new and germane to the sociological study of work as such. In the present study, I have noted some such findings in the section on colleagueship. Here I would like to point out certain other findings that seem to have no analogue in the literature of occupational sociology.

(1) *The work situation.* We saw that the hustler must be not only a skilled player, but that he must be skilled at pretending *not* to have great playing skill. The latter requirement is one thing that distinguishes him from the usual con man (who often, on the contrary, feigns more expertise than he has). And it also distinguishes him from the usual professional gambler. The latter indeed sometimes pretends to be other than he is and disclaims real skill ("I guess I'm just lucky tonight"), but he relies basically on playing skill alone, or else on a combination of playing with cheating skill—being able to switch dice into and out of a game, or to deal seconds or thirds or bottom cards, etc. Pretending to lack of skill is not a basic requirement of the gambler's job, as it is for the hustler. As far as I know, this hustling reliance on competence at feigning incompetence is unique, and nowhere treated in the occupational literature.

(2) *Careers.* Certain occupational roles require youthfulness by definition (e.g., acting juvenile parts), and thus enforce unusually early retirement.[42] In certain other oc-

---

[41] Forrest Bogan and Harvey Hamel, "Multiple Jobholders in May 1963," *Monthly Labor Review* (U.S. Dept. of Labor), Vol. 87, No. 3 (March, 1964), p. 249.

[42] The earliest documented retirement of this kind I have run across is the following: "Chattanooga, Jan. 7 (UPI)—

cupations (airline pilots, for example) age-related career contingencies also force early retirement. It is common to cite competitive sports or games requiring high physical skills as examples of this type—but pool or billiard playing doesn't fit the pattern. And because such faulty generalizing about sports occurs not only among occupational sociologists but among the populace at large, sometimes old age actually helps the hustler in his con.

In textbooks and treatises on the sociology of work, the attention paid to the moonlighter is notable for its scantiness. To the extent that occupational sociologists have studied the subject, they agree with Wilensky's conclusion that the moonlighter "is a man caught in a life-cycle squeeze—he has many dependents."[43] But this pattern obviously doesn't apply to hustlers—nor, for that matter, to the aforesaid typists and shopgirls who moonlight in prostitution.

(3) *The external world.* We saw that changes in American sporting life over the past three decades have severely damaged the hustler's work situation and career. These changes have reduced the number of places he can hustle in, the time-span in which he can stay unknown, the number of people he can hustle, and the average amount of money he can get from someone he hustles. Hustling is a dying trade.

Whenever an occupational group faces a disappearance or major decline of the market for its skills and a consequent inability to make ends meet, we conceptualize this situation as "technological unemployment." But this concept doesn't fit the situation of hustlers at all well. They suffer not from a shift in technology but from a shift in America's demographic structure, i.e., the decline of the

---

Chris Haley retired from county government service yesterday at the age of 9. Chris had been drawing names for Hamilton County grand jurors since 1959. The law requires such tasks to be performed by children under 10. The boy will be 10 in March." From the New York *Daily News,* January 8, 1964, p. 42.

[43] Wilensky, *op. cit.,* p. 110.

bachelor subculture that populated poolrooms so heavily, and secondarily from a shift in fashion, i.e., the decline in the average amount of money bet on poolroom games. In origin, the hustler's problem is utterly unlike that of, say, the order clerk displaced by the introduction of electronic data processing. There is nothing whatever in the present technological structure of our society to prevent hustling (and poolroom life generally) from having or regaining its former place in America. It would seem, then, that occupational theory needs to complement the notion of "technological unemployment" with notions such as "demographic unemployment" and "fashion unemployment."

A more general lesson of this essay is that sociology has unduly neglected the study of people who engage in sports or games for their livelihood. The sociological reason for this neglect is that sociology is compartmentalized into "fields" that tend to make such people, for all their visibility to the sociologist as citizen, invisible to him in his role as sociologist: such people are neglected by students of leisure because the latter are by definition concerned with sports involvement only in its impact on avocational life; and because sports involvement is for the very great majority of people strictly avocational, and those who earn a living at it constitute a minuscule fragment of the labor force, the study of the latter is neglected by occupational sociologists. Thus a largely unexplored area of social research consists of the people who work at what most of us play at.

Appendix: The Hustler and His Argot

Outsiders usually find a deviant group's argot to be one of the most interesting things about that group. But analysis of the argot requires an amount of space disproportionate to its importance in an over-all account of the group. To attenuate this conflict I have followed David Maurer's practice (in *The Big Con*) and relegated argot analysis to an appendix. Moreover, what follows is in no sense a

full-scale study of hustlers' argot; it does not even contain
a full vocabulary list. Instead, it examines the argot merely
in its more sociological aspects—in its relation to hustling
life and to the structural and functional features of argots
in general.

A myth that dies very hard, even among linguists and
social scientists, is that the special language or slang developed by a socially deviant group functions importantly
to protect the group, has secrecy as a primary motive and
mainspring. It dies hard because any outsider quickly no-
tices on first acquaintance with such language that (a) it
has terms for various shady processes and techniques,
(b) it has terms to distinguish insiders from outsiders,
and (c) he can easily be spotted as an outsider because
he doesn't know, or misuses, some of the language. "Common sense" tells him that all this greatly aids group secrecy.
But all it shows *eo ipso* is that the argot of any special
group (deviant or otherwise) includes many terms for
things peculiar to that type of group, is in good part a
technical vocabulary that must be learned. The hustlers'
argot is no exception.

Like all other American deviant argots I know of, it
also reveals numerous facets that testify against a "secrecy"
interpretation. Some examples: (1) Hustlers always use
their argot among themselves when no outsiders are present, where it could not possibly have a secretive purpose.
(2) The argot itself is not protected but is an "open secret,"
i.e., its meanings are quite easily learned by any outsider
who wishes to learn them and is an alert listener or
questioner. (3) The argot is elaborated far beyond any
conceivable need to develop a set of terms for deviant phenomena, and even far beyond any need to develop a full-
scale technical vocabulary (which subsumes the terms for
deviant phenomena).

That last point indicates the true mainsprings of argot:
in various specialized groups, be they deviant or merely
specialized occupational groups, argots develop partly to
provide a shorthand way of referring to technical processes
but partly also as an elaborately inventive, ritualistic, often
rather playful way of reinforcing group identity or "we-

feeling." Thus the argot of hustlers sets them off not for the purpose of secrecy, but rather by way of helping their sense of colleagueship and *esprit de corps*.[44]

Any secrecy function the argot serves is incidental, a bonus as it were, and hustlers certainly do not count on it. The hustler, like the members of secret societies discussed by Georg Simmel, knows that the only way to maintain group secrets is to keep his mouth shut about them in the presence of outsiders—not discuss them even in esoteric terms, which would, if anything, only make the outsider highly suspicious. For this reason hustlers actually use their argot much less when outsiders are present than when they are absent. To the very small extent that hustlers' collaborative swindling (dumping) requires some secretive communication in the presence of the swindled, such communication is, as we have seen, carried out not via argot at all but by a pre-arranged *ad hoc* signal ("the office") that is not standard argot and in fact is usually nonverbal.

[44] Linguists commonly distinguish between two types of specialized slang: (a) a noncriminal group's specialized slang, called *argot,* which of course is unintelligible to outsiders (and thus may occasionally be used for secrecy), but nevertheless is developed and used primarily to meet the need for technical terms and secondarily as a way of bolstering group solidarity; and (b) a criminal group's specialized slang, called *cant,* which is designed and used primarily to make the group's conversation unintelligible to outsiders.

This distinction may have some validity when applied to the criminal speech of certain other countries in certain historical periods, but it is often uncritically assumed to hold good for American criminal speech also (see, for example, H. L. Mencken's *American Language,* 4th ed., p. 578). A lot of myth and nonsense about American criminals' so-called "cant" has been generated by linguists bookishly familiar with the history of specialized slang but unfamiliar with the actual lifeways of American criminals. I contend that "cant," in the linguists' sense of the term, has not been demonstrated to exist, and cannot be demonstrated to exist, for any American criminal group whatsoever.

An honorable exception among linguists is David Maurer. His discussion of the language of con men in his *The Big Con* (New York: Pocket Books, 1949, pp. 282–88) is, with one exception noted below, a model of sociological sense.

The lexicon of hustler argot overlaps that of some other argots. First, there is considerable overlapping with general poolroom argot. I estimate that most regular poolroom players understand at least a third of hustler argot. (And since the portion they understand is not restricted to "innocent" technical terms but includes such items as "fish," this is further evidence against a secrecy function.) Hustler argot subsumes that of the poolroom world; it is poolroom argot plus about twice as many additions and elaborations. And, as one would expect from the fact that hustlers have a greater sense of collective identity than poolroom habitués in general, that portion of the argot understood by non-hustlers isn't used by them with anywhere near the frequency that hustlers use it.[45]

Secondly, and quite understandably in view of the nature of hustling life, there is lexical admixture from other professional criminal argots, especially gamblers' argot. The most important such term is "action," used variously in the senses of "a bet" or "betting" or "an opportunity to bet" or "a situation involving betting." As the reader may have gathered by now, it is the most ubiquitous argot word in hustler speech. Some other criminal terms used by hustlers are: "the office"; "the wire" (in the phrase "to send" or "give" someone "the wire," to tip him off—not in the professional con man's sense); "score" (noun: an amount of money or goods won or taken; verb: to win or take money or goods); "mechanic"; "yard" ($100); "the joint" (jail), etc.

Finally, one should note—though it is technically part of general slang admixture rather than argot—that a huge dimension of the hustler lexicon is in the use of obscene exclamations ("motherfucker," "rat bastard," "cock-

---

[45] A portion of poolroom argot, and consequently of hustler argot, is also used by that dwindling band of upper-class billiard players who play entirely or almost entirely in private men's clubs. For example, I find the hustler term "shortstop" (meaning an excellent player but of the second rank, one who can stop all but the top players) used in a billiard book issued by an upper-class club. [*Amateur Billiard Championship of America (Class A): A Souvenir. . . .* (New York: Knickerbocker Athletic Club, 1899), p. 18].

sucker," "*chinga su madre,*" etc.). The hustler is particularly given to these exclamations when he unintentionally
misses a shot. His use of such terms is far more frequent
than one would expect simply from his lower-class origins.
There are two reasons for this: (a) In general, obscenities
are used oftener in the poolroom than elsewhere in lower-
class life, because the main inhibition against their use (for
all classes) is the presence of women—and the poolroom,
like the army, is ordinarily an all-male institution. (b) The
hustler spends more time than anyone else in this non-
inhibiting milieu of the poolroom, and thus tends to develop
greater habitual use of obscenity than other poolroom
players. For these reasons also, when a woman does enter
an action poolroom it is the hustlers who are likely to feel
most resentful, for they suffer the greatest inhibition of
their characteristic mode of discourse.

An argot has a geography, which means not merely
that it is used in various localities of a country but that
typically its content varies a bit, at any given time, from
one locality to another. Such variation takes two main
forms: (a) The same thing may be referred to differently.
Thus in one locality the usual criminal term for police
may be "the Man," in another it may be "the fuzz," in another "the nabs," in another "busters," etc. (b) The same
term may be used for different things. Thus the term "gunsel" among Illinois criminals means a homosexual who
takes the female role, but among California criminals it
means an armed robber. Both kinds of variation occur not
only from one city to another, but in larger cities they
sometimes occur from one neighborhood or friendship
clique to another. Hustler argot seems unusually bare of
such variations; the only significant exception is that one
kind of hustling game is usually called "one pocket" in
some cities and "pocket apiece" in others. The argot is
strikingly uniform from one city to the next and, within
large cities, from one poolroom to the next.

It is tempting to attribute this relative uniformity to intercity and inter-poolroom communication, to the fact
that hustlers possibly move about oftener than members
of most other argot-using groups. But intercity communi-

cation is not sufficient to deter the preserving of local linguistic patterns. (For example, many linguists once assumed that the rapid spread of radio ownership in the
1920's and 1930's would tend to level out American regional differences in pronunciation and semantic patterns,
but the *Linguistic Atlas of the United States and Canada*
abundantly disproved this assumption.) Rather, it seems
attributable mostly to the hustler's strong traditionalism
—something that will emerge more clearly when we look
at the argot historically.

An argot varies in time as well as space. Over the years
it adds and drops words; and some other words, though
they remain in the argot throughout, have their meanings
changed. (For example, the criminal term "gunsel," some
of whose current meanings are given above, once meant
—among other things—an apprentice safecracker.) Such
historical change is more rapid in argot than in the language at large (though less rapid than change in general slang); compendia of argot get out of date much
sooner than a general dictionary does. Furthermore, the
argots of socially deviant groups (e.g., drug addicts, jazz
musicians, professional criminals) tend to change even
more rapidly than argots of respectable trades; when an
argot word of such a group gets to be common coin among
outsiders, the insiders often replace it—again, not for purposes of secrecy, but by way of reaffirming their separate-
ness and "in-groupness." (Thus, only outsiders these days
still refer to a marihuana cigarette as a "reefer.") But
despite these strong predisposing factors, the hustlers'
argot shows hardly any evidence of historical change.

Of course the argot of pool and billiard hustlers didn't
spring full-formed from Zeus's head; there must have been
a developmental period in which words were added and
others dropped. But this period, whenever it was, certainly antedated World War I. For as far back as I have
been able to trace the argot of hustlers—about sixty years
—it has been remarkably stable. During this entire time it
seems that: (a) no new words have been introduced;
(b) no words have become obsolete; (c) no words are
obsolescent (used or understood only by oldtimers); (d)

only one word has become more generalized in its meaning; and (e) only three words have become more specialized in their meanings.

I believe this is related to the strong element of traditionalism in hustler ideology, to the fact that the hustler has more awareness of, involvement with, and reverence for his outstanding predecessors and their accomplishments than other kinds of deviants have for their historical counterparts—more than the usual professional criminal or drug addict; more, even, than the homosexual or jazz musician.[46] Certainly it is not due to any lack of linguistic inventiveness or playfulness on the hustler's part (as we shall see when we consider hustlers' nicknames).

A stigmatized group counter-stigmatizes by having at least one pejorative term for outsiders as a class. Outsiders (in this context think of all non-hustlers, in or out of the poolroom world) are likely to encounter this term at least as frequently as any other in the argot; that is why the term applied to outsiders by, for example, jazz musicians and many criminal groups, "squares," is now understood by nearly all outsiders and is indeed used by so many of them that it has ceased to be just an argot word and has become part of general American slang. A few argot words for outsiders, though, remain fairly esoteric, e.g., the homosexual term "jam." Hustler argot is unusual in that its term for outsiders, "suckers," is properly speaking not an argot word at all; that is, it did not originate with hustlers, or even in other deviant groups that use it,

[46] The homosexual's interest in famous predecessors tends to be limited to citing them for the purpose of self-justification. The jazz musician's interest in famous predecessors or their accomplishments tends to be limited to those few major breakthroughs of the recent past, such as the innovations of Charlie Parker, from which current developments are deemed to stem. (Jazz fans are often more involved with past history—much to the annoyance of the musician, who would prefer that his questioner stop bugging him to recall details of a recording date of 25 years ago and concentrate instead on current sounds.) The historical attitude of most pool and billiard hustlers is quite different; even teenage hustlers are often full of respectful and prideful lore about their forebears.

but was adopted from general American slang. This possibly may relate to the fact, noted earlier, that hustlers are unusually indifferent to the opinions of those who put them down, and hence would feel little need to develop counter-stigmatizing terms of their own.

Criminal or quasi-criminal groups commonly have a name for those outsiders considered to be prospects, for their actual or potential "victims." This is especially so for deviants who do their "victimizing" in a primary, face-to-face situation. Thus the con man has his "mark," the prostitute has her "john" or "trick," etc. But the hustler has no such special term. A few decades ago, when pool hustlers were also (and usually) called pool "sharks," their actual or potential victims were often called "fish." But for fifteen or twenty years now the term "shark" has not been used in this sense among hustlers themselves and among poolroom habitués generally (though it is still so used among older outsiders whose acquaintance with poolrooms ended years ago), and the term "fish" has been restricted to cover only a small minority of victims—those rare ones who keep returning for more beatings.[47] (The hustler's "fish" is thus comparable to the con man's "addict" rather than his "mark.") Today, hustlers use the term "sucker," which formerly had only one meaning (outsiders as a whole, i.e., all non-hustlers), indiscriminately to refer to (a) outsiders as a whole or (b) that particular class of outsiders who are actual or potential victims. Which of these meanings it has depends on the

[47] "Shark" survives in poolrooms with a specialized meaning as a transitive verb: to "shark" one's opponent means to upset or distract him while he's shooting, for example, by making a sudden movement in his line of sight when he is aiming. In addition to the specialization of "shark" and "fish," the word "hustler" itself has taken on a specialized meaning among hustlers. When they referred to themselves as "sharks" in the old sense, they often used "hustler" in the general slang sense of anyone who's alert and willing to take on any sort of odd job for a quick buck; now, of course, they use "hustler" in the narrower meaning of a member of their profession. For the early usages, and the period of overlap between the meanings of "shark" and "hustler," cf. Vogeler, *op. cit., passim.*

context, and in some contexts it can mean both at once (as in one hustler's remark to me, "The trouble today is that most of the suckers are wise.")

Perhaps the most striking aspect of the pool and billiard hustlers' argot is its development and use of nicknames. Well over half of all full-time hustlers have nicknames which they use regularly. My impression is that the percentage of them who have nicknames is not only higher than among either professionals or hustlers in other sports, but is higher than in any other adult group in America except for certain criminal groups (notably con men). A few hustlers acquired their nicknames in their pre-hustling childhood or adolescence—this is especially likely if the nickname refers to a physical characteristic of the hustler—but the good majority acquired such names after they entered hustling.

The following are the nicknames of some hustlers recently or currently active: Brooklyn Jimmy, Cornbread Red, Spanish Eddy, Sleepy, Blueshirt, Glendale Johnny, Fats, Wimpy, Harry the Russian, Snake, Whitey (three hustlers), Connecticut Johnny, Detroit Whitey, Brooklyn Johnny, Jersey Red, Blacky, Fifth Avenue Red, Miami, Shoes, Cicero, Gigolo, Subway, Country, Peter Rabbit, Weenie Beanie, Skinny Eddy, Squirrel, Fast Eddy,[48] Gypsy (two hustlers), Tallahassee, Boston Shorty, Rockaway Abe, Brooklyn Charlie, Johnny Irish, Big Gene, Charlie the Hat, the Knoxville Bear,[49] Derby, Dago Frankie, Lefty (three hustlers), Iron Joe, Bob the Destroyer, Jimmy Sure-Shot, Daddy Warbucks, and Tommy the Sailor.

Nicknames formed on similar principles were borne by hustlers active before 1920: Cowboy Weston, Boston Whitey, the Sicily Kid, Seattle Slim, Farmer Jones, Johnny Icewater, West Coast Willie, Dago Joe, Bowery Al.[50]

---

[48] Fast Eddy was nicknamed after the character in the movie *The Hustler*—but ironically, for when he was first learning the game he was noted for the speed with which he would lose his paycheck.

[49] The Knoxville Bear is, however, more frequently referred to among hustlers by his real name, Eddy Taylor.

[50] These nicknames of pre-1920 hustlers are taken from Vogeler, *op. cit.*, p. 346.

I had assumed at first that certainly this part of the argot, if no other, was used for purposes of secrecy or disguise. A nickname, I thought, would help a hustler to con because he, whose poolroom reputation is known via his nickname, could disguise his identity from the non-hustler by introducing himself by his real name (could con by "honestly" introducing himself). This hypothesis was completely disproven. The hustler doesn't keep his nickname from his opponent or anybody else in the pool-room; he is always pleased to use it and be referred to by it. For example: at the start of a game with a hustler I'd seen but never met, I introduced myself by saying, "I'm Ned," and the hustler replied, "They call me Shoes." Most hustlers never use their real names (except occasion-ally with outsiders encountered outside the poolroom), not because these need to be hidden but simply because they prefer to be nicknamed. Like many other argot terms, these nicknames exist because, to quote the words of more than one hustler, "they lend a little color to the game."

This is to say that the hustler's nickname is a *monicker,* not an *alias.* True enough, the monicker of a hustler (or other criminal) may incidentally aid him when he is being sought by police, for the latter may be seeking him only under his real name whereas most of his colleagues and friends have never heard that name and know him only by his monicker. It is also true that hustlers sometimes have to dodge the police because of trouble over their criminal moonlighting jobs. But the hustler (or other crimi-nal) trying to avoid arrest never depends on his monicker for this purpose; on the contrary, when on the lam and faced with any situation in which he must give his name—e.g., meeting new people, renting a room, buying a plane ticket—he uses neither his real name nor his monicker but temporarily adopts yet another name, a true alias.[51]

Although the chief reason for hustlers' use of monickers

[51] Unfortunately David Maurer's discussion of monickers (*op. cit.,* p. 286), in failing to note the functional distinction between a monicker and an alias, misleadingly conflates the two.

is, as indicated above, the furtherance of *esprit de corps,* additional factors bolster such use. Taken together, they probably account for the extremely high percentage of hustlers—old and young alike—with monickers. (a) Hustlers are overwhelmingly from the lower class, which makes more frequent use of nicknames in adulthood than other classes. (b) The hustlers' world overlaps other criminal circles that have high monicker rates (especially, other types of gamblers). (c) Hustlers are historically minded, and the use of monickers is one way of maintaining a long-standing craft tradition (the old-time hustlers also had monickers). (d) The monickers may also reflect a continuance of certain male-alliance aspects of adolescence. Relevant here is the fact that the poolroom world—at least the world of action rooms—is exclusively male, except on infrequent occasion.[52]

[52] After this book was in press one hustler, whose monicker is "Fats" and who alleges he is the model for "Minnesota Fats" in *The Hustler,* published a book of reminiscences: Minnesota Fats with Tom Fox, *The Bank Shot and Other Great Robberies* (Cleveland: World Publishing Company, 1966). Fats is a delightful storyteller, but his imagination and ego have resulted in a book that presents, along with much fact, much fiction as if it were fact.

Research Method, Morality, and Criminology

Experience with adult, unreformed, "serious" criminals in their natural environment—not only those undertaking felonies in a moonlighting way, such as pool hustlers, but career felons—has convinced me that if we are to make a major advance in our scientific understanding of criminal lifestyles, criminal subcultures, and their relation to the larger society, we must undertake genuine field research on these people. I am also convinced that this research can be done by many more sociologists, and much more easily, than the criminology textbooks lead us to suppose.

No criminology textbook, on balance, encourages such field research; most criminology textbooks actively discourage it; no criminology textbook pays attention to techniques for solving problems connected with it; every criminology textbook to discuss it is concerned above all to offer copouts for avoiding it. This chapter tries to remedy such defects.

The reason for these defects is not far to seek. Field study of adult criminals requires among other things giving up, indeed carefully avoiding, any and every kind of social-work orientation (such as a concern to "rehabilitate" criminals); but in sociology's struggle to become a science it has been precisely criminology, of all the subfields of sociology, that has been least successful in freeing itself from traditional social-work concerns.

In the years immediately ahead that struggle may be
even more difficult, because of a recent retrograde development: lately a number of sociologists themselves have joined
forces with social workers to promote extra-scientific goals
in the name of science and have saddled us with new
euphemisms for these goals, such as "applied sociology"
and "action research." Some sociologists have come to this
from mistaken conceptions of science, others from being
tired of being tired radicals, and others from an appraisal
of where most of the grant action is. Whatever the motive,
they are wrong, and below I shall have to animadvert on
their views insofar as these views affect criminology. But
let us look first at the criminology textbooks.

I

Criminology textbooks can be roughly grouped in three
basic categories, according to the means they employ to
cop out.

The simplest technique, and in a way the most effective,
is for the textbook writer to be so generally negligent and
imprecise about research methods that no serious comparison or even description of different methods is offered,
and consequently the troublesome question of whether field
research might sometimes be the method of choice need
never arise. This is seen, for example, in Marshall Clinard's
Sociology of Deviant Behavior.[1] But it is atypical. The
fact that statistics on crime in general, and on convictions
in particular, are so obviously defective in so many ways—
something no criminologist can avoid seeing and having
to discuss—causes most textbook writers at least to break
silence on this question.

A second mode of evasion, intellectually the shoddiest,
illustrates the special kind of blindness that can sometimes
be induced by a "labelling" stance.[2] It is represented at

[1] This is also true, despite its promising title, of the same
author's "Research Frontiers in Criminology," *British Journal
of Delinquency,* VII (October, 1956), pp. 110–22.

[2] For additional remarks on difficulties with the application
of labelling theory, see Chapter 5.

its ingenious best, or disingenuous worst, in the way Richard Korn and Lloyd McCorkle delimit the subject matter of their *Criminology and Penology:*

> Faced with evidence that large numbers of persons commit violations for which they are never prosecuted, we are led to the further conclusion that the *actual, objective extent of law breaking may, in itself, be an unreliable index of criminality.* This conclusion is suggested by the recognition that criminality itself (as distinguished from law breaking) is a matter of social stigmatization and official action in the first place. . . . An act of actual law breaking does not become criminal in any realistic social or legal sense until and unless it is conventionally defined and officially acted upon.[3] [Italics in original.]

We need not deny the important consequences of either conventional definitions or official actions to see that the foregoing point of view is, first of all, a cover-up for the fact that most sociologists find it too difficult or distasteful to get near adult criminals except in jails or other anticrime settings, such as the courts and probation and parole systems.

Secondly, and more importantly, it is an abdication of sociology's role as a special discipline able uniquely to discover certain kinds of knowledge and understandings of social life—abdication in favor of a misguided "democratic" notion that a society's official acts and conventional public definitions really tell us what the society is all about, and that the sociologist's main job is to count and codify them.

[3] Richard Korn and Lloyd McCorkle, *Criminology and Penology* (New York: Holt, Rinehart & Winston, 1959), p. 11.

Other texts using the Korn-McCorkle mode of copout sometimes do so via their definition of crime rather than of the criminal. Thus for Walter Reckless, the only "real" crimes are those that are officially recorded; see his *The Crime Problem* (New York: Appleton-Century-Crofts, 1961, 3rd ed.), pp. 23, 27. Still other criminology texts, such as the one by Ruth Cavan, dodge the issue by never coming to grips with the problem of definition at all. Some of these texts partake also of the first mode; in fact, Korn and McCorkle, when it comes to description and comparison of research methods, are fully as vague as Clinard.

The latter kind of operating definition of sociology, a very common one, produces nothing but hackwork, a flood of books whose conclusions are remarkable for little besides utter banality; which is why the intelligent layman so often decides that except for the statistics and the jargon, he has been a sociologist all his life and didn't know it.

If, on the other hand, sociology is what my teacher Louis Wirth used to claim it is, the study of how society is really run as distinguished from how the society's civics textbooks say it is run, then—Korn and McCorkle to the contrary—it is exactly the discrepancies between law breaking and law enforcement that constitute one of the most central topics of criminology. But we are never going to know much about that topic, or many another, until we get out of the jails and the courts and into the field. Of course our ignorance can remain blissful if, like Korn and McCorkle, we use labelling theory as a form of verbal magic to convince ourselves that the only "real" criminal is a caught criminal, one whom law enforcers have obligingly placed where it is convenient for criminologists to study him.

II

Fortunately, most criminologists are not magicians, and the typical criminology text is given rather early on to moaning and groaning about the fact that criminals and the things they do are not well represented by official crime statistics. (This fact is then usually ignored in the later chapters.)

We still have much to learn on this matter of bias in official records. (Especially, when it comes to assessing historical trends, I think we have much to learn from professional historians' techniques of weighing sources.[4]) But the better criminologists are trying hard. The trouble is

[4] For a brilliant example of how a historian can dissect the biases in official crime records and illuminate a good deal of social reality in the process, see Margaret Gay Davies, *The Enforcement of English Apprenticeship: A Study in Applied Mercantilism, 1563–1642* (Cambridge, Mass.: Harvard University Press, 1956), *passim*.

that they are overly grateful for small gains, and thus get trapped in halfway houses. Two of these halfway houses are quite seductive.

One halfway house, whose foundations were firmly built by Edwin Sutherland's work on white-collar crime, comprises research that ferrets out new information by looking beyond police and court statistics to the records of acts punished by other governmental agencies of social control. Its definition of crime includes *mala prohibita* as well as *mala in se,* which, lawyer-sociologist Paul Tappan to the contrary, makes good juridical sense as well as good sociological sense.[5] Marshall Clinard's study of wartime pricing and rationing violations, *The Black Market,* is an excellent example of this kind of research. A recent offshoot of this Sutherland tradition is Mary Owen Cameron's study of shoplifters, *The Booster and the Snitch,* extraordinarily valuable because it uses, for the first time in criminology, data to be found in the records of private police (in her study, records of department-store detectives), which reveal many acts that are *mala in se* but nevertheless don't show up in official statistics.

A second halfway house consists essentially of using survey research methods to collect statistics on crime. The inchoate beginnings of this approach are in the special

[5] Paul Tappan's "Who is the Criminal?," *American Sociological Review,* XII (February, 1947), pp. 96–102, restricts crime to acts "adjudicated as such *by the courts*" (my italics) so as deliberately to exclude corporate violations of law, or of governmental directives issued under authority of law, that are adjudicated by non-court regulatory agencies of the state. Most jurists as well as social scientists, however, would agree with C. S. Kenny's *Outlines of Criminal Law* that crimes are simply "wrongs whose sanction is punitive and is in no way remissible by any private person," regardless of the type of enforcement machinery. Max Gluckman's *The Judicial Process Among the Barotse of Northern Rhodesia* (Glencoe, Ill.: The Free Press, 1955), from which I take Kenny's definition of crime, also notes approvingly (p. 346) Kenny's point that crimes are "tried by different procedures before various tribunals, and sanctioned in many degrees by various kinds of punishment and moral reprobation." On this view, Sutherland's "white collar crime" is most definitely crime.

crime surveys undertaken by some states in the 1920's,
but the modern scientific foundation was laid principally
by James Short and F. Ivan Nye, who demonstrated that
intelligently constructed anonymous questionnaires, intelligently distributed in schools, could be used to gather
important and valid data on the distribution of delinquent
acts among those who had not been adjudicated as delinquents.[6] Criminologists have been slow to develop possible variations of this method in the study of adult crime,
and we don't really know to what degree it would work
with adults. But it is an intriguing possibility to be explored.
[*Addendum, 1968:* Since the foregoing was written, the
National Opinion Research Center has done important survey research on crime victims, which reveals that under-
reporting of crimes to the police is fantastically greater
than anyone had suspected.]

Halfway houses are of course better than the tents of
reliance only on official crime statistics. It is also obvious
that the number of criminologists is limited, that these
halfway houses (and others) could have many rooms added
to them, and that such construction work could keep every
criminologist usefully busy for years. But this would hardly
be the best allocation of manpower, because these are still
halfway houses and we should also be constructing houses
that take us all the way.

It is all very well to draw a fuller quantitative picture of
the numbers and kinds of criminals or criminal acts. But
we cannot use this to dodge what is the ultimate, qualitative
task—particularly regarding career criminals, whose importance to any theorist of human behavior, not to mention
the rest of society, is so disproportionate to their numbers:
providing well-rounded, contemporary, sociological descriptions and analyses of criminal lifestyles, subcultures,
and their relation to larger social processes and structures.

That is just where criminology falls flat on its face. Especially in the study of adult career criminals, we over-

[6] Cf. James F. Short, Jr., and F. Ivan Nye, "Reported Behavior as a Criterion of Deviant Behavior," *Social Problems,* 5
(Winter, 1957), pp. 207–213, and the references therein to
other articles by these authors.

depend on a skewed sample, studied in non-natural surroundings (anti-crime settings), providing mostly data recollected long after the event.

Apropos of that last point: Criminologists can tell you about Sutherland's "Chic Conwell," but they can't give you comparable data on professionals of today, still less the many other kinds of data on professionalism in crime that Sutherland never got to at all; criminologists can tell you much (though by no means all) about the Capone mob or Luciano mob in the 1930's, but on organized crime today they are no better than Will Rogers (all they know is what they read in the newspapers) and are inferior to any good crime reporter (who knows a lot that can't be put in the newspapers). We are always going to be in this spot—always slowly fitting together a jigsaw puzzle that is decades out of date, and never even knowing if we have all the pieces, or the right pieces—unless we change our research methods.

This means—there is no getting away from it—the study of career criminals *au naturel,* in the field, the study of such criminals as they normally go about their work and play, the study of "uncaught" criminals and the study of others who in the past have been caught but are not caught at the time you study them.[7] We know how much valuable knowledge and insight has been gained from field study of all sorts of other people. We even know it in the case of juvenile delinquents, and even in the case of mildly criminal adults engaged in "victimless" crime, such as drug users, homosexuals, and prostitutes. There isn't the slightest reason to suppose that adult felons are an exception.

We know also, or ought to know by now, that data gathered from caught criminals, for reasons in addition to and quite apart from possible sampling bias, are not only

[7] By an "uncaught" criminal I do not mean someone who has never had contact with the police; any career criminal is almost certain to be picked up for questioning sooner or later, and indeed one hallmark of the professional is that he plans for this contingency. Rather, I refer to the fact that many career felons have never been convicted of anything more than a single petty offense, and the fact that many others have never been convicted at all.

very partial but partially suspect. These are data that are much too heavily retrospective; data from people who aren't really free to put you down; data often involving the kind of "cooperativeness" in which you get told what the criminal thinks you want to hear so you will get off his back or maybe do him some good with the judge or parole board; data from someone who is not behaving as he normally would in his normal life-situations; and, above all, data that you cannot supplement with, or interpret in the light of, your own direct observation of the criminal's natural behavior in his natural environment.

To put the argument another way: Animal behavior has a narrower range of determinants than human behavior, is much less complex and variable. And yet, in recent years, animal ecologists have demonstrated that when you undertake "free-ranging" study of an animal in his natural habitat, you discover important things about him that are simply not discoverable when he is behind bars.[8] Obviously we can no longer afford the convenient fiction that in studying criminals in their natural habitat, we would discover nothing really important that could not be discovered from criminals behind bars. What is true for studying the gorilla of zoology is likely to be even truer for studying the gorilla of criminology.

III

And so we come to the third kind of copout to be found in the criminology texts, one that is fairly intelligent on this matter of field research: it grants the potential value of such studies, regrets the lack of them, and then proceeds, sadly but firmly, to give sophisticated rationalizations as to why nothing much can be done about this unfortunate lack. Here the leading text, as in so much else concerning criminology, is by Edwin Sutherland and Donald Cressey.

The main obstacle to studying criminals in the field, ac-

[8] Cf. George B. Schaller, *The Mountain Gorilla: Ecology and Behavior* (Chicago: University of Chicago Press, 1963); Irven DeVore (Ed.), *Primate Behavior: Field Studies of Monkeys and Apes* (New York: Holt, Rinehart & Winston, 1965).

cording to Sutherland and Cressey, lies in the fact that the researcher "must associate with them as one of them." Few researchers "could acquire the techniques to pass as criminals," and moreover "it would be necessary to engage in crime with the others if they retained a position once secured."[9] Where Sutherland and Cressey got this alleged fact they don't say and I can't imagine. It is just not true. On the contrary, in doing field research on criminals you damned well better *not* pretend to be "one of them," because they will test this claim out and one of two things will happen: either you will, as Sutherland and Cressey indicate, get sucked into "participant" observation of the sort you would rather not undertake, or you will be exposed, with still greater negative consequences. You must let the criminals know who you are; and if it is done properly (more on this below), it does not sabotage the research.

Another mistaken Sutherland-Cressey claim about field research on career criminals is that "few of them [criminals] would permit interrogations regarding their earlier lives or would volunteer information regarding the processes by which they became criminals."[10] A few won't but most will—they will, that is, if you aren't pretending to be "one of them." Some examples: A syndicate criminal connected with illegal control of bars and nightclubs has described to me how he entered his line of work. (The process was in all essential respects comparable to an upper-class youth "going into daddy's business.") A long-time professional burglar has described to me his teenage apprenticeship to an older burglar. (The apprenticeship took place with his father's knowledge and consent, the father's chief concerns being that the older burglar not make a punk out of his son and that he teach him how to stay out of jail.) A man in charge of a numbers operation grossing millions each year has described to me his entire career from the time he became completely self-supporting at the age of 12. It might also be noted that two of the aforementioned people have never been convicted of anything, and the third,

[9] Edwin Sutherland and Donald Cressey, *Principles of Criminology,* 6th ed. (Philadelphia: J. B. Lippincott, 1960), p. 69.
[10] *Ibid.,* p. 69.

over a career of more than twenty rather active years, has done less than three years' time.[11]

Although criminologists need not "acquire the techniques to pass as criminals," there is another matter of individual competence that excludes, or rather should exclude, a number of potential researchers; but it narrows the field in only limited degree. The problem, which criminology texts ought to talk about but don't, inheres in that requirement of telling criminals who you are. In field investigating, before you can tell a criminal who you are and make it stick, you have to know this yourself—know, especially, just where you draw the line between you and him. If you aren't sure, the criminal may make it his business to see that you get plenty shook up, really rack you up about it. I shall come back to this matter later. My point here is that field research on criminals, to judge from reactions to my classroom pitch about the need for it, seems especially attractive to people who are still trying to find out who they are. I have had to learn to discourage converts who are going through various identity crises, and to indicate bluntly that for them field research on criminals is a good thing to stay away from. Unfortunately, it is often the people best able to overcome moralism and achieve genuine empathy with criminals who are most vulnerable to allowing empathy to pass into identity.

But that "screening" problem aside, most criminologists can intelligently, safely, and successfully undertake field study of adult criminals if they put their minds to it. In what follows I shall discuss problems connected with this research method and techniques I have found useful for

[11] In addition to the general propensity he may have for "putting on" outsiders, many a criminal is given specifically to exaggerating his own importance and skill—and so a criminal's statement that he has done little or no time should be checked with especial care. Often this can be done via simple cross-checking: do A's statements about himself and B and C square with what they say about A and themselves, etc. Another useful technique, which should be used sparingly if you want to be able to continue using it, is to have someone with access to law enforcement services check the informant's record for you.

solving them; illustrate some gains in knowledge that can be made by means of this method; and counter some additional objections to this kind of research.

IV

Most difficulties that one meets and solves in doing field research on criminals are simply the difficulties one meets and solves in doing field research. The basic problem many sociologists would face in field work on criminals, therefore, is an inability to do field work. I cannot try to solve that problem here, but shall briefly indicate what I think is its nature before discussing problems peculiar to research on criminals.

Successful field research depends on the investigator's trained abilities to look at people, listen to them, think and feel with them, talk with them rather than at them. It does *not* depend fundamentally on some impersonal apparatus, such as a camera or tape recorder or questionnaire, that is interposed between the investigator and the investigated. Robert E. Park's concern that the sociologist become first of all a good reporter meant not that the sociologist rely on gadgets to see, hear, talk, and remember for him; quite the contrary, it asked the sociologist to train such human capacities in himself to their utmost and use them to their utmost in direct observation of people he wants to learn something about. But the problem for many a sociologist today—the result of curricula containing as much scientism as science—is that these capacities, far from being trained in him, have been trained out of him. He "knows" that Park-style sociology produced merely "reportage" (this is less than a half-truth at best) and insists that the real way for him to learn about people is to place one or more screens between him and them. He can't see people any more, except through punched cards and one-way mirrors. He can't talk with people any more, only "survey" them. Often he can't even talk *about* people any more, only about "data." Direct field study of social life, when he is forced to think about it at all, is something he fondly labels "soft" sociol-

ogy, as distinguished from his own confrontation of social
reality at several removes, which in his mysterious seman-
tics is "hard" sociology.

Colleagues in older disciplines have begun to give up
such scientism—for example, psychologists studying child
development have lately come out of the laboratory in
droves to look at the child in his natural habitat—and when
sociology has finished anxiously proving it is scientific it
too will abandon scientism.

In what follows I shall take this problem of trained incapacity for field work as already solved. This means I
shall assume, at the outset, that the sociologist is not a man
who needs an NIMH grant to find a criminal, that he can
humanly relate to non-sociologist humans and by asking
around can quickly get introduced to a career criminal or
at least find out where one or more can be met.

But suppose he finds, say, a tavern where a jewel thief or
loan shark or fence hangs out, and has him pointed out or
is even introduced. What then? The problems have just
begun.

Perhaps the largest set of problems arises from the fact
that a criminal judges the judges, puts down the people who
put him down. Any representative of the square world
initially encounters some covert if not overt suspicion or
hostility; it is best to assume such feelings are there (in the
criminal) even if they don't show, and that you are not
going to get far unless and until you overcome those feelings. This problem, although it exists in studying a criminal
enmeshed with the law, is usually magnified in dealing with
an uncaught criminal in his natural surroundings, for the
following reasons: (1) You are more of an intruder. As
far as he is often concerned, it's bad enough that he has
to put up with questioning when in the hands of the law,
and worse when squares won't even leave him in peace in
his own tavern. (2) He is freer to put you down and you
are more on your own; you have no authority (police,
warden, judge, parole board) to back you up. (3) There is
more of a possibility that he might be hurt by you, that is,
he has more to lose than someone already in jail.

At least potentially going for you, on the other hand, is

the fact that because you are not working in a law-enforcement setting you might *possibly* be all right; and the sooner you firmly establish in his mind that you are not any kind of cop or social worker, the sooner that fact begins going for you.

The following paragraphs will not solve for every researcher these and related problems, but will give some procedures—in no special order—that I have found useful to overcome such problems and often to prevent them from arising in the first place. They should be understood as a first attempt to state formally what I have arrived at on a more or less intuitive and trial-and-error basis in dealing with uncaught criminals. They might not work for every researcher, but I think they would work for most.

1. Although you can't help but contaminate the criminal's environment in some degree by your presence, such contamination can be minimized if, for one thing, you use no gadgets (no tape recorder, questionnaire form) and, for another, do not take any notes in the criminal's presence. It is quite feasible to train yourself to remember details of action and speech long enough to write them up fully and accurately after you get home at the end of the day (or night, more typically). Historians accept an account by a disinterested eyewitness written immediately after the event as decent evidence, even when by an untrained observer, and there is no good reason to deny validity to similar accounts by trained observers.

2. Most important when hanging around criminals—what I regard as the absolute "first rule" of field research on them—is this: initially, keep your eyes and ears open *but keep your mouth shut*. At first try to ask no questions whatsoever. Before you can ask questions, or even speak much at all other than when spoken to, you should get the "feel" of their world by extensive and attentive listening—get some sense of what pleases them and what bugs them, some sense of their frame of reference, and some sense of *their* sense of language (not only their special argot, as is often mistakenly assumed, but also how they use ordinary language). Even after all this has been learned, if the researcher is a compulsive talker or otherwise longwinded,

if he can't shut up for considerable periods, he will be seriously handicapped; his sheer verbosity, even if in "correct" language, will bother most informants (as it will lower-class people generally).

Until the criminal's frame of reference and language have been learned, the investigator is in danger of coming on too square, or else of coming on too hip (anxiously overusing or misusing the argot). The result of failure to avert such dangers is that he will be put on or, more likely, put down, and end by provoking the hostility of his informant. True, sometimes a skillful interviewer can deliberately provoke hostility to good effect. But that technique is difficult except after long experience with the particular type of deviant one is studying; and in any case, outside of anti-crime settings it should be tried, if at all, only with milder kinds of deviants.[12]

3. Once you know the special language, there is a sense in which you should try to forget it. You cannot accurately assess any aspect of a deviant's lifestyle or subculture through his argot alone, although many investigators mistakenly try. (This sort of thing disfigures David Maurer's *Whiz Mob,* for example, a work much inferior to *The Big Con.*) Such attempts result in many errors, because there is often a good deal of cultural lag between the argot and the reality.

One cannot, for instance, assume that every important role in a deviant subculture is represented by a special term. An example: A distinctive role in the male homosexual subculture is played by that type of woman, not overtly lesbian, who likes to pal around with male homosexuals

[12] For a hilarious, but genuine, verbatim transcript of an interview in which the deviant's hostility is deliberately and usefully provoked by the interviewer, cf. "Terry Southern Interviews a Faggot Male Nurse," *The Realist,* No. 43 (September, 1963), pp. 14–16.

[*Addendum, 1968:* Paul Krassner, editor and publisher of *The Realist,* assures me that the interview cited above is a total fraud. So let the foregoing paragraph serve as a tribute to the literary skill of Terry Southern—and as an object lesson in the need to check the validity of sources, even "primary" sources.]

and often serves as a front for them in the heterosexual world; but although this role has, according to older homosexuals I know, existed for decades, it is only within the past several years that homosexual argot has developed special terms for such a woman (today eastern homosexuals often refer to her as a "faghag" and western homosexuals refer to her as a "fruit fly").

Conversely, the widespread use of a term for a deviant role is not always a good clue to the prevalence or even the existence of role incumbents. An example: In the American kinship system, the three basic types of incest are brother-sister, father-daughter, and mother-son. We have a common term, originating in Negro subcultures and now part of general American slang, to designate one partner in the third type ("motherfucker"), and no special terms for the other types. But the facts of American incest are the reverse of what the language might lead one to believe: brother-sister and father-daughter incest are frequent, whereas mother-son incest is so extraordinarily rare that the staff of the Institute for Sex Research, when I queried them about this a few years ago, had found only one case that they regarded as genuine.

Thus the presence or absence of special language referring to deviance is conclusive evidence for nothing except the presence or absence of such special language. It may sensitize you as to what to look for in actual behavior, but the degree of congruence between the language and the reality of deviance is an empirical matter to be investigated in each case.

Also, the researcher should forget about imputing beliefs, feelings, or motives (conscious or otherwise) to deviants on the basis of the origins of words in their argot. Whether the etymologies are genuine or fancied (what linguists call "folk" or "false" etymologies), they tell us nothing about the psychic state of the users of the words. One form of analysis, a kind of parlor version of psychoanalysis, implicitly denies this. I have seen it seriously argued, for example, that heroin addicts must unconsciously feel guilty about their habit because they refer to heroin by such terms as "shit," "junk," and "garbage." Actually, the use of any such term by a heroin addict indicates, in itself, nothing whatever about his guilt feelings or the lack thereof, but merely that he is using a term for heroin traditional in his group.

At best, deviant argot is supporting evidence for behavioral phenomena that the investigator has to pin down with other kinds of data.

4. In my experience the most feasible technique for building one's sample is "snowballing": get an introduction to one criminal who will vouch for you with others, who in turn will vouch for you with still others. (It is of course best to start at the top if possible, that is, with an introduction to the most prestigious person in the group you want to study.)

Getting an initial introduction or two is not nearly so difficult as it might seem. Among students whom I have had perform the experiment of asking their relatives and friends to see if any could provide an introduction to a career criminal, fully a third reported that they could get such introductions. (This experiment also produced rather startling information about parental backgrounds of some of today's college students!) Moreover, once your research interests are publicly known you get volunteer offers of this sort. From students, faculty, and others, I have had more offers of introductions to career criminals—in and out of organized crime—than I could begin to follow up. And that is hardly anything compared to introductions obtainable via criminal lawyers and crime reporters (to say nothing of law enforcement personnel).

Be that as it may, there are times when you don't have an introduction to a particular scene you want to study, and you must start "cold." In such a situation it is easier, usually, to get acquainted first with criminals at their play rather than at their work. Exactly where this is depends on your individual play interests. Of course, initiating such contact means recognizing that criminals are not a species utterly different from you; it means recognizing not only that there but for the grace of God (or whoever else you think runs the show) goes you, but that you do have some leisure interests in common with criminals. It means recognizing the reality of a criminal's life (as distinguished from the mass-media image of that life), which is that he isn't a criminal 24 hours a day and behaves most of the time just like anyone else from his class and ethnic background.

In fact, one excellent way of establishing contact involves a small bit of fakery at the beginning, in that you can get to know a criminal on the basis of common leisure pursuits and *then* let him know of your research interest in him. (But this latter should be done quite soon, after the first meeting or two.) Where and how you start depends, other things being equal, on what you do best that criminals are also likely to be interested in. For example, in trying to make contact with criminals in a neighborhood new to me, I of course find it best to start out in the local poolroom. But if you can drink most people under the table, are a convivial barroom companion, etc., then you should start out in a tavern. If you know horses, start out at a horse parlor. If you know cards, ask around about a good poker game. If you know fighters, start out at the local fight gym.

5. If you establish acquaintance with a criminal on some basis of common interest, then, just as soon as possible, let him know of the differences between you if he hasn't guessed them already; that is, let him know what you do for a living and let him know why, apart from your interest in, say, poker, you are on his scene. This isn't as ticklish as it seems to people who haven't tried it—partly because of that common interest and partly because the criminal often sees, or can easily be made to see, that there may be something in it for him. For example, he may have some complaint about the outside world's mistaken view of him that you, as someone who has something in common with him, might sympathetically understand and correctly report. (Sometimes these complaints are in fact accurate—as, say, when a pimp complains that, contrary to public impression, his girls drum up their own business.) Or he may want to justify what he does. (For example, a numbers operator justified his activity to me on the basis of a localistic sort of patriotism; he feels that he, like local bookies, benefits local businessmen because when a player wins he spends some money with a neighborhood merchant before blow-

ing the rest in further gambling, whereas racetracks merely drain money out of the neighborhood and in fact out of the city.) Or he may be motivated by pride and status considerations, e.g., want to let you know that his kind of criminality is superior to other kinds. (Examples: A burglar tells me his line of work is best because "If you do it right, there are no witnesses." Another, indicating his superiority to pimps, told me that among his colleagues a common saying about a girl supporting a pimp is that "Maybe she'll get lucky and marry a thief." And a robber, indicating his scorn of con men, proudly informed me of one of his scores that "I didn't *talk* him out of it—I *took* it off him.")

These and similar motives are present not far below the surface in most criminals, and are discoverable and usable by any investigator alert for them.

6. In studying a criminal it is important to realize that he will be studying you, and to let him study you. Don't evade or shut off any questions he might have about your personal life, even if these questions are designed to "take you down," for example, designed to force you to admit that you too have knowingly violated the law. He has got to define you satisfactorily to himself and his colleagues if you are to get anywhere, and answering his questions frankly helps this process along.

Sometimes his definitions are not what you might expect. (One that pleased but also disconcerted me: "You mean they pay you to run with guys like me? That's a pretty good racket.") The "satisfactory" definition, however, is usually fairly standardized—one reason being that you are not the first non-criminal he's met who didn't put him down and consequently he has one or more stereotyped exceptions to his usual definitions of squares. And with a bit of experience you can angle for this and get yourself defined as, for example, "a square who won't blow the whistle" or "a square who likes to play with characters" or "a right square."

One type of definition you should always be prepared for (though it is by no means always overtly forthcoming) is the informant's assumption that you want to be like him but don't have the nerve and/or are getting your kicks vicariously. Thus one of the better-known researchers on drug addiction has been described to me by junkies as "a vicarious junkie," criminals often define interested outsiders as "too lazy to work but too scared to steal," and so on. This type of definition can shake you if there is any truth in it, but it shouldn't; and indeed you can even capitalize on it by admitting it in a backhanded sort of way, that is, by not seriously disputing it.

7. You must draw the line, to yourself and to the criminal. Precisely where to draw it is a moral decision that each researcher must make for himself in each research situation. (It is also to some extent a decision about personal safety, but this element is highly exaggerated in the thinking of those who haven't done field work with criminals.) You need to decide beforehand, as much as possible, where you wish to draw the line, because it is wise to make your position on this known to informants rather early in the game. For example, although I am willing to be told about anything and everything, and to witness many kinds of illegal acts, when necessary I make it clear that there are some such acts I prefer not to witness. (With two exceptions I have had this preference respected.) To the extent that I am unwilling to witness such acts, my personal moral code of course compromises my scientific role—but not, I think, irreparably.

8. There is another kind of compromise that must be made, this by way of keeping faith with informants. As the careful reader of some other parts of this book will gather, in reporting one's research it is sometimes necessary to write of certain things more vaguely and skimpily than one would prefer. But that is more of a literary than a scientific compromise; there need be no distortion of the *sociological* points involved.

9. Letting criminals know where you draw the line of course depends on knowing this yourself. If you aren't sure, the criminal may capitalize on the fact to maneuver you into an accomplice role.

The possibility of such an attempt increases directly as his trust of you increases. For example, I knew I was really getting somewhere with one criminal when he hopefully explained to me why I would make a fine "steerhorse" (which in his argot means someone who fingers a big score for a share of it). To receive such indication of "acceptance" is of course flattering—and is meant to be—but the investigator must be prepared to resist it or the results can be far more serious than anything he anticipates at the beginning of his research. I have heard of one social worker with violent gangs who was so insecure, so unable to "draw the line" for fear of being put down, that he got flattered into holding and hiding guns that had been used in murders.

10. Although I have insisted that in studying criminals you mustn't be a "spy," mustn't pretend to be "one of them," it is equally important that you don't stick out like a sore thumb in the criminal's natural environment. You must blend in with the human scenery so that you don't chill the scene. One consequence is that often you must modify your usual dress as well as your usual speech. In other words, you must walk a tightrope between "openness" on the one hand and "disguise" on the other, whose balancing point is determined anew in each investigation. Let me illustrate this with an example.

During the summer of 1960, in the course of the research reported on in the next chapter, I spent much time with people involved in heroin use and distribution, in their natural settings: on rooftops, in apartments, in tenement hallways, on stoops, in the streets, in automobiles, in parks and taverns. (The way I wrote up my material at the time —which I have left essentially unchanged for its republication in this book—is one example of what I mean about keeping faith with informants.) On the one hand, I did not dress as I usually do (suit, shirt, and tie), because that way of dressing in the world which I was investigating would have made it impossible for many informants to talk with me, e.g., would have made them worry about being seen with me because others might assume I represented the law. But on the other hand, I took care always to wear a short-sleeved shirt or T-shirt and an expensive wristwatch, both of which let any newcomer who walked up know immediately that I was not a junkie.

11. A final rule is to have few unbreakable rules. For

example: although the field investigator can, to a large extent, plan his dress, speech, and other behavior beforehand so as to minimize contamination of the environment he is investigating, such plans should be seen as provisional and subject to instant revision according to the requirements of any particular situation. Sometimes one also must confront unanticipated and ambiguous situations for which one has no clear behavioral plan at all, and abide the maxim *On s'engage et puis on voit.*

So much for the abecedarium I have evolved in studying criminals outside of jails. Obviously it is not exhaustive. But I hope it will encourage other sociologists to study adult criminals in their natural settings. A bit more needs to be said, however, about what the criminal's "natural setting" actually means.

Studying a criminal in his natural setting means not only studying him outside of any law-enforcement context. It means studying him in *his* usual environments rather than yours, in his living quarters or streets or taverns or wherever, not in your home or your office or your laboratory. And it means you mustn't "schedule" him, mustn't try to influence his shifting choices among his environments or interfere with his desire either for mobility or immobility. If he wants to sit in front of his TV set and drink beer and watch a ballgame for a couple of hours, so do you; if he wants to walk the streets or go bar-hopping, so do you; if he wants to go to the racetrack, so do you; if he indicates (for whatever reason) that it's time for you to get lost, you get lost.

Involved in all this is much more than making him feel comfortable and establishing "good rapport" (although that is of course important). Such free-ranging study, as the animal ecologists call it, is concerned to avoid as far as possible any serious disruption of his daily routine. (It will often thoroughly disrupt *your* daily routine; that's one of the unavoidable prices of this research method.) It thus provides a fluid research situation consisting of a series of *natural* events in the life of your subject (for example, his running into friends), which (1) allows you to make observations about his lifestyle you ordinarily wouldn't make,

(2) causes you to think of important questions about him that ordinarily you wouldn't think of, (3) causes him to think of relevant things to tell you that he otherwise wouldn't think of, and (4) causes him to make explanations of certain events to you that he ordinarily wouldn't make.

Given the known results of comparable field research on animals and on humans, and given the known and suspected qualitative as well as quantitative defects of research on people in jails, there is every reason to hope that field study of career criminals would bring us much in the way of genuine additions to knowledge. Just how much remains to be seen. In the meantime, let us look at one rather small example concerning professionalism in crime.

V

As a result of getting to know a professional heavy man in his own environment I was able to observe quite naturally, and quite naturally remark upon, the fact that his revolver seemed unusual. (It was a .38 that had been remounted on a .44 frame.) This so pleased him that he not only explained the gun's origin but, with very little additional prodding on my part, I was able to elicit from him the following attitudes concerning this tool of his trade. (For the sake of brevity I run his remarks together by omitting my responses to them.)

> The only pistol you can count on is a revolver. Every real character [criminal] knows that. So do the cops. Did you ever see a cop with an automatic? When you read about a job where an automatic was involved, you know the guy was an amateur. Sometimes an automatic won't go off. Yeah, not very often, but it happens. Once is all you need. When you pull that trigger your life depends on it. You can't take that chance. You don't have that worry with a revolver. And a revolver is balanced better. You can be more accurate with it.
>
> Another thing, when you read about guys using .45's and such. That's just amateur stuff. You're giving up accuracy for a lot of power you don't need. Sure, maybe

it makes sense for an FBI man to use a .357 Magnum sometimes, 'cause sometimes he has to knock down a door and things like that. For me a .38 is plenty. But you can't go much lower. A .32 is the bottom. You want a gun that if you have to shoot somebody, he goes down. Take a .25; that's a gun that's fit for nothing but a lady's purse.

Most times what you're supposed to do is just throw down on somebody [point the gun at him]. You don't really use that pistol if you don't have to. That's show-off stuff too. And when you use it you don't shoot if you don't have to. You have to fade enough heat without maybe killing somebody, so what you do is you try to slap somebody 'cross the head with it. That's another reason for a revolver. You slap somebody 'cross the head with an automatic, that mechanism gets loose and starts rattling, and maybe it jams next time.

Possibly the same information about professional ideology and technology might have been elicited from someone sitting in jail, but what evidence we have indicates otherwise. I am scarcely the first criminologist to have talked with such a criminal, and moreover I am not an especially skillful interviewer, yet this kind of material cannot be found in previous criminological literature (at least, after much searching I cannot find anything like it). Why not? The most reasonable conclusion is that the novelty of the data derives from the novelty of the situation, from the free-flowing sequence of natural events in the criminal's life within which my observations and verbalizations were embedded and within which they could reinforce each other.

The remarks of a professional heavy man quoted above perhaps typify the attitude of such a craftsman toward the tools of his trade, and perhaps they do not. We don't know. That is in fact my complaint: we just don't know, and we will never know unless criminologists bestir themselves to do field studies of a good number of such criminals.

Given a cumulation of field researches, however, we would scientifically "know" a great deal more than we do now. That brings me to another copout concerning field study, which is succinctly formulated by Sutherland-Cressey and garbled in some other texts (for example, Taft and

England): "One individual could not build upon the work
of another to a very great extent, for precise, controlled
techniques of observation could scarcely be employed."[13]

In countering this view I note, firstly, that providing "precise, controlled techniques of observation" which can be
exactly duplicated by other investigators is a problem
hardly unique to field research. It is just as much of a problem in the study of criminals who are seen in jail, or in the
office of a parole officer, or in one's own office, or even in
the experimental laboratory. And if this criticism applies
to field research, it applies *a fortiori* to the cumulation of
knowledge by means of retrospective autobiographical data
such as form the basis of Sutherland's *The Professional
Thief*.

Secondly, to make an absolute fetish of "precise, controlled techniques of observation" is to put the cart before
the horse. It often is, in the jargon of sociology, a dysfunc-
tion of the bureaucratizing of our profession, the converting
of a means into an end in itself so that the attainment of
the original end is subverted. That is why some non-
sociologist investigators of crime who know nothing of this
fetish, such as the English teacher David Maurer in his
The Big Con and the newspapermen Ed Reid and Ovid
Demaris in their *The Green Felt Jungle*, have, for all their
sloppiness and naiveté from a sociologist's point of view,
produced valuable studies of career crime that put the
criminologist to shame. (Rather, such books ought to make
the criminologist feel ashamed of himself, but unfortunately
they don't.)

Thirdly, to impose on the field worker some of the controls that purists want—to insist that different field researchers studying, say, loan sharks, must each ask their subjects
exactly the same questions in exactly the same order in
exactly the same words (or worse yet, insist that the subjects must fill out questionnaires or talk into a tape machine
or that the researcher take notes in their presence)—is severely to contaminate the very thing we want to study, the
reactions of people *in their natural environment*. Sociology

[13] Sutherland and Cressey, *op. cit.,* p. 69.

isn't worth much if it is not ultimately about real live people in their ordinary life-situations, yet many of the "precise, controlled techniques of observation" introduced by the investigator produce what is for the subject anything but an ordinary life-situation.

Fourthly, for all the variety of "natural environments" in which different investigators of loan sharks would find themselves, and thus the necessary *and desirable* differences in investigators' procedures (when to ask questions and when to shut up, what words to use, and so on), there would remain a large amount of comparability. Sutherland and Cressey notwithstanding, we could get knowledge of a genuinely cumulative kind, for example, an increasingly accurate notion of the typical pattern of loan sharks' relations with police. We might even one day arrive at the millennium: an accurate estimate of the size of the universe (all loan sharks) and the degree of representativeness of the sample, and be able to formulate that "typical pattern" in a way satisfying to the hardnosed statistician. But we will never come close if we never try.

In sum, the "scientific" objections to field research on criminals that one finds in Sutherland-Cressey and other texts are either no objections at all or apply to all sorts of other sociological research and boil down to the truism that our research methods in general fall short of perfection. The regularity with which criminologists focus on alleged scientific objections to field research, and the regularity with which they ignore or barely hint at the obvious *moral* objection to such research, suggests that the issue of morality is really what bothers them most. The moral issue deserves closer examination than the criminology textbooks give it.

VI

If one is effectively to study adult criminals in their natural settings, he must make the moral decision that in some ways he will break the law himself. He need not be a "participant" observer and commit the criminal acts under

study, yet he has to witness such acts or be taken into
confidence about them and not blow the whistle. That is,
the investigator has to decide that when necessary he will
"obstruct justice" or have "guilty knowledge" or be an
"accessory" before or after the fact, in the full legal sense
of those terms. He will not be enabled to discern some
vital aspects of criminal lifestyles and subcultures unless
he (1) makes such a moral decision, (2) makes the criminals believe him, and (3) convinces them of his ability to
act in accord with his decision. That third point can sometimes be neglected with juvenile delinquents, for they know
that a professional studying them is almost always exempt
from police pressure to inform; but adult criminals have
no such assurance, and hence are concerned to assess not
merely the investigator's intentions but his ability to remain
a "stand-up guy" under police questioning.[14]

To my knowledge, Lewis Yablonsky is the only criminologist who has had the good sense and emotional honesty
to object to such research primarily on moral grounds. He
claims that the views expressed in the foregoing paragraph
(as originally published), and any similar views, go too far
from a moral standpoint. According to Yablonsky, non-
moralizing on the part of the researcher, when coupled
with intense interest in the criminal's life, really constitutes
a romantic encouragement of the criminal.[15]

Not so. To be sure, the research involvement I recommend is hardly uninterested; but also obviously, it tries to
be as far as humanly possible *dis*interested, a scientific
undertaking concerned neither to confirm the criminal in
his criminality nor to change him, but to understand him.
Furthermore, if the sociologist himself has any lingering
"romantic" view of criminality, there is nothing so effective
as close association with criminals to get him over it, be-

[14] The foregoing paragraph was originally published, in
slightly different form, as a footnote I contributed to Howard
Becker's *Outsiders* (New York: The Free Press of Glencoe,
1963), p. 171.

[15] Lewis Yablonsky, "Experiences with the Criminal Community," in Alvin Gouldner and S. M. Miller (Eds.), *Applied
Sociology* (New York: The Free Press, 1965), p. 72.

cause criminals themselves—at least those who are beyond the novice stage and seriously committed to crime as a career—are usually quite hardheaded and unromantic about it all. In any case, the criminal scarcely needs the sociologist to make him feel important as an object of romantic interests when, every day, every TV set in the land blares forth such messages for those criminals interested in picking up on them.

It is possible—highly doubtful, but possible—that a few criminals might become more set in their criminality, to some minuscule degree, by the mere fact that my type of investigating is totally unconcerned to "reform" them or "rehabilitate" them or "make them see the error of their ways." But in the first place, such unconcern is qualitatively different from positive encouragement or approval. (Indeed, part of what I conceive to be proper research technique with criminals, as indicated previously, involves letting them know who you are and what you do for a living, which means letting them know that your value choices are different from theirs.) Secondly, the burden of proof rests upon those who claim that abstention from moralizing by the field investigator has any significantly encouraging effect on criminals' lifestyles, and they have not supplied one bit of such proof. Finally, our society at present seems plentifully supplied with moral uplifters in any case, so one needn't worry if a few sociological students of crime fail to join the chorus.

VII

And there are only a few such sociologists. Unfortunately, Yablonsky's outlook prevails among those sociologists who define themselves as criminologists. The great majority of criminologists are social scientists only up to a point—the point usually being the start of the second, "control of crime," half of the typical criminology course —and beyond that point they are really social workers in disguise or else correction officers *manqués*. For them a central task of criminology, often *the* central task, is to find

more effective ways to reform lawbreakers and to keep
other people from becoming lawbreakers.[16]

If a man wants to make that sort of thing his lifework
I have no objection; that is his privilege. I suggest merely
that he not do so in the name of sociology, criminology, or
any social science. I suggest that he admit he is undertaking such activity not as a social scientist but as a technolo-
gist or moral engineer for an extra-scientific end: making
people obey current American criminal law. This is not
to deny his right as an ordinary citizen to be "engaged"
and make value judgments about crime, politics, sex, religion, or any other area of moral dispute. Rather, it is to
deny that everything appropriate to one's role as ordinary
citizen is appropriate to one's role as scientist, and to insist that making such value judgments is not only inappropriate to the latter role but highly inimical to it.

To locate such inimical effect one need look no further
than Yablonsky's own admission that in his work with

[16] An awareness that criminology is dominated by self-
styled sociologists who are basically social workers perhaps lies
behind the Columbia University sociology department's long
refusal to harbor criminologists and its correlative banishment
of them to the School of Social Work. Such awareness on Robert Merton's part, at least, would logically follow from his negative evaluation of his early "slum-encouraged provincialism of
thinking that the primary subject-matter of sociology was cen-
tered in such peripheral problems of social life as divorce and
juvenile delinquency." (See his "Introduction," *Social Theory
and Social Structure* [Glencoe, Ill.: Free Press, 1949], p. 17.)
The mistake made by Columbia's sociology department is that
in throwing out criminology as a major sub-field it abandons a
beautiful sociological baby to drown in all that social-work
bathwater.

Given the perspectives within which delinquency and crime
are almost always studied, it is obvious why Merton might
regard them as "peripheral problems of social life" rather
than fundamental social processes of central concern to sociology. But it is also obvious that, in every society, among the
really fundamental social processes are those which involve
transgression of the society's moral norms by some people
and reaction by others to such transgression, and indeed that
these processes bear crucially on the most fundamental sociological question of all, the question of how social order is
possible.

juvenile delinquents "some gang boys who met with me almost daily—some over several years—never fully believed that I was not 'really a cop.' "[17] Any student of deviance who confounds the roles of social worker and sociologist ("the dual role of practitioner-researcher," as Yablonsky puts it) is bound to elicit that sort of response and have his research flawed by it. And if failure to solve this problem is serious in the scientific study of delinquents, failure to solve it in the study of adult career criminals is catastrophic.

The failure derives from what is truly a romantic ideology, one common to "applied sociologists": a sentimental refusal to admit that the goals of sociological research and the goals of social work are always distinct and often in conflict. The conflict happens to be extremely sharp in the case of adult felony crime. The criminologist who refuses fully to recognize this conflict and to resolve it *in favor of sociology* erects a major barrier to the extension of scientific knowledge about such crime and such criminals.

But what of one's duty as a citizen? Shouldn't that take precedence? Well, different types of citizens have different *primary* duties. And our very understanding of "citizenship" itself is considerably furthered in the long run if one type of citizen, the criminologist, conceives his primary duty to be the advancement of scientific knowledge about crime even when such advancement can be made only by "obstructing justice" with respect to particular criminals in the short run.

Many an anthropologist has been able to advance the state of knowledge only by keeping faith with people who radically transgress the moral norms of his society, that is, by refusing to turn them in to colonial officials and their cops, so I fail to see why the criminologist shouldn't do the same. Of course, if someone really wants to behave toward the savages as a missionary rather than as an anthropologist, if he really wants to be a superior sort of social worker or cop or therapist rather than a sociologist, there is no denying him this right; but at least let him own up to what he

[17] Lewis Yablonsky, in Gouldner and Miller, *op. cit.,* p. 56.

really is and stop fouling the waters of science with muck about "the dual role of practitioner-researcher."

I would not wish to be understood as claiming that the criminologist, in his role as criminologist, must ignore value judgments. On the contrary, he might scientifically deal with them in several ways well known to sociology. For example, he could study how a society came to have the particular moral norms that it has, or study the unanticipated consequences of these norms for the society, or study the differential distribution and varying intensity of these norms within different subcultures of a complex society. The sociologist or criminologist can, as a scientist, do the foregoing things and more with respect to values. But if some people claim that whatever the law may say at the moment, it is "right" (or "wrong") to do this or that and they act in accord with their value judgment, one thing the sociologist or criminologist can not do, directly or indirectly, is to gainsay them and interfere with their lives in the name of his science. The social scientist has no business attempting to "adjust" people to the moral norms of his society or any other.

Max Weber, in emphasizing that sociology must be value-neutral if it is to be genuinely scientific, long ago made the key distinctions between one's role as ordinary citizen and one's role as social scientist. Our allegedly sociological students of crime, however, have forgotten Weber's lesson if, indeed, they ever learned it.

It is hard to blame them when they see other social scientists directly criticize Weber's fastidiousness about value-neutrality out of a gluttonous desire to have their cake and eat it, to be moralizers and scientists at once. But the criticism levelled at Weber on this matter, whether by "natural law" ideologues such as Leo Strauss or "applied sociology" ideologues such as Alvin Gouldner, comes to no more than the statement that the value-neutral ideal is impossible of full attainment and that even the great Max Weber could not always keep his personal values completely out of his scientific work. Such criticism is quite true and equally irrelevant: although the ideal is indeed not fully attainable, there are radically different degrees of approximation to it that are attainable, and these quantitative differences add up to a significant difference in quality; which is to say that if we try like hell we can come very close to the ideal and enormously improve the state of our science thereby. But the critics of Weber aren't interested in trying. They apparently believe that because we cannot be virgin pure with respect to value-neutral social science we might as well be whores.

Actually, two related modes of sociological inquiry can prod us toward objectivity. One, indicated above, consciously excludes value judgments to a degree that comes close to the Weberian ideal, so much so that it can even produce findings which go against the personal values of the investigator. (For example, Chapter 5 reports conclusions about highly erotic art that seem to me inescapable as a sociologist but that I personally regret having to report —because they give ammunition to censors, whom I detest.) The related mode, suggested to me by Howard Becker and illustrated in Chapter 2, counterbalances the values of one's society—and the investigations by social workers or "applied sociologists" of one's society—by using an "anti-social" perspective, e.g., by viewing society as a "problem" for the deviant rather than the other way round. Although such counterbalancing need not be restricted to criminology—one could, for example, sympathetically study the racist's "problem" of how to check desegregation and increase racial discimination—it is likely to have especially salutary effects there. This route to value neutrality I find adumbrated not in Max Weber's work but in Friedrich Nietzsche's *Genealogy of Morals*:

> It is no small discipline and preparation of the intellect on its road to final "objectivity" to see things for once through the wrong end of the telescope; and "objectivity" is not meant here to stand for "disinterested contemplation" (which is a rank absurdity) but for the ability to have the pros and cons in one's power and to switch them on and off, so as to get to know how to use, for the advancement of knowledge, the *difference* in the perspectives and psychological interpretations. . . . All seeing is essentially perspective, and so is all knowing. The more emotions we

allow to speak on a given matter, the more different eyes we train on the same thing, the more complete will be our conception of it, the greater our "objectivity."

VIII

My complaint, however, is basically Weberian in origin: I object not that criminologists have an anti-criminal moral code but that it is misplaced morality, acted upon within the scientific role instead of being kept firmly outside it. Such misplacement is not only inappropriate to scientific endeavor but clearly detrimental to it: I have tried to show that although criminologists sometimes give lip service to the scientific ideal of dispassionately studying criminals in the open, they immediately subvert that ideal. Obviously they do so out of fear of being caught with their anti-criminal values down. Their misplaced morality leads them, in practice, to pass up the field study of criminals, to invent various rationalizations for avoiding it, to exaggerate its difficulties, and to neglect some fairly obvious techniques for avoiding these difficulties.

But if the criminologist wants to help build a real science—for example, if he wants to go beyond his ritualistic wailing over the inadequacies of retrospective data and official statistics and really do something about these inadequacies—he might ponder the reaction of Bronislaw Malinowski, over forty years ago, to a similar situation that then obtained in anthropology:

> We are obviously demanding a new method of collecting evidence. The anthropologist must relinquish his comfortable position in the long chair on the veranda of the missionary compound, Government station, or planter's bungalow, where, armed with pencil and notebook and at times with a whisky and soda, he has been accustomed to collect statements from informants, write down stories, and fill out sheets of paper with savage texts. He must go out into the villages, and see the natives at work in gardens, on the beach, in the jungle. . . . Information must come to him full-flavored from his own observations of native life, and not be squeezed out of reluctant informants as a trickle of

talk. Field work can be done first or secondhand even among the savages, in the middle of pile dwellings, not far from actual cannibalism and head-hunting. Open-air anthropology, as opposed to hearsay note-taking, is hard work, but it is also great fun. Only such anthropology can give us the all-round vision of primitive man and primitive culture.[18]

Until the criminologist learns to suspend his personal distaste for the values and lifestyles of the untamed savages, until he goes out in the field to the cannibals and headhunters and observes them without trying either to civilize them or turn them over to colonial officials, he will be only a veranda anthropologist. That is, he will be only a jailhouse or courthouse sociologist, unable to produce anything like a genuinely scientific picture of crime.

IX

But if one refuses to be a sociologist of the jailhouse or court system, takes Malinowski to heart, and goes out into the field, there is risk involved. At least I have found this so in my own experience. It is the sort of risk that writers of criminology texts, for all their eagerness to put down field work, surprisingly don't mention: most of the danger for the field worker comes not from the cannibals and headhunters but from the colonial officials. The criminologist studying uncaught criminals in the open finds sooner or later that law enforcers try to put him on the spot—because, unless he is a complete fool, he uncovers information that law enforcers would like to know, and, even if he is very skillful, he cannot always keep law enforcers from suspecting that he has such information.

Although communication between someone and his wife or lawyer or doctor is legally privileged (these people cannot be required to divulge the communication), there is no such status accorded a communication between anyone and the criminologist. The doctrine of legally privi-

[18] Bronislaw Malinowski, *Myth in Primitive Psychology*, 1926; as republished in his *Magic, Science, and Religion* (New York: Doubleday Anchor Books, 1954), pp. 146–47.

leged communication has so far been extended only to
cover certain of those other professionals (nurses, priests,
psychotherapists) who are in a "treatment" relationship
with clients. Possibly the social-worker sort of criminologist dedicated to "rehabilitating" criminals might find shel-
ter under this legal umbrella, but the scientific criminologist presumably could not. If the latter criminologist stood
fast on his obligation to protect informants in the face
of law enforcers' demands that he tell all, the guiding judicial precedents most likely would be the cases of journalists who have done likewise in legally unprotected situations, and he would be held in contempt of court. I know
of no instance where this has actually happened; but if a
significant number of criminologists began doing the kind
of research I recommend, we would probably get an instance soon.

On the other hand, few criminologists are soon likely to
undertake serious field research on serious adult criminals.
The odds are great that nearly all criminologists, even
those not desiring to be social workers, will continue to
complain about the defects of our data on crime and criminals but will also continue to duck the best way of overcoming these defects—some, perhaps, because they wish
to avoid the contingency of being put on the spot by law
enforcers; others, certainly, because of unreal estimates
of danger to their personal safety; and most, probably, because of guilt feelings involved in obtaining information on
felons and their felonies that one knows would be useful
to law enforcers but does not report. If the very few of
us concerned to do such field research are ever to convert
most of our colleagues, we will have to abate their fears
and ease their consciences a good bit more.

Either we will have to force and win a legal test case on
this matter of research privilege for criminologists (I for
one would be willing to be the guinea pig), or, in the more
likely event that no judicial basis can be found for such a
test case, we will have to obtain new statutes. Should we
manage by either method to get the communication between criminal and criminologist accorded the same legal
status as that between criminal and lawyer, then field re-

search on adult criminals would really come into its own, for we would at once have provided the necessary stiffening of criminologists' spines and have removed the biggest single obstacle to cooperation from our research subjects.

However, I see no reason to be hopeful that we will be granted this legal privilege, and in fact am quite pessimistic. In the foreseeable future, field research on criminals will have to be carried out under the hazards and handicaps that now obtain. But even under present conditions such research can be done. And if we are serious about studying crime scientifically, it must be done.

Addendum, 1970: A textbook criticized in the foregoing pages, Sutherland & Cressey's *Principles of Criminology,* has now appeared in its 8th edition (1970); it was revised by Donald Cressey (as was the 6th edition from which I quoted). The 8th edition repeats the earlier editions' rationalizations for avoiding field research, with one significant addition: Mr. Cressey footnotes the existence of *Hustlers, Beats, and Others,* and his reference to that footnote reads, in its entirety, "Moreover, when confidence men study other confidence men by this method [field research], it is impossible to determine whether the published conclusions are social science or part of a confidence game."

Apart from the author's errors of fact (I am hardly a confidence man) and of elementary logic (Mr. Cressey needs to learn about the *argumentum ad hominem*), one should note how Mr. Cressey dealt with my specific criticisms of his work: he could not bring himself to mention, much less reply to, a single one of them. One could scarcely hope for a clearer illustration of how criminologists cop out on the question of field studies.

The Village Beat Scene: Summer 1960*

Now, it is obviously easier to recognize ideologies where-
ever they are strongly institutionalized or highly verbal.
. . . The true meaning of ideology for identity formation,
however, can be fathomed only by descending into those
transitory systems of conversion and aversion which exist
in . . . adolescence. Such implicit ideologies are often
overtly and totally unideological; yet they often exist as
the most vital part of a young person's or group's life, as a
basis for a tentative and yet total orientation in life, without the knowledge or, indeed, curiosity, of the adults
around them.

ERIK ERIKSON[1]

* This chapter originally appeared in *Dissent,* Vol. 8, No. 3
(Summer, 1961), pp. 339–59. I have added to the text and notes
at several points; these additions are indicated by brackets.
Readers interested in other of my views on this subject
should consult: (a) my reply to Norman Mailer's "The White
Negro" and his rejoinder to me, *Dissent,* Vol. 5, No. 1 (Winter,
1958), pp. 77–81, both of which are reprinted in Mailer's
Advertisements for Myself (New York: Putnam, 1959), pp.
365–71; (b) my debate with Irving Howe in *Partisan Review,*
Vol. 27, No. 2 (Spring, 1960), pp. 379–83.
[1] "Identity and Totality," in *Human Development Bulletin,
Fifth Annual Symposium* (Univ. of Chicago, 1954), p. 68. A
full psychological analysis of the beats, which I do not attempt,
should in general proceed along Eriksonian lines. But in view
of the significant minority of beats in their thirties and forties,
it should place greater stress on the persistence in more or less

This essay is both more and less than a portrayal of the beats of Greenwich Village and its environs. More, because much of it holds good for beats elsewhere. Less, because I have not depicted some of the Village beat world's well-publicized aspects, but have tried for completeness only in regard to the changes that have taken place in that world since my last acquaintance with it (1957). I use the word "beat" for brevity and ask readers to note that it obscures as much as it illuminates.

I

The individuals in question resent any label whatever, and regard a concern with labelling as basically square. But insofar as they speak of themselves generically and are forced to choose among evils, they prefer the word "beat." Until recently "hipster" meant simply one who is hip, roughly the equivalent of a beat. Beats recognized that the hipster is more of an "operator"—has a more consciously patterned lifestyle (such as a concern to dress well) and makes more frequent economic raids on the frontiers of the square world—but emphasized their social bonds with hipsters, such as their liking for drugs, for jazz music, and, above all, their common scorn for bourgeois career orientations. Among Village beats today, however, "hipster" usually has a pejorative connotation: one who is a mannered showoff regarding his hipness, who "comes on" too strongly in hiptalk, etc. In their own eyes, beats are hip but are definitely not hipsters.

Although beats are characteristically ignorant of history, even of their own history, most know the oft-discussed origin of "beat" as applied to the postwar disaffected. But all are in the dark about "hip." The few Village beats with any opinion suppose that it comes from the "hep" of early 1940's jivetalk. Actually "hep" and "hip" are doublets; both come directly from a much earlier phrase, "to be on the hip," to be a devotee of opium smoking—dur-

---

chronic form of some psychic states characterizing acute adolescent phenomena.

ing which activity one lies on one's hip. The phrase is obsolete, the activity obsolescent.

As early as 1938 David Maurer noted that due to the rapid decline of opium smoking much of its argot was being loosely transferred to other types of drug taking, "frequently without a full knowledge of the original meanings of the words transferred."[2] Today's use of "hip" extends this process, for now the word has the generalized meaning of "in the know" and even among beat drug users doesn't always refer specifically to knowledge of drugs.

II

Paradoxically, nearly all articles on the beats neglect the thread that colors beat life: the overwhelming majority of beats are *not* exhibitionists or publicity-seekers but precisely the opposite. Articles by beat writers, who belong nearly always to the publicity-seeking minority, implicitly deny this fact. And square writers, who as often as not simply lift their material from beat writings, don't know this fact, or minimize it because it is unexciting, or explicitly deny it. One of the rare exceptions is Caroline Bird, who nearly four years ago correctly noted of the beat that "his main goal is to keep out of a society which, he thinks, is trying to make everyone over in its own image. . . . He may affect [distinctive dress] but *usually prefers to skulk unmarked.*"[3] Today, despite the attention given to beats in the mass media, despite the consequence that some beats now resemble professional "angry young men" securing toeholds in the lower levels of our "establishment" (the slicker cheesecake magazines) and yearning for our peculiar version of the aristocratic embrace (*Life*), Miss Bird's observations are still generally valid.

[2] Cf. Maurer's "Argot of the Underworld Narcotic Addict: Part II," *American Speech,* Vol. 13 (October, 1938), p. 179, fn. 3. Cf. also Alfred Lindesmith, *Opiate Addiction* (Bloomington, Indiana: Principia Press, 1947), p. 215.

[3] "Born 1930: The Unlost Generation," *Harper's Bazaar,* February 1957. My italics.

Nearly all Village beats most of the time and most of them all of the time want not even a hostile relationship with squares. They restrict their relations with squares to that bare minimum needed to live at all. Many a beat, sociable enough with other beats, goes for weeks at a time without engaging in a single real conversation with a square, his "conversation" with squares being limited to the few ritualistic phrases required to make food purchases, etc. Moreover, the large majority of beats do not flaunt their physical presence before the public gaze. Most beats dress in an ordinary lower-class manner, distinctive only to middle-class eyes. A substantial minority, between a fourth and a third, also wear various kinds of badges (beards, typically) but usually do so as a ready means of identifying themselves to one another and to promote a "we" feeling, not out of a desire to call the attention of outsiders to themselves. Most of even this badge-wearing minority want to remain quite inconspicuous as far as squares are concerned. Their badges are meant for fellow beats, and were worn long before publicity made the squares aware of them; it will hardly do to call these beats "exhibitionists" just because squares have lately stolen their signals. These fundamental points are garbled or suppressed, when known at all, as more and more writers discover a market for articles on "colorful" beats.

It is indeed obvious to the tourist that some beats need frequently to proclaim their negative identities by costume and behavior designed to shock. But that is no reason for even our social scientists to remain merely tourists and write, for example, as if beats typically were devoted to "conspicuous consumption of the self"—an absurdity comparable to suggesting that most homosexuals are drag queens.[4] To describe only what is more or less deliberately

[4] [The quoted phrase and related nonsense may be found in Ernest van den Haag's "Conspicuous Consumption of Self," *National Review*, Vol. VI, No. 23 (April 11, 1959), pp. 658–60. The phrase (and concept) appears to be an unacknowledged borrowing from Anatole Broyard's "A Portrait of the Hipster," *Partisan Review*, Vol. XV, No. 6 (June, 1948), p. 727; Broyard correctly applied it to the typical hipster of the early

exposed to tourist view is to forget that the cool world is
an iceberg, mostly underwater.

III

There has been in three years a great proliferation of
Village coffee shops, chiefly because square patronage
makes them profitable. New York's beat scene has become a major tourist attraction, just as happened earlier in
San Francisco. [In the summer of 1960 the Village beat
scene was at its very peak because, among other things,
most of the San Francisco beats had by then become so
harassed by tourist hordes and police that they fled to
New York.[5] Shortly after this study was finished the same
thing happened in Greenwich Village; the exodus of Village beats to the lower East Side—already begun at the time
of my study—entered full swing, the tourists and the
"ethnic" teenagers noted elsewhere in this study took their
place, and the Village became more and more folked up.
The beat subculture in its original form still survives in
parts of the lower East Side and elsewhere—although,
for reasons too complex to relate here, on a greatly diminished scale. Suffice it to say that the beats have been largely
absorbed by their "hippie" descendants.]

But an important secondary reason for the coffee shops
is that in the last three years the attitudes of beats in their
thirties have spread rapidly downward all the way to very
young teenagers (13–15 years old), who need these shops
because they are too young to fake their age in bars. About
a fourth of those under 16 are fully beat and have totally
abandoned, among other things, such square institutions
for teenagers as parental home and school. The remainder
are quasi-beat, not so much because they have doubts about
beat life as because they are not yet able completely to
escape parental control.

1940's, whose lifestyle was in key respects different from that
of the beats a decade later.]

[5] [An excellent description and discussion of the beat exodus
from San Francisco is Ralph Gleason's "Begone, Dull Beats,"
New Statesman, June 2, 1961, p. 868.]

Some newer coffee shops are on the lower East Side (out of the Village proper) and a couple of that neighborhood's restaurants have also become fairly beat. In part this is the result of low-income Villagers moving eastward in the face of rising Village rents. But these shops cater also to beats from various parts of the city who want to avoid Village tourists. These beats, together with many others who go to Village coffee shops entirely or almost entirely during non-tourist hours, and still others—including most older beats—who rarely go to coffee shops at all (a great portion of beat social life takes place at private parties), comprise the large majority of beats.

IV

Many beats are teenage runaways, but hardly any are being sought by the police; apparently most come from families that would just as soon be rid of them. But Village beats, teenagers and otherwise, are not predominantly of lower-class parentage. Roughly 35 per cent are from the lower class and 60 per cent or a little more from the middle class. There is also a sprinkling (about 5 per cent) of upper-class renegades; as a group they seem the most psychologically disturbed of all beats and as often as not are remittance men, i.e., are sent money by their parents to stay away from home.[6]

The composition of the Village beat population today, compared with that of three years ago, shows several other changes in addition to the greatly increased number of young teenagers. A dozen or so Italian neighborhood kids are breaking away from Italian community values (always opposed to Village bohemians) and are attracted to the beats. And some Puerto Ricans are beginning to enter the beat scene; previously the only "American" group one found them in was the homosexuals.

[6] The above percentages are tentative estimates, based on quite sketchy material concerning family origins. I used the following rough-and-ready class definitions: lower-class origin if parents' annual combined income was under $4500; middle class, $4500–$9000; upper class, $9000 or more.

Although a number of beat writers are of Jewish origin, the proportion of Jews among the white male beats has severely declined in the past three years, and in the Village beat scene they now seem to be considerably under-represented. Jewish women, on the other hand, are if anything over-represented. Otherwise there seems nothing unusual about the religious origins of the beats.

A few of the newer beat women are worn-out ex-prostitutes from the Times Square area, in their early twenties, who realized they had nothing to show for several years of hustling—no love, no money, no friendships. They want to escape the hustling scene but of course have difficulty adjusting to a square scene, and hence are attracted to the beats, toward whom they are motherly. Conversely, a few beat men hustle themselves a couple of nights a week in uptown homosexual bars, making enough money to stay straight in the Village the rest of the week. In one way this last is typical of the odd job the beat takes when, despite all his efforts to avoid it, he must work: he doesn't want to be *seen* working by other beats, and prefers a job away from the beat scene (except that it is considered all right to work in a beat coffee shop).

But the biggest change in the composition of the Village beat scene, and in Village life generally, is the far greater absolute number and far greater percentage of Negroes.

Until about three years ago [i.e., until 1957] there were few Negroes in the Village and they were forced to have their own bar, Johnny Romero's. Romero's paid off the syndicate after several broken windows reminded the owner of this civic duty, and of course paid the police, but was eventually closed because it got too hot to handle (one of the bar's prostitutes was discovered to be a juvenile runaway from a prominent family).

Today, hundreds of Negroes can be found in any number of Village coffee shops and bars, some of which, e.g., Polelle's,[7] function mainly as places for Negroes who

[7] In this essay Village commercial establishments frequented by beats appear pseudonymously, except for one bar now defunct.

want white girls to pick up same. The Negroes around Polelle's haven't much in common except such desires, and range from very beat to Ivy League types. The only thoroughly beat Negro scene is the Maracanda, where most of the clientele are junkies and Charlie Parker is the squarest thing on the jukebox.

V

On the increase in the Village and its east-side adjunct are beats with literally no place to live, without even a slum sleeping-room. I'd guess that at any given time these homeless beats number not less than 150.

To sleep, some drop in on friends who live in cheap lofts; often there will be ten or twelve people sleeping on a loft floor. Or they sleep in tenement hallways—the top landing, just inside the door to the roof, being the usual choice for beats (unlike homeless alcoholics, who usually must choose the less secure ground level because they can't make it up the stairs). In warm weather there are rooftops; or parks, where one has a 50–50 chance of not being awakened by the police. And some beats sit out the wee damp hours in Smith's, one of the restaurants in the area.

For several years Smith's has been a favorite place for junkies and marihuana smokers to meet their connections. But it has been very hot ever since the police stationed an informer there and one night arrested eleven people, and since then it has had a fink or more or less permanent detail. The first fink uncovered by the beats and junkies was replaced; but at this writing the police haven't bothered to replace his replacement, and the current fink, who is known as such to all the regular customers and knows that he is known, often gets baited with stage whispers of "Can anybody turn me on?" etc.

VI

Naturally, the Italian residents of the Village are going down fighting.[8] The older ones, upset by the noise and the

[8] "Italian" refers mainly to Sicilians, the dominant Village ethnic group, whose criminal minority controls Village night-

Negroes, this summer petitioned their political chiefs to
do something—whereupon two of the most prominent coffee shops were closed by the Fire Department for violations, one of them later being permitted to reopen at half
its former capacity. (The shops selected were of course
non-Italian, though hardly any commercial establishment
within blocks of the area doesn't have fire violations.)
However, contrary to the opinion of some beats, it is
doubtful that the syndicate had anything to do with the clos-
ings, for long ago the syndicate put aside its anti-Negro
feelings in favor of its commercial interests and declared
itself in for a piece of the beat pie. Except for a few upper-
class places north of Washington Square, every Village
coffee shop or bar or restaurant, beat or non-beat, pays
"grease" to the syndicate as well as to the cops.[9]

Many younger Italians of course make violent efforts
to roll back the beat invasion, especially during summer
with everyone in the streets. Most of the violence is di-

---

life and is prominent in the national crime syndicate, not to
Neapolitans living south of the Village.

[9] Syndicate enforcement methods are the well-publicized
strongarm ones. Less known are the police methods for handling those who contribute too little or the rare idealist who
contributes nothing at all. These methods are nonviolent, flexible, and various. Among them are "disorderly premises" (almost anything will make it stick), "finding" heroin in the place
—one astonished response: "Man, don't crucify me, you know
I only smoke pot"—and having a New York newspaper
columnist blast the place until the owner comes across or the
police are "forced" by the publicity to raid him.

Given the system's values, the method chosen usually represents a quite rational police estimate as to how severely the
holdout needs to be punished—whether it is best to just scare
him, or have him fined, or cause him expensive repairs, or
close him for a bit, or have the State Liquor Authority lift his
liquor license, or send him to jail. Occasionally irrational factors are involved, such as one cop's invariable method of operation or another's sadism. Much less frequently, there is also
an "outside" factor, e.g., public outcry leading to pressure from
high brass, or an owner's strong political connections, or the
owner of, say, an established homosexual bar being outbid by
someone else who wants to obtain the local homosexual
business.

rected against Negroes and much of it is focused in and near the main beat crossroads, Washington Square Park. The kids under twelve usually restrict themselves to throwing water bombs and feces down on the beats from Macdougal Street rooftops; but more than occasionally beats are also slugged by junior hoodlums from the local Catholic Youth Organization—described by one beat as America's only juvenile gang with a lawyer on retainer. The daily newspapers, except for the New York *Post,* ignore such things as much as they can, and even the *Post* dare not offend part of the readership by mentioning the C.Y.O.; nor, for that matter, can the *Village Voice.*

I summarize one of many incidents:

> A beat couple are set upon and stomped by the C. Y. O. gang. The police arrest the beats along with some of their attackers. The beats of course can't make bail. As a result of the beating the girl has a miscarriage while in the Women's House of Detention. The cops, discovering that the girl is underage, point out to the couple that if anyone talks about the miscarriage they will have to charge her as a sexual delinquent and him as contributing to her delinquency. At the hearing everyone plays it cool and all are released. But the police have the judge lecture the male beat that he is barred from the Village and will be rapped the next time he's found there, so now he stays east of Third Avenue. This has raised his status in the eyes of some: "A way out bit, man. I mean, lots of studs've been eighty-sixed from bars but he's the first one eighty-sixed from the whole fucking Village."

Some beats have correctly observed that opposition to them is in part displaced hostility toward another "invading" group that the Italians can't fight effectively because it is too rich: the uptown squares who are tearing down low-rent Village housing, moving into fancy buildings that Italians can't afford, and in the process of wresting local political control from the DeSapio machine.

VII

Beats avoid work. Contrary to what I expected among the non-junkies, this avoidance is typically not a rationalization for any kind of work incapacity (such as one finds in, say, the neurotic sleeper who can't get up in the morning), but is almost always a matter of conviction pure and simple. This conviction is so strong that many beats are willing to starve for it. Consequently, even among the non-junkies there is widespread malnutrition, and some instances of beat "passivity" seem to owe as much to lack of food energy as anything else.

Since an important factor in some kinds of retreatism is an inability to meet job norms (whether legitimate or criminal), it should be emphasized that beats typically can meet such norms but voluntarily choose not to do so. True, most beats are decidedly neurotic; and because they generally refuse their chances for either job training or college education, they can get only low-skilled jobs. But their intelligence and native talents are likely to be superior when not average, and their neuroses usually do not as such incapacitate them for holding jobs. Furthermore, their ideological refusal to work is not essentially a product of neurosis, even for the most neurotic of them, but is largely cultural in origin. (In this respect beats remind one of professional criminals, who may or may not be neurotic but whose neuroses usually have little to do with the genesis of their criminality.)

[Sociologists' response to the foregoing paragraph—or rather their total lack of response to it—greatly disappointed me. At the time of original publication I assumed sociologists would fasten on that paragraph above all others, since it was the first writing to question the general applicability of the double-failure theory of retreatism—and to do so on the basis of genuine field study of a genuinely "retreatist" delinquent subculture. But nobody picked up on it.]

Unlike most of their age-mates, beats are keen critics

of the society in which they have grown up. Their anti-work ideology is not nearly so much a sign of inability to accept the reality principle as a sign of disaffiliation from particular, mutable realities. Sensible of America's inequitable distribution of income *and* its increasing depersonalization of work and leisure *and* its racial injustices *and* its Permanent War Economy, the beats have responded with the Permanent Strike. This response happens to be tragically mistaken, destructive of the self as well as incapable of provoking social change; but it is a virtuous error, arising out of dismay at things that are rotten in the social fabric.

A few beats live off parents or girlfriends and are "social parasites" as pure as anyone living off dividend checks. Most beats scuffle; they take jobs temporarily when all else fails,[10] but exist most of the time by combining panhandling, quick moves from one pad to another to beat the rent, a complex round of borrowings and repayments, short cons such as selling marihuana that is heavily cut, and so on. This freedom from routine work is bought at an enormous price: not only does scuffling often consume more time and brainpower than a square job,[11] but its effect on leisure is more stultifying than any job dissatisfaction would be.

Beats believe that voluntary poverty is an intellectual gain; they gain by giving up the evil effects of meaningless work, gadgetry and the mass media. But the net effect on their leisure is that even the most ardent intellectuals among them often can't spare the carfare to get to the

[10] Beats quit jobs as soon as possible, seldom working a total of four months per year. But most beats of several years' standing have at one time or another—usually just once—tried the expedient of working barely long enough in a given year to be eligible for unemployment compensation. Informants recently on the west coast say that because Hawaii is now a state and one can collect unemployment benefits there, it is, among those beats who can scrape up boat fare, becoming increasingly popular as against Mexico.

[11] This and other intelligent objections to the beat lifestyle can be found in the anonymous "open letter to the beats from a spy deep in enemy territory," *Beatitude* No. 15, June 1960 (San Francisco), pp. 17–20.

better free libraries and concerts and art exhibits, seldom
can attend cultural events for which admission is charged,
and never can build up reasonable book and record libraries
of their own. Their meager amount of intellectual consumption is not only questionable as such, but of course
also stunts their growth as intellectual producers. "Holy
poverty" enforces comparative poverty of the mind.

A number of times I used the above argument with
beats, and got variants of one response: better to have a
poorer intellectual life than get caught up in the rat race.
And with the rare beat who conceded that the rat race occasionally could, with much prodding, be made to yield
up work meaningful in itself, the argument quickly became the old interminable one about the virtues of remaining simon pure vs. "boring from within," with the beat
being confirmed in his purity as approaching daylight reminded me to stagger off for a couple of hours' sleep before rejoining the rat race.

VIII

I looked hard for changes in the beat attitude toward
politics, but found instead confirmation of my old impression that it is wrong to describe the beats as apolitical
lumpen who are potential fascists (Malaquais) or potential
socialists (Mailer).

Far from being *lumpen,* beats are more keenly aware
of the range of political alternatives than is the average
voter. They are not apolitical but consciously and deliberately *anti*political, which is something else entirely, and,
as a common attitude, something new in American history.
Beats suffer not from political apathy but from political
antipathy. They totally "resign" from society in so far as
this is possible, not least of all from its politics, and reject
extreme political sects with no less vigor than they reject
major parties.

It might seem reasonable to call the beat an anarchist,
for he objects to representative government on the same
ground that Proudhon did, i.e., that no man can truly "rep-

resent" another man's thoughts and feelings—but more important is the fact that the beat doesn't want to promote anarchism or any other ism.[12]

All this has some virtues of its defects. If it means that the beat rejects any rational political planning, it means equally that he is not going to be a sucker for any charismatic leader whether of the right or left. [Here I was wrong. A little while after this study was made, some beats became enamored of Fidel Castro, and not only because of his tweaking the lion's tail: they also concluded that he must be hip and use marihuana because he sported a ragged beard and refused to wear a suit.[13] These beats became quickly disenchanted with Castro as soon as his particular brand of authoritarianism set in.] Of course the beat is pleased to see beat attitudes spread, but he isn't interested in joining any organized social movement toward that end. Each of the three words "organized social movement" sounds obscene to the beat's ears.[14] And though naturally

[12] In this respect as in some others, it is misleading to rely on the beat literary record, where one can, occasionally, find a quasi-political stance. Those who see the beats exclusively through their literature should remember that over 90 per cent of the beats neither write for publication nor wish to do so.

[13] [This beat error was overmatched at the time by *Playboy* dimwits, who concluded that John Kennedy must be hip and use marihuana because of his Hollywood friends and some other matters.]

[14] In view of my earlier finding (*Dissent,* Winter, 1958) that the beats are not totally atomized individuals but instead form a subculture, they must of course have some social organization. But it is of the most tenuous sort. The beat group approximates the *primitive band* as described by Ralph Linton: a group of fairly constant membership larger than the family, compact, nomadic but exploiting a fairly well-defined territory, socially self-sufficient and facing inward, without *rites de passage,* without formal governmental machinery, etc.
The last two features (perhaps the last three) distinguish the beat group sharply from the gang. Although Lewis Yablonsky in "The Violent Gang" (*Commentary,* August, 1960) claims that today's gang "lacks all features of an organized group," he goes on to contradict himself by describing types of gang officers and their duties, etc. The very concept of office is nonexistent in any beat group. [This difficulty with Yablonsky's view of the gang has since been noted independ-

amused to see some of his fellows such as Allen Ginsberg achieve notoriety and shake up the squares, he doesn't regard Ginsberg or anyone else as his "spokesman" (much less "leader") in the sense that squares conceive of spokesmanship. The beat's only spokesman is himself.

American intellectuals, and those of European origin especially, misunderstand this because they are prone to see every irrational excrescence in American political life as a sign of fascism round the corner (recall the panicky over-interpretations of MacArthur's "triumphal" return from Korea, etc.). To those who insist on finding a German ancestor for the beats, I would suggest that the proper ancestor is not the storm trooper but rather the philosopher-poet Friedrich Nietzsche, who correctly described himself as "an ardent anti-antisemite," as "opposed to everything that calls itself *Reichsdeutsch*," and as "the last anti-political German."

If the three hundred and more beats I talked with are in any way representative, then many of their journalistic detractors—sometimes misled by ambiguities in Norman Mailer's "The White Negro"—have made utterly false equations between the teenage hoodlum and beat worlds. These armchair social analysts need to catch up with current sociological theory and learn the differences between "conflict" and "retreatist" delinquent subcultures. Even more, they need to stop bombinating *in vacuo* and actually meet the people they write about—if only to learn that for every beat who is unusually given to violence there are at least two dozen beats who are sincere pacifists.

IX

In the Village beat world, as in all bohemias by definition, the socially disapproved forms of sexual behavior are tolerated if not encouraged. And as one would expect in the current bohemia, interracial intercourse is particularly frequent.

ently by Ralph England, in *American Journal of Sociology*, Vol. LXX, No. 5 (March, 1965), p. 630.]

What one would not necessarily expect is the peculiar pattern that homosexual behavior takes among the beats. Proportionately, the amount of such behavior seems as high as in the non-beat world even though the beat whose outlets are entirely or almost entirely homosexual is proportionately very much rarer than his non-beat counterpart. In other words an extraordinary number of male beats, whites as well as Negroes, are fully bisexual or in some cases polymorphous perverse.[15] They accept homosexual experiences almost as casually as heterosexual ones. Even beats with numerous and continuing post-adolescent homosexual experiences typically do not feel the need to define themselves as homosexuals and create some sort of beat wing of the homosexual world. Nor do they give up heterosexual involvements. Beats not only tolerate deviant sex roles but, to a much greater extent than previous bohemians, display a very high tolerance of sex-role ambiguity.

Most likely this subcultural trait was originally transmitted to the white beats by Negro beats, for not only do Negroes set much of the tone of beat life, but Negro culture has always had a higher tolerance of sexual ambiguity than white culture, and also the non-beat white groups showing high tolerance (e.g., seamen, ex-convicts) have had a special conditioning factor—prolonged absence from women—that is lacking in the beat world.

The unusual breadth of beat sex life is accompanied by very little depth. All types of beats at all age levels fail to establish deep and lasting sexual relationships. Lack of virility, however defined, is a frequent problem among the white males (and a characteristic of all long-time junkies); this substantial minority is essentially passive. The majority of beats, conversely, engage in an endless series of short-term affairs that bespeak much more of acting out than of action. Their bed-hopping "genitality" comes about precisely because they too are sexually impoverished—"or-

[15] In terms of the Kinsey heterosexual-homosexual rating scale from zero to six, beats show an unusual clustering at points two, three and four. Cf. Alfred Kinsey, Wardell Pomeroy and Clyde Martin, *Sexual Behavior in the Human Male* (Philadelphia: W. B. Saunders, 1948), pp. 638–41.

gastically impotent" in Reich's terms—and have yet to discover that in sex life there is no automatic passage from quantity to quality. Consequently, even among the oldest beats it is uncommon to find a couple who have been living together more than two or three years; and as often as not, such couples have managed to stick together only by replacing sex with the symbiotic cement of mutual drug addiction.[16]

X

For obvious reasons beat drug-taking is a furtive affair, and hence few outsiders realize that it is a totally pervasive part of beat life, both as an activity and as a topic of conversation. The illegal use of drugs is one of the handful of things that characterize all male beats with very rare exceptions, and a good majority of the females. But contrary to some popular views, (a) the majority use non-addicting drugs exclusively and (b) the majority of such users do not eventually go on to use addicting drugs and become junkies.

I talked with about 285 male beats and directly or indirectly queried about 205 concerning their possible illegal use of drugs, of whom only 14 denied any such use whatever; of about 25 female beats queried, out of about 40 I talked with, 9 denied illegal use of any drug.[17] Some beats who denied such use were doubtless lying. Although for most beats I did not obtain data on frequency of use, it seems certain that the majority use drugs at least once every couple of days, whether the drugs are addicting or non-addicting or a combination. Many younger beats have

[16] This is not to imply that junkie couples achieve long-run stability (the reverse doubtless is true), but rather that in its *initial* phases mutual addiction "helps keep the family together."

[17] The figures are exact for those denying illegal use of drugs; the other figures are estimates, as I didn't start keeping strict count of these until part way through my investigation. My talks with beats were not formal interviews and varied considerably in length. With some beats in the sample I spent less than five minutes; with others, more than thirty hours.

been thoroughly socialized to drug-taking without ever having been socialized to drinking, and are teetotalers when it comes to alcohol.

Beats do not constitute the majority of those who use drugs illegally, but their lives often intersect with that majority at the points of supply. Consequently much of the information below, though gathered from Village beats, deals with general New York drug distribution.

A. Addicting Drugs. Heroin is the drug of choice among beat junkies, though a few are hooked on barbiturates. The other addicting opiates and synthetics—morphine, codeine, demerol, dolophine, pantopon, etc.—are all used freely by junkies when available, but in the Village they are available less often than heroin or barbiturates, and no beat junkie seems primarily addicted to one of these drugs as such; rather, these drugs are used in addition to heroin or as substitutes for it.

Opium itself is often available. However, it is expensive ($15–20 for a *toy,* a ball about the size of a large pea) and beats regard it as something to try once for kicks but otherwise not worth the price—partly because it is less powerful than its main derivatives and partly because there is rarely an opium layout and experienced preparer available. A few beats claim there is still one old-style "opium den" in Chinatown, which admits no whites or Negroes and very few Chinese. Although disappointed at being barred, they admire the Chinese for playing it so cool.

Apart from questions of secrecy, it is hard to estimate the percentage of junkies among the beats because there are marginal cases (those who use addicting drugs occasionally but have not become addicts) and because some addicts cannot yet admit to themselves, much less to an outsider, that they have been hooked. I counted as junkies not only those who indicated they were, but all admitted users of addicting drugs who indicated they had ever experienced withdrawal discomfort, whether or not they indicated that drugs had been taken to relieve such discomfort, and regardless of frequency of use.[18] By this criterion,

[18] A partial justification for this procedure is the statement of Lindesmith, *op. cit.,* p. 75: "The writer has never heard of a

among Village beats under 20, about one out of fifteen is a junkie; between 20 and 25, about one out of eleven; over 25, about one out of nine.

Off and on during the past year—though not at present —there have been in the Village severe shortages of heroin. Users unanimously state that this has not been due to an increase in Village arrests but entirely to another factor: some time ago the syndicate decided to pull out of the drug business temporarily—this is partly what the Apalachian meeting was to be about—because of successful government prosecution of some very big shots (notably Stromberg and Genovese).

Negroes and Puerto Ricans controlled some distribution in their neighborhoods but were not equipped to fill entirely the hole that the syndicate pullout left in their own supplies, much less take over distribution elsewhere. Apparently Negro and Puerto Rican areas at first felt the pinch as much as the Village, not merely because of the syndicate pullout but because many more white junkies began trying to score from them. Indeed, some white Village pushers and users of heroin moved to the racially mixed areas of the upper West Side and lower East Side.

When the syndicate pulled out, for some junkies there was at first total panic; their connections simply had no junk. Now all junkies can obtain heroin regularly again—a few believe that syndicate members previously unassociated with the drug traffic are entering it—but complain that the price has risen steeply in the form of greater dilution. (In the absence of actual analysis of drug samples, such statements should be treated with caution. Complaints about increasing dilution are always common among junkies, the main reason being the junkies' increasing tolerance of drugs.) Three junkies say that there have been a sharply increased number of sick junkies unable to support their habits at former levels, trying to taper off on such things as Cocinil, and hitting drugstores so often that some stores

user who, having experienced the full intensity of the withdrawal symptoms in full knowledge of their relation to the absence of opiates, did not become an addict."

have been totally "burned down," i.e., refuse to supply even non-prescription items to known junkies.

[Shortly after this study was made, Vito Genovese was convicted on federal narcotics charges. Some time later, the most prominent figure in Greenwich Village organized crime, Anthony Strollo ("Tony Bender"), permanently disappeared, and crime reporters said this was retribution for his having refused the demand of higher-ups that he be cooler about heroin distribution and take the financial losses involved.]

B. Non-addicting Drugs. Beats frequently use non-addicting and non-hallucinatory stimulants, such as dexedrine; but their use of non-addicting drugs focuses invariably and overwhelmingly on the hallucinogens. Among these, marihuana is the drug of choice. Marihuana smokers also use peyote, hashish, and synthetic mescalin in that order of frequency. Recently a few marihuana smokers have experimented with using peyote exclusively for extended periods. Cocaine is seldom used because it is expensive and the "high" it produces does not last long; beats say it is a rich man's drug, used mostly in wealthy show business and criminal circles.

Beats who use no illegal drugs are few. To estimate the proportion using marihuana, it would not be far wrong to simply reverse the above estimates concerning beat junkies. Thus, among beats under 20, marihuana smokers would outnumber junkies nearly fourteen to one; between 20 and 25, nearly ten to one; over 25, nearly eight to one.[19]

[19] These estimates differ astoundingly from those usually found in the literature on narcotics, where it is typically estimated that about 91½ per cent of all New York drug users known to authorities use addicting drugs and about 8½ per cent use non-addicting drugs such as marihuana. Cf. *Second Interim Report of the State of New York Committee on Narcotic Study,* Legislative Document (1958), No. 16, p. 12.

There are several possible reasons for the discrepancy, all of which might be operative here: (a) Though I tried to secure a representative sample of beats, junkies may have been slightly under-represented. (b) Some beats who are junkies doubtless kept this fact hidden from me. (c) Beats are somewhat unrepresentative of New York drug users generally, because nearly

About a dozen men and two women stated that most beat women smoke marihuana but few are real "potheads" (devotees of marihuana), and that most smoke it mainly because their men do.

Although beat heroin users and beat marihuana smokers are part of one subculture, they tend to split into two separate groups when it comes to the specific activity of taking drugs, each developing its own customs.

As Howard Becker has shown, marihuana smoking is a group activity in which the psychic response to the drug in large part has to be taught to the newcomer.[20] (It appears that marihuana is a drug in which tolerance not only does not go up, but as a result of learning actually goes down.) Beat marihuana smokers not only confirm this, but indicate that even after the user has internalized the group's norms and thus can get high alone, his drug-taking continues to have a much more social quality than that of the heroin user. One made a remark that would be almost inconceivable from a heroin user: "Sometimes it's okay to get high

all the junkies attracted to New York from the rest of the country (New York is now estimated to have between one-third and one-half of America's junkies) probably go to non-beat circles. (d) The number of New York marihuana smokers may indeed be several times the number of junkies, but the latter pose such a severe problem that narcotics police must give them near-total attention, and hence marihuana smokers rarely come to the attention of the authorities. (This would follow from the beat testimony cited below, which there seems no reason to doubt, concerning the pattern of narcotics arrest.) (e) Additional support for the view that marihuana smokers may greatly outnumber junkies is that the latter often must turn to crime to support their habits and/or turn themselves in for treatment—both of which bring them to the attention of the authorities—whereas marihuana smokers do neither.

The one other comparative survey of drug use I know of that does not depend on arrest rates also finds that marihuana smokers outnumber heroin users, though the differences are not nearly as startling. Cf. Charles Winick, "The Use of Drugs by Jazz Musicians," *Social Problems*, Vol. VII, No. 3 (Winter, 1959–60), especially p. 242.

[20] Howard S. Becker, "Becoming a Marihuana User," *American Journal of Sociology*, Vol. LIX (November, 1953), pp. 235–42.

by yourself, but then I always like to go out and bounce it off other studs." Beat statements about group marihuana-using sessions and group heroin-using sessions consistently indicate a far greater degree of mutuality in the former, particularly with regard to both verbal and nonverbal sharing of drug-induced psychic states.[21] It is possible that this mutuality has a strong latent homosexual component and that this is what bars most female beats from full participation; the four beats I asked about this thought there was something to it.

Narcotics police in the Village, say the beats, used to spend all their time chasing junk (addicting drugs). Marihuana users were safe if they stayed on their own scenes, and were arrested only if they were discovered accidentally —typically if they were on a junk scene when the police came looking for junk. This is still generally true, but beats note that in the past year there have been two major Village raids on strictly marihuana-smoking groups. And the police forced the one coffee shop that earlier this summer was selling peyote openly (not against New York State law) to discontinue sales, by invoking a city health ordinance concerning potentially poisonous foods.

During the past four months (May through August) there have been recurrent shortages in the Village marihuana supply. These shortages have been more frequent and of longer duration than heroin shortages, a situation the beats say is truly extraordinary: "Man, there's never been anything like it. All the smack you want and a complete pot panic."[22] To obtain marihuana at all, beats have sometimes been forced to buy it in a form (already rolled into "joints," rather than loose) and at a price (75 cents

[21] This psychic sharing among marihuana smokers reaches its peak in the "contact high." Cf. Winick, *op. cit.*, p. 244.

[22] "Smack" is one of several terms for heroin. Marihuana is usually "pot," though "boo" and other terms are sometimes heard. "Panic," usually in the form of "there's a panic on," means that there is a drug shortage. The argot is of course subject to rapid change. For humorous effect, beats will sometimes use a term that is no longer current except among square writers: "Got a reefer, man?"

or $1 per joint) that they say are usually reserved for the rich college crowd. There are many stories about marihuana being cut with bay leaves, oregano, etc., and about an increase in the number of "burns" (in which someone who claims he can obtain drugs takes money in advance and never returns).[23]

Beats feel that the marihuana shortages, unlike those of heroin, have little to do with the syndicate lying low, for the distribution of marihuana has always been almost entirely independent of syndicate control. The consensus is that marihuana supplies have not decreased, and may even have increased, but in recent months have had to be spread over a suddenly expanding market.

The horde of new teenage beats, many just arrived in the Village this summer, nearly all use marihuana.[24] More-

[23] Some older drug users say the greater number of burns is due to the increased mobility of today's beats. Beats are in fact more mobile than old-style hoboes. Not only do they shuttle between New York and California, but they have their own "international set" whose principal stopping places are in Mexico, the Balearic Islands, Tangier, and Paris.

[24] In the opinion of some beats, which I share, the new teenage beats will end up producing proportionately fewer junkies than older groups have done. This is *not* because they are aware that "just fooling around" with heroin almost always leads to addiction, for there is hardly a heroin addict alive who didn't know that to begin with. It is rather that among beats today the use of heroin has lost much of its glamor, is less often considered a requisite of being hip, and frequently is even considered "uncool." A similar change seems to have taken place in the ideology of jazz musicians. Cf. Winick, *op. cit., passim.*

[*Addendum, 1968:* The above prediction about the diminishing proportion of junkies was fully borne out. The beats of the early 1960's, and their immediate "hippie" successors, went less and less for addicting drugs, and indeed developed an elaborate ideology which promulgated "mind" drugs and put down all "body" drugs (by which they meant not only the usual addicting drugs, such as heroin and the barbiturates, but also those drugs, non-addicting in ordinary use, that can produce physical dependence with prolonged use of heavy doses —such as alcohol and the amphetamines). About 1966, however, this ideology began to break down and the fad of injecting amphetamines, particularly methedrine, spread among the hippies. Heroin also made a bit of a comeback, though reaching

over, while the Village beat market has been expanding, some of its normal supplies have been deflected to new markets elsewhere. Beats say that the use of marihuana in white non-beat circles was until recently pretty much restricted to jazz musicians and theater people, but that in the past year it has been spreading rapidly in the worlds of advertising, radio-TV, college students, etc.—the *Playboy* readership, essentially—and that some suppliers formerly in the Village have shifted to the favorite hangouts of these groups because they pay more. It is said that some ex-Village pushers of marihuana and hashish now work the fancy uptown East-Side bars, and that earlier this summer two Village pushers took off for Provincetown when they discovered that what would be a $5 bag of marihuana in the Village was selling for $15 to the Provincetown sports-car set.

[The beats' most enduring imprint on American culture appears, in retrospect, to have been precisely this diffusion of marihuana use to many circles of middle- and upper-class whites outside the jazz world. Such contemporary white use, although now self-sustaining and still growing, stemmed largely from public attention given to beat practices and beat literary proselytizing on the matter. The accompanying chart—which represents, as nearly as I can determine at this time, the history of marihuana use in America—illustrates the role of the beats as the key transmission belt for the current white use of marihuana.

---

nothing remotely like the popularity it had enjoyed among the beats of 1960.

All of this indicates not only that, contrary to the Federal Narcotics Bureau, there need be no "graduation" from non-addicting to addicting drugs. It also indicates, contrary to what many sociologists believe, that whether or not someone goes from non-addicting to addicting drugs does *not* depend essentially on whether he is heavily involved in "the drug-using subculture." Rather, it seems that the use or non-use of addicting drugs is a matter of shifting fad and fashion in the drug-using subculture itself, and whether someone ever uses these drugs depends on—among other things—the particular point in time at which he is socialized to and participates in that subculture.]

THE SPREAD OF MARIHUANA USE IN AMERICA*
Culture Contact, Differential Association, and Subcultural Diffusion

MEXICO

SOUTHWESTERN U.S.

(introduced about 1910 by Mexican laborers; becomes established among Mexican-Americans; sporadic cowboy use, but doesn't become established there)

NEW ORLEANS

(introduced to Negroes, via Mexican-Americans, by 1920)

URBAN NEGRO LOWER CLASS, SOUTH & NORTH

(well established by mid-1920's; rapid spread begins about 1931)

WHITE LOWER CLASS IN RACIALLY MIXED NEIGHBORHOODS (some by mid-1930's, but mostly since late 1940's)

NON-MUSICIAN WHITE ENTERTAINERS (some by early 1930's; mainly nightclub & stripper subcultures—incl. criminals & prostitutes assoc. with those industries—but also some movie, circus, & legit theatre people)

NEGRO JAZZ MUSICIANS** & NEGRO FANS (simultaneously with other Negroes, as above)

WHITE JAZZ MUSICIANS & WHITE FANS (some by mid-1920's, esp. in Chicago; rapid spread among white musicians in mid-1930's, but not among fans until "hipsters" of early 1940's and "beat" fans from about 1948 onward)

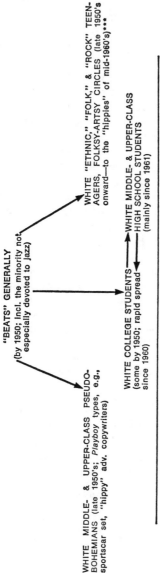

"BEATS" GENERALLY
(by 1950; incl. the minority not especially devoted to jazz)

WHITE "ETHNIC," "FOLK," & "ROCK" TEEN-AGERS, FOLKSY-ARTSY CIRCLES (late 1950's onward—to the "hippies" of mid-1960's)***

WHITE MIDDLE- & UPPER-CLASS HIGH SCHOOL STUDENTS (mainly since 1961)

WHITE COLLEGE STUDENTS (some by 1950; rapid spread since 1960)

WHITE MIDDLE- & UPPER-CLASS PSEUDO-BOHEMIANS (late 1950's; *Playboy* types, e.g., sportscar set, "hippy" adv. copywriters)

*This chart derives to a small extent from printed sources (e.g., Mezz Mezzrow's *Really the Blues*), but is based mainly on information given me by present and former marihuana users of long standing (three of whom were smoking marihuana in the 1920's).

**The earliest of many jazz records whose titles refer to marihuana is Louis Armstrong's *Muggles* (OK 8703), recorded December 7, 1928. ("Muggles" is an obsolete argot term for marihuana.) The titles of three earlier jazz records refer to other drugs: Josie Miles's *Pipe Dream Blues* (1924), Duke Ellington's *Hop Head* (1927), and Victoria Spivey's *Dope Head Blues* (1927). I take these from Charles Delaunay's *New Hot Discography* (New York: Criterion Music Corp., 1948), but have not been able to check through Brian Rust's later and fuller discography.

References to marihuana also occur in the lyrics, but not the titles, of other jazz records, e.g., Bessie Smith's *Gimme a Pigfoot* (1933) and Joe Marsala's *Salty Mama Blues* (1940).

***Innumerable post-1960 references to marihuana can be found in recordings by white "folk" and "rock" singers (Bob Dylan, the Rolling Stones, *et al.*).

The beats managed to do what some scientific investigators of marihuana had tried but failed to do: they convinced many sectors of the American public that the Federal Narcotics Bureau's myths about marihuana—the notions that marihuana is a significant cause of crime, insanity, and heroin addiction—were indubitably myths.[25]

Some other hallucinogens not mentioned in my study were taken up by the beats in 1961 and have since then spread elsewhere. But recent publicity about increasing use of the most powerful such drug, LSD-25, has tended to obscure the fact that marihuana use has been, and still is, increasing much more. From estimates made for me by students on several college campuses, I would judge that among college students the number of regular marihuana users is at least twenty times the number of regular LSD users—and this despite the fact that over half the college marihuana users apparently have also tried LSD at least once.

With the rise of marihuana use among college students has come its acceptance, in a sense, by college administrators. Especially in the large schools, officials tend increasingly to "look the other way" and do nothing whatever about marihuana-using students unless pressured by police or parents or newspaper publicity.

Proselytizers for marihuana—beats, hippies, and college users alike—interpret all this to mean that marihuana will

[25] [Although the better-educated segment of the public is now aware of the myths for what they are—knows, for example, that the myriads of college students who currently smoke marihuana are not thereby "led to" heroin addiction—this has in no wise lessened the efforts of the Federal Narcotics Bureau to perpetuate the myths and otherwise to suppress the scientific evidence of marihuana's harmlessness. The Bureau's undiminished efforts have led a number of sociologists, including myself, to come round to the view long maintained in heroic isolation by Alfred Lindesmith of Indiana University, viz., that some Bureau officials are not dedicated truthseekers having honest differences of opinion with the academic investigators, but, on the contrary, dedicate themselves first and last to extending the power of the Federal Narcotics Bureau—to the extent of deliberate falsification of evidence.]

be adopted by ever-widening segments of the population and one day replace liquor in the affections of most Americans. But the social scientist knows that a trend does not always remain a trend, and indeed often reverses itself. And with respect to trends concerning marihuana, the scientist must take account of *all* the facts, some of which the propagandists conveniently ignore.

Proselytizers are unhappy when confronted with such facts as these: in societies where alcohol and marihuana start out competing on fairly equal terms, the alcohol often drives out the marihuana (as in present-day Mexico); marihuana clearly supplants alcohol only in societies with strong religious prohibitions against alcohol (notably Islamic countries); even such countries, as they "modernize," tend to use alcohol and pass and enforce laws against marihuana (the clearest example is Turkey). Finally, in regard to America's current "trend" toward marihuana, we should keep in mind that the only age-group being affected in significant degree is the one most given to fads; smoking marihuana may be to this college generation what swallowing goldfish was to another, and college students of 20 years from now may have as little interest in marihuana as did college students of 20 years ago.]

XI

Almost all Village beats technically are literate, and some whites have even attended college, but at best a sixth are habituated to reading (none seem addicted) and far fewer are concerned with writing. (Most square articles on "the beats" go astray because beat writers, being highly visible, get all the attention and thus a small and atypical part is taken for the whole.) Among the minority who could be called regular readers, the "literary" materials read consist almost wholly of writing by romantic hedonists, much of it third-rate or worse and nearly all of it contemporary.

Interest in Zen passed its peak over a year ago and has radically declined. In the Village at least, Zen now appears to have been a beat fad whose only lasting significance in

American intellectual history is that it (along with jazz-cum-poetry) marks the first time that a west coast bohemia exerted a major influence on an eastern one. About the only carryover from earlier mystical concerns is that some beats continue to take an interest in divination; but formerly beats used the *I Ching, or Book of Changes* for this purpose, whereas now one finds the use of Tarot cards or some Harlem-derived routine.

Insofar as most beats, whites and Negroes alike, can be said to have a dominant intellectual interest, it is jazz music. And the jazz world is the single non-beat segment of American society that often attracts beats. (Their admiration for it is not requited, to judge by musicians' complaints.) The nature and depth of the beats' relation to jazz have remained unchanged over the past three years, except that these years have produced some new heroes (e.g., Ray Charles) and a new villain (for some beats, Ornette Coleman has replaced Dave Brubeck as the arch-fraud).

Although the white beat's attraction to the jazz world is often the very core of his "white Negro" role, there is little uniquely "beat" about all this. Such involvement is socially not very different from the relationship of adolescent whites to Negro jazz in several American non-beat and pre-beat bohemias. [Even the "white Negro" concept itself is old. A critic noted in 1930 that white jazzmen of the early 1920's, such as Bix Beiderbecke, "felt as a reality the spirit of Negro blues. Indeed, such bands as the Wolverines were called 'white niggers.' "26] For example, nearly twenty years ago [i.e., 1942], when I was v.-p. of my high school jazz club, a 13-year-old zoot suiter, we often used to make the Harlem "balcony scenes"—boosting old Bessie Smiths and Hot Fives from the balcony of the Rainbow Music Shop before the wartime scrap drive wrecked the supply, going wild in the Apollo Theatre's sweet-smelling second

26 [Charles Edward Smith, "Jazz," *The Symposium*, Vol. 1, No. 4 (October, 1930), p. 509. When the traveler Richard Burton, during his youthful service in the Indian Army, went among the natives disguised as a native, his fellow-officers derisively dubbed him "the white nigger." Cf. Frank Harris, *Contemporary Portraits* (New York: Brentano's, 1920), p. 193.]

balcony—odoriferous from pomade and pot, though we didn't know about the latter at the time—to a Basie-Millinder twin bill. And we traveled Swing Street when it still swung (where half the time we'd get kicked out despite our borrowed I.D.'s), to hear Billie Holiday at the Onyx Club or Art Tatum at the Three Deuces. Today, the big boosting scenes are Goody's and the Colony instead of the Rainbow; Swing Street has been replaced by scattered Village clubs; the white intellectual jazz mentors are Nat Hentoff and Martin Williams instead of Ralph Berton and Gene Williams; there are goatees instead of 12-inch peg pants, etc. But apart from the music itself, and the fact that now one merely listens to it at Birdland instead of stomping to it at the Savoy, not much has really changed. [*Addendum, 1968:* One of many notable differences between today's hippies and their beat progenitors is of course the hippies' absorption with white "rock" music and their relative lack of interest in Negro jazz, except for blues. On the other hand, many things originating in Negro life have been so thoroughly taken over by the white culture that we have merely lost sight of their Negro origins—and this applies to white "rock" music as much as anything else.]

XII

A few beats, invariably among the youngest, are not so much interested in jazz as in the folk music of the "ethnic" set. But all beats reject the folksy-artsy group as people because in fundamental attitude the latter, despite the number of Negroes among them, are un-or anti-beat.[27] The Village devotees of ethnic music are historically minded, scholarly, middle-class youths, mostly Jewish, who are trying to disown their parents' culture not by becoming beat but rather by proving that ancient proverb, "New York ain't America."

[27] When the Fire Department raided beat coffee shops, the proprietor of The Folklore Center on Macdougal Street went so far as to issue a mimeographed broadside (dated June 12, 1960) praising this action and condemning the beats. Shortly thereafter he had his window broken.

The intersection of beat and "ethnic" circles, and indeed of Village social circles generally, can be seen at its warm-weather wildest in the hundreds of people who on Sunday afternoons gather round the children's wading pool in Washington Square Park. The circles here are as much concentric as intersecting.

The inner circle consists of people who arrive by 1:00 P.M. and thus get seats on the rim of the pool and on the steps leading down into it; this circle is a mixture of early-rising square Villagers, many of whom have brought their children to wade, and beats who get there early because they've been up all night. (The beats used to get high and roll around in the pool with the kiddies, fully clothed, until the Park Department enforced the rule restricting the pool's use to those under 12 years of age.) Surrounding this is a second, standing circle of clusters of folk and hillbilly performers and their listeners: uptown tourists and new-style rich Villagers, "ethnic" teenagers, Italians, a few beats. Around this is a third circle, also quite mixed but consisting mostly of beats asking each other what's happening, tourists with cameras trying to elbow their way into the second circle for a good shot, and tight-trousered Village homosexuals walking their dogs and cruising each other.

XIII

In going through a good-sized collection of beat and semi-beat little magazines, published in various cities here and abroad, I have been unable to find 150 writers who by any definition could be called beat. Given the fact that beat writers are not notably reluctant to take the first things that pop into their heads and send them out to the world (if only via the mimeograph machine), and that on a most conservative estimate there cannot be less than 2000 beats in New York alone, it would be charitable indeed to say that a tenth of the beats are concerned to write. But today in the Village and elsewhere, significantly more beats are writing than was the case three years ago, and it seems that now at least as high a proportion of them are writing

as was true of earlier bohemians.[28] In four or five cases
their motives are not of the highest—come to no more than
the knowledge that one can pick up some change by re-
citing shockers to tourists in coffee shops—but most are
sincere about their writing, and in any event whatever
literary talent there may be among the beats now stands a
good chance of being discovered.

Most beat literature is poor when it is not godawful. And
this is certainly true of its best-publicized examples, which
have been surpassed even by the minor Victorians: James
Thomson's poetic howl of urban despair, *The City of
Dreadful Night,* is greater by far than anything Ginsberg
offers,[29] and in on-the-road literature the genuine gusto
of George Borrow, for all his prudishness, is preferable to
the faked-up fervor of Kerouac. As for the beat talk of
achieving a "breakthrough" with respect to the old literary
forms: this should be translated simply as "breakdown."
The beats have not significantly extended the range of the
old forms. And their contribution in the way of a new art
form, if one can call it that, consists of bad poetry read to
bad jazz, with not even an integration of the badnesses.
That last point seems to have been realized by the beats
themselves, for jazz-cum-poetry recitals occur infrequently
these days.

Though a few beats regard Ezra Pound as one of their
literary mentors, they see only the *épater l'académicien*
side of him and don't dare face up to such typical Poundian
dicta as: "Saxpence reward for any authenticated case of
intellect having stopped a chap's writing poetry! You might
as well claim the railway tracks stop the engine. No one

[28] Still far less than 10 per cent, however. In thinking of
past bohemias we tend to recall only accomplishments and
forget that for, say, every Village bohemian of the 1930's who
actually sat down and wrote, there were several others just
talking about it and a couple of dozen others doing not even
that. Artists by definition know how to play, and hence attract
many people who want to play all the time, which in turn
makes it harder for artists to get their work done.

[29] *Howl* will remain important in our literary history as the
most influential programmatic statement of a beat worldview.
I deny merely that it is good poetry.

ever claimed they would make it go." Beat writers start
with a great deal against them. They are victims of a primi-
tivist ideology that, in its oversimplified anti-academicism
and anti-historicism, prevents many of them from reading
much at all, prevents most of the others from reading anything written earlier than the day before yesterday, leads
them into false and fatuous notions of "spontaneity," and
keeps them from fully learning the technical skills involved
in their art and fully exploiting whatever talents they may
have. [In an interview granted in March, 1962, Pound himself put down the limited artistic purview of the mindless
howlers who would misappropriate him. *"Interviewer:*
'You have given advice to young writers all your life. Do
you have anything special to say to them now,' *Ezra Pound:*
'To improve their curiosity and not to fake. But that is not
enough. The mere registering of bellyache and the mere
dumping of the ashcan is not enough. In fact the University
of Pennsylvania student *Punchbowl* used to have as its
motto, 'Any damn fool can be spontaneous.' "30]

The "spontaneity" nonsense may be discerned not only,
or even primarily, in Kerouacian prose, but in the myriad
beat poems written according to the new poetic that has
received its most erudite expression in the "write like you
breathe" and "composition by field" prosodic theory
Charles Olson has elaborated.31 Granted the obvious integrity of Olson himself, it remains true that "the importance of any theory," as P. W. Bridgman once remarked,
"is what it actually does, not what it says it does or what
its author thinks it does"—and that Olson's theory functions
as a copout for poets with tin ears, with a defective sense
of rhythm and structure. The theory put into practice gets
rid of "artificiality" by getting rid of art.

And yet, the beat literary scene is not nearly as dismal
as it was in 1957. For there *are* beats with genuine literary
ability, and despite their cockeyed theories this ability is

30 ["Ezra Pound: An Interview," *Paris Review,* Vol. 7, No.
28 (Summer-Fall, 1962), pp. 28–29.]
31 Cf. Olson's essay reprinted in Donald Allen, ed., *The.
New American Poetry, 1945–1960* (New York: Grove Press,
1960), pp. 386–97.

occasionally beginning to show itself. During the past three years the beats have produced some permanently valuable additions to American letters. (This is more than can be said for the entire output of some literary schools. Try reading, say, *Proletarian Literature in the United States*.) Among these writings are Gregory Corso's poem "Marriage," John Rechy's "The Fabulous Wedding of Miss Destiny" (one of the most dazzling American stories in years, and so genuinely distinctive that the editors of *Best American Short Stories, 1960* couldn't bear to put it in their also-ran list of "distinctive" stories, much less give it honorable mention or reprint it), and Jack Gelber's play *The Connection* (which acts much better than it reads).[32] And because the beats, unlike their French existentialist cousins and rather like the earlier Dadaists, see "the absurd" in its comic implications as fully as its tragic ones, a good deal of beat literature that fails as Art is quite enjoyable as Wisecrack.[33]

The beat writer with the most raw potential is Gregory Corso. True enough, he lacks a couple of technical craft skills (which can be taught) and sometimes falls into the worst clichés of thought as well as style. But unlike our slick young technicians Corso shows some real talents (which cannot be taught): he often does have something to say, usually makes you feel that *he* feels what he's saying, and displays in abundance a virtue that is the keystone of fine poetry—loving, imaginative play with language. Whether he will surpass the limits imposed by beat ideology or remain an extraordinarily gifted primitive is problematical.

[32] Corso's poem is most readily available in Allen, *op. cit.*, pp. 209–212. Rechy's story is in *Big Table*, Vol. 1, No. 3 (1959), pp. 11–39. *The Connection* is published by Grove Press. [Rechy's story has since been republished as part of his novel, *City of Night* (New York: Grove Press, 1963), pp. 102–129. I think it is the best part of the novel.]

[33] A recent example is "Wailing Wall for Richard Gumbiner —last seen," by Pierre Delattre and Alan Dienstag, in *Beatitude* No. 16 (July, 1960, no paging). This is the San Francisco magazine, not the rival *Beatitude* No. 16 published in New York by a defecting editor from San Francisco.

XIV

Both white and Negro beats are notably given to calling a spade a spade. One would never catch them describing race relations as "intergroup" relations even if they knew the term, nor describing the lower class as the "working" class or old people as "senior citizens." But this forthrightness of speech and attitude, laudable as it may be, is not accompanied by much clarity of vision. Nowhere is there greater disparity between beat theory and practice than in the role that Negro beats, wittingly or unwittingly, are forced to play for white beats.

The several white beats I met who knew my earlier critique of them—unfortunately I met no Negro beats who knew it[34]—all disputed my claim that they accept the Negro only for his "Negro-ness" (as bringer of marihuana and jazz, etc.) and thus practice an inverted form of "keeping the nigger in his place." According to them, they really do accept the Negro in his totality. Maybe so; but I doubt it. White beats should be given credit for the best of conscious intentions, but it is disheartening how often their actions confirm that old Negro proverb, "Whenever you see a white man with a colored man, the white man wants something from the colored man."

To see that Negroes living in the interracial beat world are still "invisible men" means to become sharply aware of something that white beats characteristically dodge: no modern urban Negro—raised as he is on white movies, white comic books, white television—can avoid internalizing white ideals, most especially can he not avoid internalizing white ideals of physical beauty, and on one level or another of his consciousness he puts himself down every time he looks in a mirror. (Hence the enormous Negro hair-straightening and skin-lightening industries, the profound

[34] Some material that follows is touchy if not downright offensive to most Negroes, beat or non-beat. As I was able to explore all of it with only three Negro beats (two agreed completely, the other hedged on some parts), it should be regarded as subject to further proof or disproof.

discrimination among Negroes themselves on the basis of skin color, the high yellow beauty on the cover of *Ebony* who gives the lie to the magazine's title, etc.) Contrary to what many white beats believe, there is hardly a Negro alive who in his heart of hearts wouldn't rather be white, and the various kinds of Negro chauvinist movements invariably represent a reaction formation against the forbidden desire to be white.

[As disproof of my claim that Negro chauvinist movements "invariably represent a reaction formation against the forbidden desire to be white," Nat Hentoff noted, in the April, 1962, issue of *Nugget,* that an increasing number of Negroes take conscious pride in being black. I replied (in *Nugget,* October, 1962, p. 8) as follows: "Mr. Hentoff's point does not at all contradict mine. I used 'reaction formation' in its technical psychoanalytic sense, which refers to an *unconscious* process. What I was trying to get at —the unconscious roots of conscious black chauvinism—is perhaps best indicated by the slip that one Negro chauvinist leader, Malcolm X, made on a TV interview program last November, in response to the interviewer pointing out that he (Malcolm) obviously had a lot of white blood in him: 'I hate every drop of black blood—I mean *white* blood— that's in me.' "]

The modern American Negro's need to be white is one culture trait that the white male beat, like most of his square white brethren, cannot emotionally accept. This comes out most clearly, though not exclusively, in beat sex life; the Negro's desire for white girls is continually and subtly opposed by the white males, whatever their conscious beliefs may be, *not* merely in the terms with which one usually opposes a sexual rival but with such remarks as "X is too hung up on balling white chicks" or "Y's trouble is that he's too fay-oriented," and so on. Thus miscegenation in the beat world is essentially a conspiracy between white females and Negro males, that triumphs over strong white male opposition only because the latter can never become fully articulate since it contradicts the conscious ideology.

In addition to the remarks of white beats quoted above, there is evidence from the Negro side that all is not well.

Every Negro knows that the white man, though he dislikes all non-whites, has especially hostile feelings toward American Negroes; he knows experientially the truth in Max Weber's remark that the difference between the white man's attitude toward Indians and toward Negroes is that the Indians were never slaves. So the Negro who finds his status intolerable sometimes concludes that if he can't change his skin, at least he can try to escape his status as an *American* Negro—can try to enter some halfway house by pretending to be a Jamaican or Haitian or whatever. Recently the most influential halfway house among Negroes has been Islam.[35] These halfway houses are part of what Franklin Frazier calls the Negro "world of make-believe" —few Negroes or whites are really fooled by an American Negro's claim to be somebody else—but they do ease the pain somewhat. Now, it happens that several prominent jazz musicians have been converted to Islam. Statistically speaking, they represent a small portion of either American Negro Moslems or jazz musicians, and yet their presence has a real meaning, which is this: even if you're a very successful Northern Negro and move in circles that include many hip white admirers and make it with some cool white chicks, you're still expected to play it like a spade and it's still a drag.

The hip attitude toward Negroes is, to be sure, not only better than the usual square rejection of them but is superior to the phoney some-of-my-best-friends-are routines (which at best let in special performers of the arts, scholarship and politics under special conditions). And this ideology does mean that white beats meet with Negroes more

[35] However, the emergence of West African nations is causing a shift among some Harlemites from a North African Moslem orientation to a West African non-Moslem one. See, for example, Priest Ofuntola Oserjeman, *Orisha: A First Glimpse of the African Religion of Brazil, Cuba, Haiti, Trinidad and now U.S.A.* (New York: Great Benin Books, African Library Series, n. d. [1960]), available from The Shango Temple, 71 East 125th Street.

often than white squares usually do. What is still questionable is the nature of these relationships.

Although the white beat grants the Negro a fuller role than other white "pro-Negro" groups do, he does it merely by compounding the limited roles those groups demand. For the white beat, the Negro fulfills the liberal's demand that he entertain plus the radical's demand that he symbolize the results of reactionary oppression plus the Harlem thrill-seeker's demand that he act out the primitive in all of us. One thing the Negro must *not* do is try to be white.

Instead of worrying about the Negro becoming "too fay-oriented" the white beats might consider accepting him in his inescapable aspect of Negro-wanting-to-be-white. They might even encourage it, for surely the only real solution to the psychological problems peculiar to the American Negro is the very solution that so worries our Southerners: miscegenation on a grand scale, the production of more and more Negroes who can pass, and ultimately the total "mongrelization" of the two races.

XV

I found it relatively easy to talk with beats, though the talk often had to be literally in their terms and representatives of the non-exhibitionist majority had to be diligently sought out: first, because they are typically more tolerant than political sectarians, more willing to accept an outsider who makes an honest attempt to understand them; second, because I agree with many of their criticisms of modern society; third, because from the onset of my own adolescence until a couple of years thereafter (at which time I enlisted in the death-struggles of Marxism), I and some of my friends went through a "white Negro" phase similar to that of many young beats today. However, if one makes it clear to the beats, as I did, that he is essentially a square, he will run into some who will give him a rough time, he will occasionally be put on (a combination of being conned and being baited). This was overcome in nearly all cases.

Generally, the only real hindrance proved to be that the beats, who by definition avoid work, are nightpeople. With respect to drugs there was the special problem that anyone investigating this area must of course convince the people involved that he is not a fink or a plain-clothesman, and I was not always able to do so. Thus the material on drugs, full as it may seem, is actually the thinnest part of my essay.

Nearly all beats I talked with at any length were told that I would write about them, and with four exceptions fairly easily accepted this. Nor was it necessary, except with a few paranoid-homicidal types, to keep from them my disagreements or the fact that what I wrote would in good part be critical.

On the Sociology of Pornography*

Samuel Johnson once informed James Boswell that he could recite a complete chapter of a book called *The Natural History of Iceland*. The chapter was entitled "Concerning Snakes," and consisted in its entirety of the following: "There are no snakes to be met with throughout the whole island." I can be similarly brief concerning studies on the sociology of pornography: there are no such studies to be met with throughout the whole of sociology.

What we do have, first of all, is an abundance of offhand "sociologizing" about pornography, on the part of contemporary journalists, cultural historians, psychiatrists, literary critics, lawyers, and judges—especially if they are of liberal inclination and don't like censorship. This material isn't worth much. In fact its chief interest for sociologists, as I shall elaborate below, is that the sociological interpretations most often found in it are demonstrably wrong.

Secondly, we have some published data on consumers of pornography and their social backgrounds. The best material of this sort, as on most matters sexual, comes (as

* Most of this chapter was presented at the annual meeting of the American Sociological Association, Miami Beach, August, 1966. I offered a sketchy first version of some of it at a public symposium, "Pornography and Literature," in which I participated with Alfred Chester, Benjamin De Mott, Ephraim London, and Hubert Selby, at the YMHA Poetry Center, New York City, March, 1966.

you might expect) from the Institute for Sex Research.[1]

Thirdly, we have a particular sociological theory—I would call it a theory of the upper-middle range—that was not developed to explain the place of pornography in society but nevertheless serves, I think, to explain that place very well.

There are many special aspects of the sociology of pornography, and in what follows I shall not even mention most of them, much less pursue them. Instead, I shall try to spell out how that theory of the upper-middle range gives a sociological overview of pornography within which more specialized investigations might proceed.

I

In his study of prostitution Kingsley Davis demonstrated, with cogent reasoning and much evidence that I cannot rehearse here, the following main argument: (a) the goals of sexual behavior in man are not inherently social; but (b) societies need to hook sexuality onto social ends, particularly the ends of bearing and raising children, by restricting the morally legitimate expression of sex to the institution of the family; and (c) this conflict between sexual inclinations and social requirements is ameliorated by prostitution, which helps to maintain the family as an institution by acting as a safety-valve for the expression of antisocial coitus—i.e., impersonal, transitory, nonfamilial coitus—that cannot be fully suppressed.[2] Davis thus sees the family and prostitution as complementary institutions, each requisite to the other.

[1] Cf. Alfred Kinsey, Wardell Pomeroy, and Clyde Martin, *Sexual Behavior in the Human Male* (Philadelphia: W. B. Saunders, 1948), pp. 363, 510; and Kinsey, Pomeroy, Martin, and Paul Gebhard, *Sexual Behavior in the Human Female* (Philadelphia: W. B. Saunders, 1953), pp. 652–72. N. B. that most Kinsey findings on male use of pornography are presented in the volume on females, along with comparative data on females.

[2] Cf. Kingsley Davis, "Prostitution," in Robert Merton and Robert Nisbet (Eds.), *Contemporary Social Problems* (New York: Harcourt, Brace & World, 1961), pp. 262–88.

I suggest that Davis's theory applies, *mutatis mutandis*, to pornography. Prostitution and pornography occur in every society large enough to have a reasonably complex division of labor; and although pornography develops in only a rudimentary way in preliterate societies (by means of erotic folktales and simple pictorial or sculptural devices), whenever a society has a fair degree of literacy and mass-communication technology then pornography becomes a major functional alternative to prostitution.

In saying that prostitution and pornography are, at least in modern societies, functional alternatives, I mean that they are different roads to the same desired social end. Both provide for the discharge of what society labels antisocial sex, i.e., impersonal, nonmarital sex: prostitution provides this via real intercourse with a real sex object, and pornography provides it via masturbatory, imagined intercourse with a fantasy object.

Although societies use both alternatives, the degree to which one is used in preference to the other seems to vary considerably from one society to the next, in ways and for reasons that remain to be investigated. There is also variation within a given society, of at least two kinds: First, there is variation in what is considered appropriate in different social situations; for example, a group of adolescent boys might collectively visit a prostitute but masturbate to pornography only singly and in private, with group contemplation of pornography serving merely to convey sex information or as the occasion for ribald humor. A second kind of variation has to do with what is considered appropriate in different subcultures. The main such variation in our own society, revealed by the Kinsey data, is that masturbating to pornographic books or pictures is largely a phenomenon of the better-educated classes; at the lower levels of our society, this is generally put down (as is longterm masturbation *per se*), and, conversely, prostitutes are visited much more often.

Prostitution, as Davis noted, presents a great paradox of social life: on the one hand it is so nearly a cultural uni-

versal[3] that it seems to fill a need endemic to complex
societies, but on the other hand the prostitute is, except
in very special circumstances, generally and highly stigmatized. Davis's theory resolves the paradox, and does
so in a way that applies equally to pornography: both
prostitutes and pornographers are stigmatized because
they provide for the socially illegitimate expression of sex,
yet their very existence helps to make tolerable the institutionalizing of legitimate sex in the family.

An additional relation between the functioning and
the stigmatizing of prostitutes and pornographers, a relation at once more general and more intimate than that
given by Davis, may be inferred from the neo-Durkheimian
theory of deviance recently proposed by Kai Erikson. He
observes:

> The only material found in a system for marking [moral]
> boundaries is the behavior of its participants; and the kinds
> of behavior which best perform this function are often
> deviant. . . . In this sense, transactions between deviant
> persons and agencies of social control are boundary-
> maintaining mechanisms. . . . Each time the group cen-
> sures some act of deviation it sharpens the authority of the
> violated norm. . . . [Instances of publicity about deviants,
> as in the old public parading of them or in the modern
> newspaper] constitute our main source of information
> about the normative contours of society.[4]

In Erikson's view, then, one function of prostitutes and

___

[3] [*Addendum, 1968:* Mario Bick has pointed out to me that
prostitution and pornography are not fully cross-cultural phenomena, and that Davis and I have been misled simply because these occur in various Eastern societies (such as China,
Japan, India) as well as Western ones. Mr. Bick notes that
(a) all the examples we can cite are from long-time monetary
economies, and (b) in non-monetary, polygynous societies such
as those of Africa, prostitution appears to be unknown before
European contact and/or urbanization, and erotic depictions do
not have the pornographic function they have in monetary
economies.]

[4] Kai Erikson, "Notes on the Sociology of Deviance," *Social Problems,* Vol. 9 (Spring, 1962), pp. 307–14.

pornographers would lie precisely *in* the fact that they are stigmatized.

II

The use of pornography is by no means limited to its role as an adjunct to masturbation. For example, as already indicated, pornography may sometimes serve rather as a sex instruction manual. (Conversely, a sex instruction manual may serve as pornography.) And sometimes pornography, far from stimulating masturbation, may be used to stimulate real intercourse, as in, say, the case of whorehouse murals from Pompeii to the present. Granted all that, and other uses as well, people given to using pornography do so for the most part as a means of facilitating masturbation. This is the primary use of pornography. It is summed up in the classic definition of pornographic books as "the books that one reads with one hand."

The consumption of pornography is a sort of halfway house between sexual intercourse and erotic response to purely private mental fantasies. Masturbation to pornography is more "social" than masturbation simply to inner pictures, i.e., pornography offers the masturbator erotic imagery that is external to himself, a quasi-real "other" to whom he can more "realistically" respond. That is why even lower-class males frequently use pornography for masturbatory release—and here the Kinsey findings need qualification—when they are deprived of their usual sexual outlets: people in prisons are overwhelmingly from the lower class, and the masturbatory use of pornography is widespread in prisons and a continual headache for any prison administrator who wants to make it one.[5] Sociologists, however, in their fascination with the way prisoners turn toward homosexuality, seem to have neglected the prisoners' turn toward pornography.

[5] Cf. Charles Smith, "Prison Pornography," *Journal of Social Therapy*, Vol. 1 (1955), pp. 126–29, and Stanley B. Zuckerman, "Sex Literature in Prison," *ibid.*, pp. 129–31. I cite these articles merely to document the widespread prison use of pornography.

As my reference to jailhouse pornography implies, a
great deal of pornography exists unpublished, in the form
of manuscript writing or drawing. Even outside the prison
context, an enormous number—perhaps even the majority
—of pornographic works are in manuscript.[6] The important thing to realize about such manuscripts is that mostly
they are produced neither for publication nor for circula-
tion as manuscripts, but for self-enjoyment. Here we have
a major difference between prostitution and pornography:
hardly any man can, as it were, be his own prostitute (although many try, by attempting auto-fellation),[7] but every
man can be his own pornographer. Even a good deal of
published pornography was written initially to aid the masturbation of the writer. For example, Jean Genet indicates
that this was why he wrote *Our Lady of the Flowers*.[8]
And it is apparently to this motivation that we owe the
pornography produced by the most noted pornographer
of them all, the Marquis de Sade. Here is a letter from
Sade to his wife, written from prison in 1783—a date, note
well, that is several years after Sade had begun writing non-
pornographic works but before he had written any pornography:

> I'll bet you thought you had a brilliant idea in imposing a
> revolting abstinence on me with regard to the sins of the
> flesh. Well, you were all mistaken. You brought my brain
> to the boiling point. You caused me to conjure up fanciful
> creatures which I shall have to bring into being.

Over the years that followed, most of them spent in

[6] This seems to be the implication of a statement about
quantities made in the Kinsey volume on females, *op. cit.*,
p. 672. See also Wladimir Eliasberg, "Remarks on the Psychopathology of Pornography," *Journal of Criminal Psychopathology*, Vol. 3 (1942), pp. 715–20, although on other
points, as note 20 below may indicate, Eliasberg is unreliable.

[7] Kinsey *et al.* report in their volume on males, *op. cit.*,
p. 510, that "a considerable portion" of males attempt auto-
fellation, at least in early adolescence, but that it is anatomi-
cally impossible for all except two or three males in a thousand.

[8] Cf. Jean Genet, *Our Lady of the Flowers* (New York:
Bantam Books, 1964), e.g., pp. 59–61.

jail, Sade devoted himself to setting down those fanciful creatures on paper. As Albert Camus put it, Sade "created a fiction in order to give himself the illusion of being."[9]

Of course Genet and Sade wrote most of their pornography while in prison. But especially when it comes to sexuality, society imprisons everyone in a number of ways; that is the starting point of Kingsley Davis's argument and mine—and also and originally and profoundly, though Davis is silent on the matter, of Sigmund Freud's. Let us now consider one of those ways—and here my point of departure is Freud rather than Davis—that seems especially germane to our subject.

III

Prostitution and pornography, as we have seen, allow the expression of antisocial sex—impersonal, transitory, nonfamilial sex. But both institutions also provide for antisocial sex in another, deeper sense—one that is merely mentioned in passing by Kingsley Davis but is nevertheless a key function of prostitution as well as pornography: these institutions permit "polymorphous perverse" and other sexual behaviors so highly stigmatized as to be labelled deviant even within the institution of marriage and morally inhibited from expression therein.

In other words, sex is socialized by being placed in a double constraint—the marital relationship on the one hand and a specified selection of possible sex acts on the other. It is important to see that the function of prostitution and pornography in alleviating the latter constraint is clearly distinct from their providing merely for coitus *per se* (real or imaginary) in an impersonal and transitory relationship.

No real house of prostitution has perhaps approached the logically ultimate one depicted in Genet's play *The Balcony*, where each client buys a custom-made social

[9] I take the Sade and Camus quotations from Georges May, "Fiction Reader, Novel Writer," *Yale French Studies*, No. 35, "Sade" (December, 1965), p. 7.

scene that conforms in all particulars to any wishful sexual
fantasy he chooses to select. But many such houses, as well
as freelance prostitutes, have specialized in catering to customers who wanted to indulge in sadism, masochism,
orgies, intercourse with children, anal or oral intercourse,
voyeurism, intercourse with the aid of mechanical con-
traptions, fetishism, and so on. Among one city's documented examples that come to mind are: London's Victorian houses of child prostitutes, including (a sub-specialty
of the house) the providing of prepubescent virgins[10]; the
advertisement by London prostitutes, in their *Ladies Directory* of 1959–1960, offering themselves in rubber or
leather clothing; and the many more advertisements, in the
same periodical, by prostitutes offering "corrective treatment" and signing themselves with such sobriquets
as "Ex-governess, strict disciplinarian" and "Miss
Whyplash."[11] In a study of 732 American clients of prostitutes (574 clients were married, 158 single), the motivation
for patronage that the clients indicated most frequently
(78 per cent of the clients) was that they "got something
different" from a prostitute, and 10 per cent of these further volunteered the information that the difference was in
the type of sexual act performed.[12] Other studies have
shown that even the prostitute having no desire to specialize must learn, and quite early in her career, that she
will encounter a goodly share of customers presenting
"kinky" or "freaky" sexual requests.[13] There is an enor-

[10] Cf. W. T. Stead's series of articles, "Maiden Tribute of
Modern Babylon," in issues of the *Pall Mall Gazette* for 1885.

[11] Published monthly in Soho, the *Ladies Directory* was trans-
parently disguised as a directory of "models" in an attempt to
circumvent the new ban on open soliciting. At least nine issues
appeared. The prosecution of its publisher is described in, e.g.,
the London *Evening Standard* of July 26, 1960.

[12] Cf. Charles Winick, "Clients' Perceptions of Prostitutes
and of Themselves," *International Journal of Social Psychiatry*,
Vol. 8 (1961–62), pp. 289–97.

[13] Cf. John Murtagh and Sara Harris, *Cast the First Stone*
(New York: McGraw-Hill, 1957), pp. 180–86; James Bryan,
"Apprenticeships in Prostitution," *Social Problems*, Vol. 12,
No. 3 (Winter, 1965), pp. 287–97.

mous amount of this sort of material on prostitution (far more than I have mentioned), but, although most of it was available when Davis wrote, he ignores all of it.[14]

For our purpose, the point is this: as prostitution goes with respect to perversity, so goes pornography—only more so. Possibly the "more so" derives from the fact that "freaky" sexual interests, being much more highly stigmatized than simple nonmarital coitus, lie closer to total repression or suppression and thus are more often banished strictly to fantasized interaction; possibly other factors account for the difference. In any event, it seems clear

[14] There are many other defects in Davis's account of prostitution. Most are matters of detail—e.g., Davis thinks the attempt to control pimps arises only with industrialized societies, though Pompeo Molmenti could have told him that in twelfth-century Venice "pimps were imprisoned, branded, tortured, and banished"—but one is crucial: Davis insists that *promiscuity* is the fundamental defining element of prostitution, with commercial and emotionally indifferent aspects of the role being distinctly secondary. But against this emphasis we can put the following considerations: (1) The typical prostitute undertakes intercourse for money or valuables. (2) Even the untypical prostitute, such as one whose prostitution is a religious duty, works for some remuneration, albeit largely for what the economist calls "psychic income." (3) Davis ignores the fact that nymphomaniacs, free souls, and others who literally "give it away" may be stigmatized by the society but are not generally classified as prostitutes either by law enforcers or by laymen (for example, cf. W. F. Whyte, "A Slum Sex Code," *American Journal of Sociology*, Vol. XLIX [July, 1943], pp. 24–31). (4) Davis also ignores the fact that, conversely, some women not promiscuous in the slightest degree, such as concubines, are usually regarded as special types of prostitutes, although they carry lesser stigma. (5) Davis finds support for his "promiscuity" thesis in the fact that the prostitute's stigma is lessened whenever promiscuity is lessened (as in the case of *geisha*, who were selective about customers); but with equal logic one can note that the prostitute's stigma is lessened whenever she is not "strictly commercial," even if she is highly promiscuous (as in the case of temple prostitutes). A definition of prostitution that would best fit all these points—while excluding the woman who "marries for money" as well as the girl who consents to intercourse only after a fancy dinner and is, as Kinsey remarks, "engaged in a more commercialized relationship than she would like to admit"—is the following: Prostitution is the granting of nonmarital sex *as a vocation.*

that although much pornography depicts sexual relations whose only deviance consists of their nonmarital status, an extraordinary amount of this material offers fantasy involvement in sex acts that society proscribes as "unnatural." The history of pornography provides endless examples, and in this regard it makes no difference whether one thinks of the "hard core" tradition from, say, the *Priapea* of ancient Rome to such current paperbacks as *Perverted Lust Slave*, or of the "art" tradition from, say, Petronius to *Histoire d'O*.

IV

From a sociological standpoint, our society's current distinction between "genuine" or "hard core" pornography and highly erotic art is specious in a more fundamental respect.

In recent years the U.S. federal courts have tended to second and extend the view—a view advanced by defense lawyers, literary critics, *et al.*—that certain extremely erotic books and films are not really pornographic because they show over-all serious artistic intent and/or contain other redeeming social virtues, that is, because they seem not to be simply "dirt for dirt's sake." The courts in various ways have reaffirmed and amplified the doctrine, first set forth clearly in Judge John Woolsey's 1933 decision on Joyce's *Ulysses* and the 1934 confirming opinion of Augustus Hand, that highly realistic descriptions of sex cannot be judged pornographic in isolation, but must be viewed within the context of the work as a whole.[15] And except for a handful of diehard clergymen, our social critics, literary scholars, journalists, and the like—our "sociologizers" about pornography—have fallen in line.[16] But

[15] Judge Woolsey's decision is most readily available in the front matter of the Modern Library edition of *Ulysses*. For Augustus Hand's superb affirming decision, which languishes unreprinted, see 72 F. (2d) 705.

[16] Among many recent examples of this kind of reasoning, the best known is probably Eberhard and Phyllis Kronhausen, *Pornography and the Law* (New York: Ballantine Books, 1959).

the sociologist, at any rate this sociologist, must disagree with such "contextual" arguments and maintain that a work like, say, Henry Miller's *Tropic of Cancer* is pornographic, whatever else it may be in addition.

Granted that in one type of sociological analysis—what is loosely called the "labelling" approach—pornography is neither more nor less than what the society's decisive power groups say it is at any given time, and if our society now chooses officially to label *Tropic of Cancer* non-pornographic, that's that.[17] Such a conceptual framework does lead to many useful discoveries, along the lines indicated by W. I. Thomas's famous dictum that if people define a situation as real, it is real in its consequences. But this mode of analysis has its limitations, as can be seen when we turn to another and equally legitimate mode, functional analysis, and define pornography in terms of what it actually does to or for society—what are its particular uses and effects on people, intended or otherwise.[18]

[17] The "labelling" viewpoint, associated with publications in recent years by Edwin Lemert, Howard Becker, John Kitsuse, *et al.,* is actually a reinvention of a viewpoint formulated and applied in sociology at least as far back as Wilhelm Lange-Eichbaum's *The Problem of Genius* (1931), and in the sociology of deviance at least as far back as Frank Tannenbaum's *Crime and the Community* (1938; see Tannenbaum on "the dramatization of evil"). As a "literary" insight into the workings of society its history goes back much further, e.g., the Spanish inquisitor Salazar Frias wrote in 1611 that "there were neither witches nor bewitched until they were written and talked about." The topic is worthy of a Shandean postscript, but I forbear.

[18] As other parts of this essay should indicate, I am hardly arguing for functionalist theory *against* labelling theory, and rather believe that the two theories apply at different levels of analysis and that both have great explanatory power. But unfortunately some "labellers," in their initial zeal for the reinvented theory, fail to see its limitations. They have overly reified W. I. Thomas's dictum, and are in danger of falling into the same trap W. Lloyd Warner fell into when he concluded that social class is "really" what people say it is.

Thomas's insight is true, but only half the truth. The other half is that social life, though profoundly affected by the participants' linguistic interpretation of it, is not identical with or completely determined by such interpretation. In other words, a real situation has some real consequences even if

Pornography obviously has many functions; and some of these are not even sexual, e.g., the providing of paid work for pornography producers and sellers, as well as for their professional opponents. But as we have seen, pornography's main function at the societal level (as distinguished from the individual-psychological level) is to help preserve society's double institutionalizing of legitimate sex—within marriage and within a specified few of the possible sex acts—by providing sexual depictions that literally drain off the other, socially illegitimate sexual desires of the beholder. Any sexual depiction (written, recorded, pictorial) that facilitates such masturbatory involvement is thus pornographic. And when pornography is defined in this way, it becomes clear that the courts and the literary critics are wrong, viz., their assumption that pornography and art are mutually exclusive is patently false. For in contemplating naturalistic erotic art, people can and do easily respond to the erotic qualities as such, in utter disregard of the "artistic context." The stock of every pornography store confirms this. Thus the user of written pornography, for example, gets his pornography from "hard core" literature or from erotic "art" literature; so far as he is concerned, the only significant difference is that in the latter he usually gets less for his money.[19]

Let me suggest at this point that my readers think back to their early adolescence and recall the so-called "dirty books" that were used for adolescent masturbation. (Rather, I ask males among my readers to do this. As the Kinsey data reveal, only a small minority of females are sexually excited by pornography, much less masturbate to it, for

people *don't* define it as real. That fact is often lost sight of by those who take a "labelling" stance (see, for example, my remarks on Korn and McCorkle in Chapter 3). It is never lost sight of by functionalists; in fact, their recognition of it underlies two of the most useful analytic concepts of modern sociology, the concept of latent function and the concept of functional alternatives.

[19] Hanan Selvin has reminded me that the strong erotic appeal, as such, of much erotic art, is also noted in Sir Kenneth Clark's *The Nude*.

reasons largely unknown.[20]) I think most will be able to recall not only "hard core" pornography, such as the little booklets containing pornographic versions of American comic strips, but also that there were so-called "dirty books" which were really for the most part "clean" and were read for their occasional "dirty pages," such as the books of Erskine Caldwell. At least, that was true not only for my own early adolescence but for that of most every other middle-class boy I knew at the time.

I know of no evidence to indicate that people erotically interested in naturalistic descriptions of sex—whatever their age—are seriously impeded by, or even give much thought to, the over-all non-erotic context in which such descriptions might be embedded; and this applies to highly artistic

[20] Note that theories of the female "role" won't do to explain this, for even when men take on all the female role attributes they can, i.e., become hyper-effeminate homosexuals, they do not give up the male's interest in pornography (though of course the object changes and so their pornography consists of erotic depictions of males). And, conversely, when women take on as many male role attributes as they can, i.e., become tough "butch" lesbians, they do not typically lose the female's disinterest in pornography.

There are indeed many pornographic "lesbian" novels, but they are fakes. They are written by men and bought by men. (Both points have been made to me by Times Square pornography peddlers, and I have confirmed the latter from observation in their stores.) The genuine lesbian novel, whether the inartistic kind such as Radclyffe Hall's *Well of Loneliness* or the artistic kind such as Djuna Barnes's *Nightwood*, does not contain naturalistic description of sex but emphasizes the emotional-psychological aspect of sexual relationships. In this respect it is similar to the romantic literature that heterosexual women enjoy (on the latter, see the Kinsey volume on females, *op. cit.,* p. 670).

Apart from disinterest by females (heterosexual or homosexual) in pornography consumption, and the fact that "lesbian" pornography is actually produced by males for males, it has also been established beyond doubt that heterosexual pornography production by females is very rare. (Cf. Kinsey volume on females, *op. cit.,* p. 672.) Yet Wladimir Eliasberg, *op. cit.,* claims a striking feature of pornographic literature is that one cannot tell whether a man or woman is either the producer or consumer.

works as well as any other. Can one seriously maintain,
for example, that most of the Americans in Paris who
smuggled back copies of *Lady Chatterley's Lover* and
Tropic of Cancer did so out of interest in the "artistic" or
"other social redeeming" qualities of these books rather
than out of "prurient interest"? Or when it comes to the
people—adolescent or adult—who masturbate to such books,
can one seriously claim that they used these works for
masturbatory purposes only so long as our society labelled
them pornographic and stopped such masturbating when the
label changed? Clearly we must modify W. I. Thomas's
dictum, which is the "labelling" dictum writ small, to read
that if people define a situation as real (erotic book X is
non-pornographic), it is real in some of its consequences
(erotic book X can be sold over the counter) but not in
others (people don't stop masturbating to it).

And clearly society has always permitted the dissemination of some kinds of material that are functionally pornographic. In our own society one of the major ways it
currently does so, as previously indicated, is to non-label
such material as pornographic if it is packaged between
significant amounts of non-erotic material—as in, say, the
pages of *Playboy*.

The social processes involved in deciding which pornography shall be permitted, and even some (though by no
means all) of the selective criteria used, are roughly analogous to the way that—as Sutherland showed us—our society
permits certain types of criminals, notably businessmen
who commit crimes in their corporate capacities, to escape
penological consequences and even public stigma.[21] The recent case of the magazine *Eros* notwithstanding, the classier

[21] Cf. Edwin Sutherland, *White Collar Crime* (New York:
Holt, Rinehart & Winston, 1949), especially pp. 42 ff. Of
course there are also special selective factors operating at more
mundane levels of pornography production. For example, in the
recent case of a Michigan hard-core pornographer who was
not only fined $19,000 but sentenced to ten years in prison, I
assume that the severity of the sentence was not unrelated to
the title of his masterpiece: *The Sex Life of a Cop*. (Cf. New
York *Daily News,* April 7, 1966, p. 13, col. 1).

the pornography the more likely it is to be permitted.[22] What is big news about the publisher of *Eros* is precisely what is big news about those price-fixing G.E. officials: such people are rarely the kind who get rapped.

V

At the same time that society permits the dissemination of pornography, it officially denounces it. There is good reason for it to do both at once: from the desire to maintain a restrictive societal definition of "legitimate" sex, it naturally follows that pornography should be stigmatized and harassed yet tolerated as a safety-valve, in the same way that, as Davis demonstrates, society stigmatizes and otherwise harasses prostitution but never really abolishes it.

And just as Davis indicates for prostitution, the stigma attached to pornography is lessened when pornography is tied to some other socially valued end, such as art or science. One important result is this: when the "situation" being defined by society is a naturalistic depiction of sex, the most real consequence of a definition that labels it something other than pornographic is to increase its pornographic use in the society by reducing the inhibitions on acquiring it. This is obvious from the libraries of countless souls who avidly buy highly erotic works that society labels "art" or "literature" or "science" or "scholarship," but who take care not to buy "real" pornography.

And if the non-labelling of an erotic depiction as pornographic actually increases its pornographic use in the society, *de*-labelling increases such usefulness still more. As any publisher can tell you (I speak as a former publisher), it is much better for sales to have an erotic book that was once labelled pornographic and then got de-labelled than to have one that never got labelled at all. Thus such works as *Lady Chatterley* or *Tropic of Cancer* are, functionally, among our society's most pornographic books of all.

All of this could, as Albert Cohen has suggested to me,

[22] On the case of *Eros* and the prison sentence given to its publisher, see, for example, *The New York Times,* March 27, 1966, p. 8E, cols. 1–2.

simply indicate that many if not most Americans label
Playboy or erotic art or sexual scholarship as "pornography" even if the courts and others don't. But such an
interpretation depends on a dubious double hypothesis—
that the courts have largely deluded themselves in claiming
to follow community opinion and have also failed to mold
opinion. It might still be truer than mine, and only empirical
data we don't yet have can settle the question. However,
I think it more reasonable to suppose this: If the behavior
of people often contradicts their attitudes (and social research is forever stumbling against that one), then it can
be just as discrepant with their labelling or definition of
the situation, and, moreover, such discrepancy is widespread in areas of life involving socially encouraged hy-
pocrisy and unawareness, as in the case of sex behavior.

And even clearer, and more fundamental, discrepancy
between social reality and the social definition or labelling
of the situation has to do with highly erotic depictions that
make no claim to art or science and are not enwrapped in
non-erotic contexts, depictions that society calls "real" or
"hard core" pornography or "dirt for dirt's sake." Such a
label means that the material is, in the words of Mr. Justice
Brennan, "utterly without redeeming social importance."
That definition of the situation is obviously upheld by the
great majority of our society; it is entertained equally by
the courts, by assorted professional experts (such as literary critics and psychiatrists), and by the lay public. It is,
nevertheless, mistaken. To the extent that society, in restricting morally legitimate sex to certain specified acts
within marriage, cannot count fully on the mechanisms of
repression and suppression, to that extent it must provide
stigmatized safety-valve institutions such as prostitution and
pornography.[23] As Thomas Aquinas put it—he was explain-

[23] The historical and comparative sociology of the part that
"safety-valve" institutions play in social control has yet to be
written. We do not even have an adequate general theory of
these functions—merely scattered remarks about *panem et cir-
censes*—although Freud has provided many psychological un-
derpinnings for such a theory. Here I note only that in our
society major historical changes in safety-valve mechanisms
have involved other than sexual institutions; for example, there

ing prostitution—"A cesspool is necessary to a palace if the whole palace is not to smell."[24]

VI

As I mentioned at the beginning of this chapter, there are many special aspects of the sociology of pornography. One involves a hypothesis I am currently testing and for which I have already found a bit of confirmation, namely, that organized crime is more and more associating itself with the production and distribution of hard core pornography, particularly but not exclusively the most profitable part of it, pornographic movies. This would represent a coming together of organized crime's traditional interest in providing illegal goods and services, with a change in American consumption patterns that is having fateful consequences for the technology of pornography: the great increase, over the past fifteen years, in private ownership of 8 mm. movie projectors.

Until roughly 1950, the pornographic movie business consisted largely in renting films for showing at stag dinners, fraternity parties, and the like, but since then it has been increasingly, and is now overwhelmingly, a matter of outright sale of prints to individual customers.[25] Consequently, over the past decade and a half, the pornographic movie business has had one of the highest growth rates of

has been a decrease in displacement of secular goals onto an afterlife (a decline in "pie in the sky" or "opium of the people" functions of religion), and an increase in spectatorship for competitive sports as a means of draining off potential public violence.

[24] This view of prostitution—which, shorn of its moralism, is the essence of Davis's sociological view—can be found in many writers beside St. Thomas, e.g., in Horace's *Satires* and Mary Wollstonecraft's *A Vindication of the Rights of Woman*. Of these functionalist explanations prior to Davis, the ablest are in Bernard Mandeville's "An Inquiry into the Origin of Moral Virtue" (his preface to the 1714 edition of *Fable of the Bees*) and his *A Modest Defence of Publick Stews* (1724).

[25] I am informed by pornography distributors in Soho, London, that a similar shift has taken place in England.

any business in the United States (legal or illegal); and
organized crime is now well aware of that fact if the general public is not. It is true that the pornographic movie
industry, like the pornography industry generally, is still
mostly in the hands of individual entrepreneurs; but if
present trends continue, investment in this industry by organized crime may one day reach the takeoff point, that
is, the stage where muscle is applied to make independents
fall in line or get out.

There are other special hypotheses about the sociology
of pornography that need investigating, dozens of them.
What I have tried to do here is offer a general framework
within which such investigations might be made.[26]

[26] *Addendum:* A detailed scholarly study of mid-Victorian
sexuality and pornography, based on the Kinsey collection,
was published after this book went to press: Steven Marcus,
The Other Victorians (New York: Basic Books, 1966). At
various places in his book Mr. Marcus discusses the relation
of pornography to Victorian society, and his concluding chapter is, in design and in the words of the publisher, "an essay
propounding a general theory of pornography as a sociological
[i.e., social] phenomenon." In this late note I cannot demonstrate, but only asseverate, that *The Other Victorians* is a prime
instance of rubbishy "sociologizing" about pornography, "sociologizing" of the sort produced by that growing band of
American literary critics who believe they are experts on society
simply because they live in it.

One brief example: Mr. Marcus seems ignorant of statistical
reasoning and, worse, of its possible relevance to his argument.
Hence one cannot learn from his book that the Victorian era's
tremendous upsurge in the growth rate of pornography publishing, which he finds so strange, was equalled and usually surpassed by increases in growth rates for every other kind of
publishing. (Indeed, he even seems innocent of the distinction
between growth and growth rate.) Nor can one learn that all
this had some relation to England's having perfected, in the
first decade of the nineteenth century, the Fourdrinier machine
for cheap papermaking, nor the fact that, over the following
decades, while England's population grew nearly fourfold its
literate population grew thirty-two-fold.

Thirty Years On

Over the past three years, as I gathered material needed to bring the preceding chapters up to date, that pile of notes and publications grew into a mountain; less hyperbolically, two full #38 cartons. It became obvious that a full-scale updating would require an epilogue almost as long as the original book—a project for which my publisher might have the stomach but I do not. Here I offer instead a selective and sometimes cursory picture of developments relating to the first five chapters that have taken place over the last three decades, plus some revision of my earlier views. In considerable part, the following survey also has the mark of the "personal essay" and is a "supplement" in the very wide sense that the term has in Diderot's titles.

A problem in addition to that of selection is this: the earlier essays are linked by the concept of "deviance," but are otherwise a miscellaneous lot. In dealing with recent changes that pertain to those essays individually or severally or collectively, this chapter needs to be more miscellaneous still. I shall begin with some general remarks and then focus on the earlier chapters more or less seriatim, although it will sometimes be necessary to abandon the latter procedure. Hold on for a jumpy ride.

One major social change that affects the interpretation of certain details in the first five chapters, so obvious that it might be overlooked, is the American economy's continu-

ous inflation—sometimes slow, sometimes rapid, but continuous—since the 1960s. All monetary amounts given in
the preceding pages—the amounts bet on poolroom games,
the dollar estimates for the social-class origins of the beats,
etc.—should be multiplied by, I would estimate, a factor of
at least eight. Your local economist can supply a more precise estimate for the year in which you read these words.

Another type of development in recent American history
affects, or should affect, one's view of the preceding chapters much more fundamentally; it has to do with their con-
necting thread, "deviance." But that is a tricky and debat-
able concept. What is "deviance" and who is "deviant"?
Before discussing the relevant social changes, I think it
needful, and helpful to the reader, to clarify that question
and try to answer it.

Sociologists, in the name of science, try to define
deviance in a value-neutral way; whatever their personal
values might be and wherever their personal sympathies
might lie, they regard "deviance" simply as what is stigmatized in a given society, and "deviants" as people who, in
consequence, encounter a good deal of stigma in that society. That view of course presupposes cultural relativism:
What is deviant in one society may not be deviant in
another, or may even be highly approved and rewarded in
another. It also presupposes historicism: In any particular
society, what is deviant in one historical period may not be
deviant in another, and vice versa.

My friend and colleague the late Erving Goffman, who
helped considerably with this book, came to question the
validity of the concept as such. In his book *Stigma* (1963)
he noted that people are stigmatized for a variety of reasons;
"deviance" didn't make much sociological sense to him
because, as he pointed out, it lumped together stigmatized
people ranging from murderers and robbers to blind people
and idiots (the "developmentally challenged" in current
social-worker jargon). What he unfortunately missed was
that some (though not most) sociologists, including myself,
had already overcome that objection by unpacking the
notion of deviance so as to exclude people who were not
morally stigmatized; that is, we excluded from our defini-

tion (and our courses on the sociology of deviance) various kinds of people, such as those unusually ugly according to a society's current standards of physical attractiveness, who might indeed be stigmatized (by for example being avoided socially or joked about or discriminated against in employment) but whose condition is generally recognized to be "not their fault."

It is almost always clear-cut as to whether the stigmatizing of a particular kind of person will be moral or not, the major exception in our society being its most prevalent type of drug addict: Sometimes alcoholics are stigmatized on moral grounds (it's their fault, they lack character) and sometimes not (it's a disease, they can't help it).

Things get more complicated in large and quite heterogeneous societies such as ours, where different social groups often differ about what is moral and immoral. The solution to that difficulty was given by "labelling theory," especially as developed by another friend and colleague, the still-kicking Howard Becker, who helped even more with this book. Becker pointed out, and backed up with much empirical detail, that when groups offer differing moral labels for a given behavior, what is crucial is the political process: Which group, in the competition, manages to get its label to stick, that is, prevail at the societal level? Competing definitions of deviance always involve an explicit or implicit struggle for power at that level.[1] In disputes about which behaviors should be labelled not only immoral but illegal, the key question is which group has the power to get its label written into law and acted upon by the society's official agencies of social control. In disputes about which behaviors should be labelled immoral but not criminal, the key question is which group has the power to have its label predominate in the mass media and in public opinion (as measured by surveys). As an example of the latter type of deviance, consider the moral stigma accorded someone who

[1] Note that our unit of analysis here and throughout is a society. It could of course be larger, say the international community as represented by the United Nations or World Court, or it could be smaller, say an ethnic community within a society.

does nothing illegal but is defined as a "user" of people or as a "sponger."

Another complication is that highly industrialized societies are the ones most subject to rapid change, not least with respect to moral stigma. Our "historicist" perspective on what is deviant may sometimes apply to the very short term only. Although some behaviors in modern societies remain morally stigmatized over long historical periods (or apparently forever), others are rapidly becoming "more" or "less" deviant than they were just a short while ago. In considering modern societies especially, we must always remain sensitive to this processual aspect of deviance.

Some radicals and multiculturalists with nonscientific agendas object to the labelling viewpoint for its supposed capitulation to the "power elite's" definition of what and who is deviant. Labelling theory does have limitations (see pp. 111–12, 193), but that is not one of them. It makes no judgment as to whether or not it is a "good thing" that certain people are stigmatized by the powers that be, but instead emphasizes the major consequences for the lives of the people who are thus stigmatized. To put that emphasis another way: W. I. Thomas enunciated the maxim that "if people define a situation as real, it is real in its consequences," and that goes double if the people doing the defining are members of the power elite. And after all, it was precisely Becker who first insisted that "deviance" is always at bottom a question of political power; even the most rabid of the "vulgar Marxists" ought to appreciate that one.

To conclude with a definition that tries to account for all the above: Deviance is what is morally stigmatized, at a particular time in a particular society, by that society's decisive power groups.

In the light of that definition, several kinds of people seen as deviant in the preceding pages are no longer so, or are very much less so. Their behaviors that were morally stigmatized have not changed; what have changed are our society's dominant attitudes toward those behaviors. A good bit of material in the earlier essays now constitutes a chapter in the "past history" of deviance in America.

The most important general shift is that America's "Puritan heritage" has been increasingly abandoned. Defenders of "family values" are outraged precisely because, over the past thirty years or more, their views of morality have counted for less and less at the societal level. Even in the Bible Belt, those views carry less weight than formerly. Before discussing specific examples, however, I must reiterate the caveat on page 171 that "the social scientist knows that a trend does not always remain a trend, and indeed often reverses itself." Note also that in recent years some kinds of people have become *more* deviant according to our definition, such as cigarette smokers, who are increasingly stigmatized on moral grounds as endangering the health of others, and whose smoking in public places has been increasingly prohibited by law; similarly, manufacturers of tobacco products are now often subject to moral stigma, e.g., as "cancer merchants."

As indicated above, some—though by no means most— of the developments noted in the following pages involve the de-labelling of behaviors as deviant. Such changes as they relate to pool playing and poolrooms, hustling, drug use, pornography, etc., are discussed later, in the sections on those topics. But here, to begin with, I shall discuss one such change, that relating to homosexuality, because it offers a cautionary lesson about historical causation.

Some of my material about homosexuality on page 79, published in 1967 and written a year or two earlier—the view of homosexuals as constituting a "deviant" subculture, the need to inform many readers about the special function of Halloween and Mardi Gras in that subculture, etc.—now seems utterly quaint in this age when U.S. Congressmen can publicly reveal their homosexuality and still get reelected. The pre-1970s blackmailing and arrest and imprisonment of homosexuals, their automatic loss of employment if their homosexuality became known at their workplaces, the frequent need of public figures to have "front" marriages (such as those of Harpo Marx or Billie Jean King), the hounding of homosexuals by self-hating closet queens (such as J. Edgar Hoover or Roy Cohn)—all that and more is gone. Religious leaders, who most people in our society regard as the ultimate experts on morality, increasingly give way on this matter, although there remain plenty of holdouts. Even the more conservative denominations now usually try at least to get round the teachings of St. Paul, who was the most influential queer-baiter of all time.[2]

What instigated that great change? The obvious answer: the June 1969 police raid on New York's Stonewall Tavern, which precipitated rioting by gays as they were being rounded up; the consequent formation over the following days of the modern Gay Liberation Movement; the latter's entry into the political process that ultimately decides whether something is "deviant"; and its increasing success in getting its definition to stick at the societal level.

But in connection with those events I should like to note something important for the history of deviance (and other things): the role of the fortuitous and quite unpredictable in human history. One does not have to be a Humean skeptic about causality to realize that the timing of many historical developments is accidental.[3] Why did that riotous response to a police raid, and the consequent founding of the Gay Liberation Movement, occur in June 1969? It doesn't explain anything to say, as gays did when I queried them about this, such things as "It finally reached the boiling point" and "We just couldn't take it anymore and began to fight back." We know that. But why *then*? Certainly, for as

[2] St. Paul's teachings on sexual morality retain and amplify what he had been taught as a Jew, Saul of Tarsus. The Jews were the first people in recorded history to define as *morally* reprehensible such things as homosexuality, masturbation, anal intercourse, and oral intercourse. The moral stigmatizing of those behaviors, making them "deviant" in our sense, is one of the fundamental contributions of the Judeo-Christian tradition to "civilization."

Another such contribution is genocide, as has been observed by Edward Said and, obliquely, George Steiner. The greatest tragic irony in history is that the inventors of genocide became its chief victims.

[3] Full awareness and appreciation of the unpredictable consequences of human action are features of the Scottish Enlightenment, as in the work of Adam Ferguson or of that Enlightened Scotsman in English clothing, Edward Gibbon.

far back as any gay can remember, there had been raids as vicious as anything the police did at Stonewall. Why wasn't the "boiling point" reached some years earlier, or some years later, or perhaps not yet? We do not know, and I think we cannot know. Among the answers that I got when asking gays about why 1969 was the turning point, an answer as good as any was "Well, honey, any year with 69 in it can't be all bad."

Contemporary journalists often refer to a "sexual revolution" as having taken place over the last thirty years or thereabouts. Yes and no. There has *not* been a "sexual revolution" in the sense that journalists and their audiences usually mean by that term. That is, there has been no demonstrable major change in the percentages of people who practice the different variations on who does what, and when, and where, and with which, and to whom; at least, there has been no major change that the scientific survey researchers have been able to detect. But there *has* been a real revolution in the moral judgments that our society's dominant power groups make about sexual behavior. In regard to sex, if anyone thirty years ago had predicted what today is permitted to be sold over the counter, talked about and seen on television, taught in our schools, etc., that person would have been regarded as crazy. Pick a newspaper— any newspaper—that has been publishing for at least thirty years and compare the sexual content of the stories, photographs, and advertisements in an issue of thirty years ago with an issue of today. You will be amazed. As Joe Namath said, I guarantee it.

I now turn to focus on the previous chapters in the order of their appearance, as far as that is feasible.

Of Pool Playing and Poolrooms

One thing that unfortunately has not changed is the paucity of statistics on the number of poolrooms, and the unreliability of the figures sometimes given. I had wanted to compare the number of poolrooms in 1970 with the number in every succeeding fifth year up to 1995, and so I asked a knowl-

edgeable official of the U.S. Billiard Association whether
the industry could supply me with those statistics or with
the data that would allow me to compile them myself. He
replied that the compiling of such statistics was not possible. I then asked if an association of billiard-equipment
manufacturers could supply accurate information on the
number of pool and billiard tables manufactured or sold in
1970, 1975, 1980, and so on—and got the same depressing
answer.

However, three developments in the recent history of
American poolrooms are generally remarked upon in the
industry (and by me): (1) The collapse of the 1960s poolroom revival, whose beginnings I pointed to in 1967 (see p.
30), did indeed take hold apace. I would estimate that more
than 85 percent of the poolrooms that opened in consequence of the success of *The Hustler* (1961) eventually
went out of business. (2) A new revival was sparked by the
success of *The Hustler*'s sequel, *The Color of Money*
(1986). (3) As far as the number of poolrooms is concerned,
that new revival has been smaller than the earlier one. That
is, fewer poolrooms have opened in response to *The Color
of Money* than had opened in response to *The Hustler*.

Not remarked upon in the industry is that as far as poolrooms are concerned—note carefully "as far as poolrooms
are concerned," whose significance will become clear
later—the revival has pretty much halted and shows signs of
weakening. The rate at which new poolrooms have opened
has gone down sharply, quite a few new poolrooms have
folded, and some others survive at least in part as "laun-
dries" for drug money. However, I think that unlike the earlier poolroom revival, this one shows signs of retrenchment
that do not presage a real collapse. For reasons made evi-
dent below, the remaining new poolrooms stand a fair
chance of staying in business.

Compared to the 1960s revival (not to mention the poolrooms from an earlier era), the new revival has a more solidly
middle-class character. This is clear both from the new
rooms' greater likelihood to be in middle-class neighborhoods than the old ones were, and from the nature of the
new clientele. To be sure, lower-class (or "working-class," if

you prefer) customers are still abundant; but now, I think at least as often as not, it is the lower-middle class that predominates (and in some "yuppie" poolrooms, the upper-middle class). That trend has been heavily reinforced by recent immigration, especially from China (including Hong Kong), Taiwan, and Korea; at least on the East and West coasts, poolroom customers now include many Asian-American youths from "respectable," upward-striving families (as well as, of course, the "unrespectable" kind).

All of that means, among other things, that the poolroom is far less dependent than it ever was on remnants of the old bachelor subculture. It also means—the most startling change to someone like me who began frequenting poolrooms more than half a century ago—that the new poolrooms almost invariably have among their regular customers a sprinkling of women. And when it comes to occasional customers, it is now not at all unusual for a middle-class male to suggest to his wife or date that they spend an evening playing pool. The yuppier poolrooms even have customers who for a special occasion will rent all or part of the poolroom and toss a pool-playing party for the couples they know.

Contrary to wishful thinking in the poolroom industry, all of that has had nothing to do with the industry's effort to "clean up the game" and improve its "image" and thereby make the poolroom a place "for the family."[4] What has made it possible is something unpredictable, noted a few pages earlier: America's rapid abandonment over the past thirty years of its "Puritan heritage." One of the most important aspects of that heritage has always been the middle-class moral objection to gambling. That has declined radically. During the past three decades virtually every state has not only tolerated gambling but increased the legal forms of it: off-track betting, bingo or card parlors, casinos, lotteries.

---

[4] Apropos of that effort, and in memoriam Jack "Jersey Red" Breit, d. 1997, I should like to record that he was the player barred from the 1963 world tournament because of his profanity and so forth (see pp. 58–59). It was a shame. Red was then at his peak and might well have won the championship.

Among the out-of-date details in the earlier chapters is my statement (p. 38) that "Every poolroom has at least one 'No Gambling' sign on display . . . "; poolrooms hardly ever bother with such signs nowadays. Moreover, a feature of the new-style poolrooms—its importance will become clearer when we consider hustling—is that nearly all of them have one or more weekly house tournaments offering substantial cash prizes. And apart from America's increasing rejection of the middle-class objection to gambling, there is that additional factor, noted above, of the influx of immigrants from countries where neither poolrooms nor gambling were stigmatized, immigrants who either are middle class or have strong middle-class aspirations.[5] In sum, today's American poolroom is a far less "deviant" institution than it has ever been.

The Color of Money, in addition to sparking an increase (which now seems to be ending) in the number of poolrooms, instigated two other developments that at this writing show no sign of weakness: (1) The adopting of pool games as one more viable (salable) type of program for TV sports channels; and (2) a major increase—which is apparently, although no one has the statistics, a far larger increase than that given to poolrooms—in the number of bars that have installed small-sized, coin-operated pool tables. Because those developments have considerable import for hustling, I will consider them in more detail later, but note here that they constitute another reinforcing factor in producing clientele for poolrooms and maintaining their interest.

Thirty years ago I noted that a research problem for the sociologist concerned with billiards or any other sport was

---

[5] As a quick index to such "middle-classness," consider the poolroom etiquette displayed by Korean immigrants. (I confess to some prejudice here because they are the saviors in America of my favorite game, three-cushion billiards.) Unlike most American players, when they get a lucky break they *always* apologize to their opponent. When Sang Chun Lee, America's best three-cushion player, makes a lucky shot, he always apologizes by holding up the palm of his hand to his opponent; when Sonny Cho, currently America's third best three-cushion player, makes a lucky shot, he always apologetically bows to his opponent.

that "America's professional historians have not done what might be deemed their part of the job" (p. 4). That is no longer the case. Sport is now a flourishing subject of research among our historians, and for more than twenty years now they have even been offering a special *Journal of Sport History*, as well as a Canadian counterpart.

Additionally, historians picked up on my complaint (pp. 22 ff.) about their neglect of the heterosexual-bachelor subculture and its former great role in American social life. Although a full-scale study of the bachelor subculture as such, in its vital relation to various social institutions (only some of which are noted on p. 23), is still a desideratum in American historiography, historians have been seriously looking at that subculture as it intertwined with sports and other aspects of American culture. In the process they have not only amplified or modified my views but have been turning up new material on billiard history itself, and devotees of that history will from now on have to keep abreast of such material. For such devotees, the most important works to date are Dale Somers's *The Rise of Sports in New Orleans, 1850–1900* (1972), Melvin Adelman's *A Sporting Time: New York City and the Rise of Modern Athletics, 1820–70* (1986), and Steven Riess's *City Games* (1989). Elliott Gorn's work, which deals with the bachelor subculture's relation to several aspects of nineteenth-century sporting life, focuses on its developing ideology of "manliness," and as one continuation of that ideology, Gorn cites, rightly I think, this book's material on pool hustlers' concerns about self-reliance, autonomy, and "heart."[6]

For the present purpose, Adelman's work is especially noteworthy because it points out a major error of omission in

[6] Elliot Gorn, "'Good-Bye Boys, I Die a True American': Homicide, Nativism, and Working-Class Culture in Antebellum New York City," *Journal of American History*, vol. 74, no. 2 (1987), pp. 388–410. Gorn provides references to other recent work, not cited above, on the bachelor subculture. See also Geoffrey Blodgett, "The Emergence of Grover Cleveland: A Fresh Appraisal," *New York History*, vol. 73, no. 2 (April 1992), pp. 132–68; Blodgett notes, p. 137, that Cleveland's political views were shaped partly by the "subculture of his bachelor friends in the hotels, saloons and livery stables of downtown Buffalo."

the first chapter of this book: Of great importance in our billiard history—one of those things so obvious that I plain for-
got to deal with it—were the billiard rooms that formerly
were a standard feature of American hotels. In the interest of
comparative history and as partial amends, I note the report
by Flaubert—no inventor of such details—of a billiard room
in Yonville's hotel, the Lion d'Or, and also transmit information from the nonagenarian painter Esteban Vicente, who tells
me that when he was growing up in Madrid, all the hotels
there had billiard rooms.[7]

In view of some other animadversions (pp. 7–8), it is also
pleasing to report that billiards at long last has a competent
bibliography: Robert R. Craven, *Billiards, Bowling, Table
Tennis, Pinball, and Video Games: A Bibliographic Guide*
(1983). As far as it goes on billiards—and it goes much far-
ther than any other source—Craven's work seems completely
reliable.

Most gratifying of all, my earlier conclusion that the
attempts at billiard historiography by players and fans represent "the lunkhead tradition of cobbling together secondary
material" (p. 5) is mostly outdated. Many devotees of the
game have now learned, at a minimum, to distinguish
between primary and secondary sources, and in consequence
have produced books of value as historiography. Among
those books are: Robert Byrne's *Byrne's Treasury of Trick
Shots in Pool and Billiards* (1982), which attempts, with surprising success, to determine who invented those shots and to
give credit where it is due; William Hendricks' *William
Hendricks' History of Billiards* (1974), overall the best treatment of its subject, especially the history of playing equipment and of the word *billiards* itself; Mike Shamos'
Illustrated Encyclopedia of Billiards (1993), crammed with
accurate information on every aspect of the game, myriad references to further information, valuable updating of Craven's
bibliography, and altogether—leaving aside instruction man-

[7] In America's sporting life, a major hotel was of course the
famous Grand Union Hotel at Saratoga, New York. For an 1875
illustration of its billiard room, see Mike Shamos' *Illustrated
Encyclopedia of Billiards*, color signature following p. 142.

uals—the one book on billiards to have if you're having only one; Victor Stein and Paul Rubino's *The Billiard Encyclopedia* (1994), a mixture of marvelous delights and maddening defects (more on both below); and Georges Troffaes' *Le Billard et l'histoire: chroniques des temps passés* (1974), a collection of key primary sources on the game's early history. In addition, Mike Shamos' column in the magazine *Billiards Digest* adds to our historical knowledge regularly.

Stein and Rubino's *The Billiard Encyclopedia* (abbreviated below as S&R) is itself a notable event in billiard history, requiring comment on its virtues and vices. A large octavo with 520 illustrations in superb color, beautifully printed in *letterpress* Monotype, it is the most lavish billiard book that there has ever been or is likely to be. It is one of those books that exemplifies what people with money can do for their chief avocational interest. (The most important such work is, I think, General Augustus Pitt-Rivers' *Excavations in Cranborne Chase*, 1887–1898, which in some ways marks the beginning of truly scientific archaeology.) And S&R, both in its text and in its illustrations, adds greatly to information about billiards. The authors spent years gathering their data, in Europe as well as America, and they give us a huge amount of billiard material that has never before been available. For their dedication, and their putting their money where their hearts are, billiard devotees throughout the world will be forever grateful.

But Stein and Rubino, unlike Byrne or Hendricks or Shamos or Troffaes, also take some giant steps backward in billiard historiography. They are old-fashioned *antiquarians* (and collectors) rather than *historians*, and that continually lands them in trouble.[8] One faults them not because their backgrounds gave them no training in modern methods of historical research, but for their negligence in not consulting a historian in order to inform themselves of such methods. They have produced a book that offers object lessons in how *not* to write history—of billiards or anything else. Because

---

[8] For distinctions between the antiquarian and the historian, see Arnaldo Momigliano's essays on historiography, especially his essay on Gibbon.

S&R will, as it should, be consulted by billiard enthusiasts for generations to come, its defects are spelled out here to head off or at least weaken their influence. To readers with minimal interest in billiard history who feel that they might not want such detail, I reiterate that it applies not just to writing billiard history but to writing the history of anything else.

Antiquarians, almost by definition, are biased in favor of claims for the antiquity of whatever it is that interests them. And so it is with Stein and Rubino. What entrances them is that historical records of games that involve a ball being hit with a stick, as has long been known, go as far back as ancient Egypt. There are countless such games in that long line of historical development. An overview of that history is Robert W. Henderson's *Ball, Bat, and Bishop: The Origin of Ball Games* (1947), which S&R raves about because of its emphasis on the ultimate Egyptian origin of all such games (including billiards).

There is of course no question that billiards did not spring forth full-formed from Zeus's head. It developed in the fifteenth century from an outdoor stick-and-ball game called *jeu de boules* or *billard de terre*, which developed from an earlier outdoor stick-and-ball game, which developed from a still earlier one, and so on back to Egypt. But Henderson, for all his talk about how such games descend from "ancient Egyptian fertility rites," is careful to make the necessary distinctions, by stating for example (pp. 121–22), that *billard de terre* "later *developed into* billiards" and was "an *ancestor* of billiards" (my italics). However, S&R tries as far as humanly possible, throughout its text, to avoid such relative clarity and to override if not obliterate such distinctions. For the authors, because they have an "antiquity of billiards" thesis on the brain, stick-and-ball games become one huge mishmash. However circumspectly Stein and Rubino might define "billiards" if you pressed them, *operationally* they define it, throughout S&R, as equivalent to that mishmash, one in which all the ingredients represent "billiards." One recalls the remark of those excellent sociologists, Gilbert and Sullivan: "When every one is somebodee, no one's anybody." If all stick-and-ball games are in some way, somehow, "billiards," then none of them is. As is well known, especially among natural scientists, when people classify things they tend toward being either "lumpers" or "splitters"; Stein and Rubino carry lumping to the point of absurdity and beyond.

As an example of the mishmash school of historical writing, consider, just for a start, this from S&R (p. 47): "The transformational lineage of billiards, from ritual to pastime and sport, is exemplified by its development in the centuries preceding the Renaissance, beginning in approximately 1100 A.D. . . . In this context, billiards' evolution from the ground to tables and the refinement of its implements are closely tied to the social history around it. The traditions inherited by the Greeks from the Egyptians and passed along to the Romans, was [sic], once again, progressing." The clumsiness of the diction and syntax may be accidental, but their deviousness and ambiguity are not. Stein and Rubino do not say flat out the nonsense that I cited on page 88, namely, that billiards was known in ancient Egypt, but they sure as hell want you to think that way; and their obfuscations will only encourage a revival of such nonsense by future writers on billiards. S&R's "historical" approach reminds one of nothing so much as that old-fashioned type of "history of ideas," now virtually defunct, in which, if only you defined your key terms vaguely enough and ambiguously enough, you could trace everything back to Heraclitus or beyond. Professional historians don't buy that sort of intellectual garbage anymore—apart from a few "Afrocentrist" crazies who want to pretend that such folks as Copernicus and Newton stole their ideas from Africa— and S&R shouldn't buy it either. Nor should we. Obviously, S&R notwithstanding, we need a definition that clearly distinguishes billiards from other kinds of stick-and-ball games. I propose the following: The term *billiards* refers to the kinds of stick-and-ball games that are played indoors, on a bounded (walled) board or table designed for the purpose, and in which you have to make your cue ball hit one or more other balls in a specified manner and with a specified result. When we thus define billiards properly, it becomes clear that the game, as I suggested on page 88 and as the careful research of William Hendricks has confirmed, began in fifteenth-century France.

Which brings me to another and worse S&R defect: its handling of evidence. The authors are among those who, as I said, have learned at a minimum to distinguish primary from secondary sources—but in their case the key word is *minimum*. Having learned the distinction, they ignore it whenever they want to push the date of billiards as far back as they can. One of innumerable examples (S&R, p. 131): "Knowledge of the game certainly arrived [in America] with the Spanish Conquistadors in the late 1500s. However, it was the early colonists of the 1600s who established billiards and gradually made it part of the country's culture." Those statements may be true and equally they may not be true. The hard fact of the matter is that no one has yet cited a primary source for billiards in America earlier than my citation of William Byrd's 1710 diary (see p. 13). S&R endlessly converts surmise and conjecture into fact, offering us the antiquated "it must have been" type of historical writing; any halfway competent historian would have told the authors to avoid this because empirical investigation often reveals that what "must have been" actually wasn't. It just won't do, like S&R, to offer "common sense" as a substitute for proof; common sense is what tells you that the sun goes around the earth. S&R also, and again without a shred of proof, lends credence to other hoary myths that even common sense would be hard put to justify, e.g., that the Knights Templars played billiards in the twelfth century. S&R utterly lacks respect for evidence, the concern to distinguish fact from fancy, which has been axiomatic among historians since as far back as George Grote's great work on ancient Greece published a century and a half ago.

S&R is unbelievably lopsided in emphasizing the history of billiards not in society but in Society. It rattles on endlessly about billiard playing by *hoi aristoi* such as royals and presidents (pp. 143–48 alone are devoted to President John Quincy Adams), but ignores as much as it can, and hurries by with generalities, playing by *hoi polloi*. For over three full centuries the lower class and the bottom half of the middle class (by anyone's definition) have produced the huge majority of pool and billiard players, but you wouldn't in a thousand centuries guess it from S&R. Not for S&R the easily

ascertainable data on that majority to be found in books ranging from Restif de la Bretonne to Robert Byrne and in hundreds of newspaper and magazine accounts, to say nothing of
such accounts as the one describing how a man was murdered
in a poolroom by being pelted to death with billiard balls. All
of those items are absent even from S&R's bibliography. And
once again, the authors reveal ignorance of modern research
methods, this time of the many advances that historians have
made in ways of getting at "history from below," such as the
study of censuses, tax records, wills, diaries, criminal court
records, and parish records.

Reflecting its upper-class bias is S&R's radical overerem-
phasis on "collectibles" (pp. 273–481!): old equipment such
as tables, balls, cue sticks, and chalk, as well as billiard toys,
images, periodicals, and books. S&R's material on collecting
old billiard books (pp. 469–74) is contributed by a British
collector, Roger Lee, whom Stein and Rubino say "is
acknowledged as England's leading billiards and snooker historian." If that is indeed the case, then English billiard historiography is now in even worse shape than I said it was thirty
years ago (see pp. 7–8). Consider this sample from Mr. Lee
(S&R, p. 471): "The first book to be devoted entirely to billiards, as opposed to single chapters in encyclopedias or
sports books, was *The Odds of the Game of Billiards* by
Bladdon in 1772. Much to my regret, this volume is not
among my billiard books, nor is *Billiards: Instructions to
Play the Game with Ease and Propriety* by An Amateur, published in 1801. I have seen them in the British Museum, and
am hoping to see them again in some obscure second-hand
bookshop . . ." In those few lines, England's leading billiard
historian manages to commit no fewer than four demonstrable errors of fact. The 1772 volume, if indeed it was actually
published (see below), was "by a Gentleman" (see p. 8); the
publisher (*not* the author) was Bladon (p. 8 again; not
"Bladdon"). Mr. Lee could not have seen it in the British
Museum because it isn't there, nor anywhere else that has so
far been discovered (my p. 8 again). It might not even have
been published, because in the eighteenth century, just as
today, publishers sometimes announced and put in their catalogues books that, for one reason or another, never got pro-

duced; bibliographers call such items "ghosts." The 1801 volume, Mr. Lee to the contrary, is titled *Game of Billiards*; when working with it in the British Museum I was careful to transcribe the title accurately because I was the first billiard historian to cite it (p. 8).

And so we come to the vexed question of John Dew's billiard treatise of 1779. (The "1799" on p. 8 is a typographical error; Louise Belden's article, cited there, actually gives 1779 as the book's date.) Was it ever really published as a separate book or not? S&R, with its usual concern for accuracy, refers to it in three different ways: "Jon [sic] Dew's *A Treatise on Billiards* (1779)" (p. 65); "a treatise in 1779 by John Dew which had originally appeared in Hoyle as early as 1775" (p. 88); and in the bibliography as "Dew, John. 'A Treatise on Billiards.' *Hoyles Games Improved*. Charles, rev. London: J. Rivington and J. Wilkie, 1779" (p. 494). The latter two listings suggest that the S&R authors could not locate a copy of Dew as a separate book and have seen it only as a chapter in Hoyle, picking up their first reference from Belden. That suggestion is reinforced by the fact that Dew's book is not only absent from all the sources I list on page 8, but also from the following: the lists of new books in the *Gentleman's Magazine* for 1779 and the *Annual Register* for 1779; the *National Union Catalog, Pre-1956 Imprints* (1971) and its supplements; the *British Library Catalogue of Printed Books to 1975* (1979 ff.). Craven wisely omits it because he has never seen a copy. Shamos wisely omits it from his supplements to Craven because he has never seen a copy. Even Roger Lee does not claim to have seen a copy. And Stein and Rubino have never seen a copy either. Heretofore, the only modern writer on billiards to have seen a copy is Louise Belden, because—she could have saved some headaches if she had told us this—it is where she worked in 1965. As I have lately discovered, the sole extant copy of Dew's 1779 treatise (as a separately published book) is in the Winterthur Library at Winterthur, Delaware. It is a duodecimo of 59 pages including plates. By courtesy of the Winterthur Library I am able to reproduce, for the first time, the title page of their unique surviving copy of the first English billiard book definitely published.

A TREATISE ON
BILLIARDS,

WITH

INSTRUCTIONS and RULES
For the following GAMES; *viz.*

The White Winning Game.

The White Losing Game.

The Red or Carambole Winning Game.

The Red Losing Game.

Fortification Billiards, with Rules and Regulations for every Method of playing the Game.

COMPREHENDING

The original RULES, regulated as they are now played, and more fully explained and enlarged;

WITH

DIRECTIONS for the Conduct of the PLAYERS and of the BETTERS, &c. never before published.

TO WHICH ARE ADDED,

The Common ODDS which are laid on the HAZARDS, as well as on the Game at BILLIARDS, from One Point being given, to Six, inclusive.

By JOHN DEW, a Marker,

Well known to be experienced in the practical as well as theoretical Parts of Billiards, upwards of Thirty Years.

LONDON:

Printed for J. F. and C. RIVINGTON, and J. WILKIE, St. Paul's Church-Yard; T. PAYNE, and SON, St. Martin's-Lane; S. CROWDER, and R. BALDWIN, Pater-noster-Row; T. LOWNDES, in Fleet-Street; T. CASLON, and B. LAW, Avemary-Lane; F. NEWBERY, Ludgate-Street; W. DOMVILLE, Royal Exchange; W. DAVIS, Piccadilly; J. RIDLEY, St. James's-Street; and W. GOLDSMITH, Pater-noster-Row. 1779.
[PRICE ONE SHILLING.]

The Hustler

In the second chapter I characterized pool and billiard hustling as an occupation in decline. Over the past three decades
it has declined still more. However, during the mid-1960s and
for some years afterward, there took place what more than
one hustler admiringly described as "the greatest hustle of all
time."

It was undertaken by the late hustler Rudolf Wanderone,
whose monicker in the trade was "Fats" or sometimes
"Broadway Fats." Willie Mosconi, the technical adviser for
the movie *The Hustler*, sometime after its release thought-
lessly remarked to a reporter that Fats was partly the model
for the movie character Minnesota Fats (played by Jackie
Gleason). All that Mosconi could possibly have meant was
that the two were similarly named or similarly obese. Fats's
personality was utterly different from that of the movie character. And Fats, even at the peak of his game, was never
among the top hustlers, much less the best; contrary to his
later claims, he often got beat for the cash. But after
Mosconi's remark, Fats, being no dummy, sued the movie
producers. The producers, no dummies either, settled out of
court. Fats, now legitimized in his new role (and newly
acquired monicker) as Minnesota Fats, was on his way—to a
lucrative career making personal appearances, endorsing billiard products, and having his own television show. All of that
hustle was greatly aided by the fact that Fats, as noted on
page 108, was a delightful storyteller.

In Fats's successful public career he never for a moment
disguised that he was a hustler and gambled for a living, in
fact he continually boasted about it—which is one more
pointer to the declining significance of old-style "family values" among America's middle class. Indeed, for many of his
new public, Fats served as something of a romantic hero:
someone who represented for the middle class, as the artist
often does (and as Paul Newman did in both *The Hustler* and
The Color of Money), a holdout individualist in the age of
organization men.

But Fats's later career, and the fact that the poolroom
revivals of the 1960s and 1980s were both instigated by

movies whose protagonists were hustlers, have taught the poolroom industry nothing about what today's middle-class public, not least its "yuppie" contingent, finds appealing. The industry's public-relations types persist in their evasions and prevarications designed to "upgrade" the game's "image" (see pp. 3–4). The p.r. men would do better, and also atone for their sins, by honoring America's recently deceased great hustler with a Jersey Red Memorial Tournament and making it the kind of tournament that Red would have wanted, meaning: (1) a tournament on 5 × 10 tables with tight pockets that was sure to separate the men from the boys; (2) with no dress code; and (3) in which no type of "action" between or among players and spectators was prohibited.

My earlier essay on hustling has two significant errors of omission—luckily no reviewer caught them—related to pool hustling in the more usual sense.[9]

The first is a con similar to, but quite distinct from, the setting up of the audience for a dump that hustlers sometimes engage in when they play each other (p. 48). In this scam, two hustlers team up, go to a strange room where they are not known, and play each other for money. One enacts the part of the "good" player and the other is the "bad" player. The good player keeps winning his games by comfortable margins—though of course he doesn't look terribly good to any excellent player—and soon the bad player quits because he has been beaten so handily or is cleaned out. The good player then looks inquiringly around the room in search of another opponent. In the process he may or may not make some noises about how good he is, but rarely has to bother with such provocation. You can write the rest of the script yourself.

In his pre-Hollywood days as a New York pool hustler, George Raft often employed that technique. He teamed up

[9] There are also errors of commission, but those are matters of detail, as in my reference on p. 78 to "Harry the Russian." The late Dan McGoorty, via Robert Byrne, kindly informed me that the player in question was always called simply "the Russian." For McGoorty's tape-recorded autobiography, see Robert Byrne, *McGoorty* (1972). It is not only the best portrayal of old-time poolroom life but one of the great American autobiographies, period. Social historians will find it invaluable.

with another hustler, Billy Rosenberg, with Raft being the "good" player and Rosenberg the "bad" one. Raft is, of course, another example of someone who retired from hustling and then did well at a different trade (see p. 86). His partner Rosenberg upon retirement did even better, becoming the songwriter and theatrical showman Billy Rose.[10]

The other big gap in the second chapter is that its scattered information on road trips is all secondhand rather than from my own direct observation; that is, I never went on the road with a hustler. I could have, and should have, but didn't. Lately that gap has been filled rather well by David McCumber's *Playing Off the Rail* (1996), although hustlers at New York City's one remaining action room question some of its details. Except for the magnificent *McGoorty*, no other consequential work on hustling seems to have been published since the second chapter; but, as you might expect, much journalistic trivia followed upon both *The Hustler* and later *The Color of Money*.[11]

Apropos of today's one New York action room: At the time of my earlier research (1962–63), two New York poolrooms had at least as much action (Hudson, Julian's), three others had much more action (Ames, McGirr's, Golden Cue), and one other—my main research site—had very much more action (711). There was also good occasional action at some other rooms, such as Lee O'Brien's (Twenty-third Street) and

[10] On the Raft-Rosenberg hustling partnership in the 1920s, see for example the periodical *Big Reel*, issue #261, February 15, 1996, p. 79. The entertainment industry's best-ever pool player, however, which is hardly surprising in view of his fantastic coordination, was Fred Astaire. Probably its best three-cushion billiard player was the co-owner of America's main circus, Henry Ringling North; in the mid-1960s I was a pretty fair player, but he clobbered me. Probably the industry's best "occasional hustler" (see p. 86) was the drummer in Duke Ellington's band, Sonny Greer. In the early days, whenever the band went broke on the road, Ellington would send Greer out to the local poolroom, and Greer would invariably return with "walking-around money" for the band. See Greer's obituary in the New York *Times*, March 25, 1980, Sec. IV, p. 21.
[11] A cut above the trivia is John Grissim's *Billiards: Hustlers & Heroes, Legends & Lies, and the Search for Higher Truth on the Green Felt* (1979). It is a curate's egg, good in parts: On the

Manny Hess's (Ninety-sixth Street—which had a fair resident hustler, "Ninety-sixth Street Whitey," although he wasn't nearly as good as the one at Julian's, "Fourteenth Street George," who in his last years transferred to Chelsea Billiards).[12]

How did that decline, almost to the vanishing point, take place? On the face of it, the middle-class de-labelling of gambling as deviant should, if anything, have increased the opportunities for hustling, that is, increased the number of suckers.

A combination of two developments—again, note well, they were unpredictable and unpredicted, like the collapse of the Soviet Union—has brought poolroom hustling virtually to its death bed.

Paradoxically, what seems to have hurt hustling most of all is precisely the decline of the middle-class aversion to gambling. Because of it, almost every poolroom now finds that it makes good business sense—keeps the customers happy and coming back—to have one or more house tournaments

---

one hand, Grissim's jazzy "hip" journalism is loaded with errors, large and small; on the other hand, the book is also loaded with transcripts, accurate as far as I can tell, from his interviews with top hustlers, and those have much important material. Trust the book's direct quotations from hustlers—as to the accuracy of the quotes, not necessarily their truth value—and use the rest with caution. One hustler's memoir, very short and very poor, is Peter Linhard's *How to Get By Without Working* (1983). Amusing comparative data, from a British woman who hustled at snooker, are in Jane Holland's "Diary," *London Review of Books*, 6 February 1997, p. 33.

[12] 711 was officially Paddy's Billiards but no one called it that; its monicker came from its location at 711 Seventh Avenue, right above the Honeymoon Lane Dance Hall (New York's last taxi-dance hall, another of those institutions that died with the bachelor subculture). Ames became nationally known via *The Hustler* ("This is Ames, Mister"), but the movie was supposed to have been, and should have been, shot at Bensinger's in Chicago. Bensinger's, which still occupied three large floors when I lived in Chicago (1948–57), had long been America's most famous action room and a "must" stop for anyone on the hustle. (The late Abe Rosen of New York told me that he had slowly hustled his way through the room in 1928.) But the producers didn't offer Bensinger enough to make it worthwhile for him to close for the shooting.

always underway. Such tournaments require from each player
a small bet (entry fee), have significant prize money added to
the entry fees by the house, and moreover are nearly always
handicap tournaments, thus assuring that every bettor has a
chance. And the handicapping is done by the house on a fair
basis (unlike the "propositions" in the hustler's "making a
game"), which is rather easy to do because players can be
handicapped with considerable accuracy (see p. 43). Some
larger poolrooms, such as the Amsterdam in New York, have
enough entrants to have separate tournaments or leagues for
beginners, intermediate players, and advanced players. In
sum: Any player who wants to gamble on his skill can now
do so almost every day of the week for a potential excellent
return on a small stake, and on terms that he knows assure
him a good chance. Why in the world should he play for
money with some stranger who might be a hustler? He
shouldn't, and doesn't. And if he should want more action
than the tournament prizes involve, he can always make a
side bet with one or more of his tournament opponents, or
play them at other times.

That reduced propensity of the suckers to be suckered is a
big "push" factor turning people away from undertaking or
maintaining a hustling career, but there is a "pull" factor that
works against it as well, namely, the increased chances to
make money by "going professional." The situation of professionals is now much better than that of three decades ago
(see p. 65). The amount of money available to them in the
form of tournament prizes—plus, for the prizewinners,
money from endorsements and exhibition fees—has sharply
improved. The reason can be given in a word: television. It is
not that the industry finally realized that a pool or billiard
game is ideal for television broadcast (see p. 20), but the fact
that television consumes material at a fantastically higher rate
than radio, and that this has, among other things, led to a radical increase in television sports broadcasts of all kinds. What
made professional tennis "big time" in terms of money, i.e.,
television sponsorship, has at last begun to trickle down a little bit to pool playing. There has also been enough sponsorship (commercials from beer companies, billiard-equipment
purveyors, casinos and hotels where the tournaments are

held, sellers of pool instruction videos, etc.) to televise women's tournaments and establish a women's professional association.[13] There is now even a tournament for "seniors," featuring such old-time greats as Boston Shorty.[14]

Which is not to say that some professional and other good players don't hustle whenever they get the chance. But they seldom get that chance. My impression—though I haven't had time to do serious research on this—is that even among the tiny band of players who still define themselves as hustlers, there are no "pure" types, i.e., that every one of them has some regular additional source of income (a permanent moonlighting job, a pension, a spouse who works, etc.).

As previously suggested, the increased market for pool tables in recent years has been partly in poolrooms and private homes, but even more in the expanded market for small-sized tables in bars. The opportunity for true hustling has greatly increased in bars. Even in the 1960s there was some opportunity for bar hustling, though only one hustler, Miami, was reputed to have done very well at it.[15]

[13] Separate tournaments for women are needed because hardly any women could compete successfully with the better men. For one thing, although the number of women who take up the game has been rising, they still are swamped by the number of men who take it up. Just as important, nearly all the women who do play get too late a start for developing fine hand-to-eye coordination (see p. 19); typically they don't start until their mid-teens or even later.
On pp. 28–29 I gave three other reasons for the dearth of good women players. The second and third, though valid at the time, obviously no longer apply. The first was cockeyed to begin with, as Robert Byrne pointed out to me.

[14] Unfortunately, none of the new-style tournaments came soon enough to help Onofrio Lauri, who perhaps held the longevity record for top pool-playing. I saw Lauri run ninety-odd balls in 1968, when he was seventy-one years old.

[15] In poolrooms it was often argued that Miami was the best one-handed hustler (p. 61); but in those disputes any old-timer who might be present (someone at least as old as the century) would invariably bring up the deceased Andrew St. Jean of Philadelphia, who, playing one-handed, had a high run of eighty-four at pool (on a 5×10 table, and with the old clay balls that don't spread apart as easily as modern balls do) and a high run of eleven at three-cushion billiards.

But few players who want to hustle avail themselves of the opportunity for bar hustling, or rather not for very long, even though the pickings are easy: You rarely meet a decent player (people are not there primarily to play pool), action is continuous because the table is coin-operated and the winner keeps the table, etc. As one former bar hustler explained it to me, it's easy to clear four to five hundred dollars per night but not really worth it. First of all, you can't hang around a bar and keep winning for more than one night; you have to be in a different bar each night, preferably in a blue-collar factory town where the drinkers gamble a lot, and that means you have to be on the road constantly. Secondly, bars and their drunks being what they are, you need somebody with you to back you up in case there are sore losers. Split two ways, four to five hundred dollars per night on average, after shelling out road expenses for car rentals, motels, etc., doesn't come to much. Moreover, even with a partner along, the chances of coming to grief are far greater than they are in any poolroom. A former bar hustler told me of one incident in which, when he and his partner were ready to leave after an evening of winning, they were held up at gunpoint by the losers and relieved not only of their winnings but of all their own money. As he said to me, "Who needs that shit?"

The implications for sociological research that I discussed at the end of "The Hustler" (pp. 93 ff.) have met with significant response from other researchers. At least one study has followed up on the "crime as moonlighting" perspective.[16] And quite a few have adopted my suggestion that the general perspectives of occupational sociology be applied to the study of career crime, the most notable being Peter Letkemann's study of burglars and bank robbers, *Crime as Work* (1973) and Robert Prus and C. R. Sharper's study of card and dice hustlers, *Road Hustler* (1977). And my observation that the sociology of sport has been neglected (p. 98) is now, I am pleased to report, quite thoroughly outdated; just

[16] H. R. Holzman, "The Serious Habitual Property Offender as Moonlighter," *Journal of Criminal Law & Criminology*, vol. 73, no. 4 (1982), pp. 1774–92.

as with the history of sport, the sociology of sport is now
flourishing as an area of serious research.[17]

Most gratifying because wholly unexpected, the second
chapter has been adopted for some occupational sociology
courses.

Research Method, Morality, and Criminology

With respect to the chapter on research methods in criminology, there has been in my view a major setback. On pages
109–10 I complained that criminology has been too much
influenced by traditional social-work concerns and "applied
sociology" ideologues. That situation seems worse than ever,
because the job opportunities and grant opportunities for
criminologists have become increasingly weighted toward
programs having to do with "administration of justice" and
the like. The truly disinterested scientific researcher on crime,
concerned neither with "rehabilitating" criminals nor with
trying to keep people from becoming criminals, increasingly
loses out for funds. Thus we have such spectacles as the head
of the University of Michigan's Survey Research Center, sup-
posedly a social scientist, each year mouthing nonscientific
government pieties about the increase or decrease in "the
marihuana problem"; he has to keep the grants flowing for
their annual survey of marihuana use.

Nevertheless, when it comes to field research on adult
felony crime—the main burden of the third chapter—there
has been much progress, i.e., a good bit of such research has
been done in the past thirty years. And because of it, the
criminology textbooks have begun to abandon their copouts
as to why such research cannot be done (see pp. 110 ff.).
Even Sutherland & Cressey—the latest edition that I have
seen is the 11th of 1992, revised by David Luckenbill—has
improved. On balance, though, it still tries to discourage field
research by retaining some of the old nonsense; e.g., it says
"one researcher cannot build on the work of another to a great
extent, for precise, controlled techniques of observation can

[17] See Paul Redekop, ed., *Sociology of Sport: An Annotated
Bibliography* (1988).

scarcely be used," completely ignoring my criticism of that
nonsense (see my pp. 132–33).

One might note here that criminology textbooks often—
Sutherland-Cressey-Luckenbill is typical—confuse matters
by conflating direct field observation with "participant"
observation. To which conflation my reply is a little yes and a
big no. In field work you do indeed, by definition, "partici-
pate" simply by your presence and your interactions with
your subjects. However, as spelled out on page 117, you need
not (though you can if so inclined) undertake the illegal acts
that are undertaken by your subjects, which is what I take
"participant" observation to mean. (On the distinction
between direct observation and participant observation, and
my employment of both when studying hustlers, see p. 34.)

In any case, a number of researchers, instead of worrying
about whether field research on "serious" criminals could be
done, have simply gone ahead and done it. It may seem invid-
ious to praise only one such research work, but I do so
because it not only has many substantive virtues (including
good writing), but because it demonstrates that such research
can be done safely by women as well as men, and at that on
quite violent crime: Laurie Gunst, *Born Fi' Dead: A Journey
Through the Jamaican Posse Underworld* (1995).[18]

The Village Beat Scene: Summer 1960

My essay on the beats dealt with them only at a particular
time and place, and also presents just a "slice" in a more
important way. For the beats were but one part of a special
subculture, which in its final phase was usually summed up
by its members as "the counterculture." One should understand the beats in that larger subcultural perspective.

A crucial defining characteristic of a subculture is one that,
as far as I can determine, is ignored in the abundant social

[18] It must be noted, though, that so far nearly all field research
on criminals has been done on nonviolent types, e.g., Carl
Klockars's *The Professional Fence* (1974) and Prus & Sharper,
op. cit. See also Robert Kelly, "Field Research Among Deviants,"
Deviant Behavior, vol. 3, no. 3 (1982), pp. 219–28; Robert
Weppner, ed., *Street Ethnography* (1977).

science literature on subcultures. Just as with a given society's culture—that society's symbolically expressed web of meanings, to use Clifford Geertz's notion of "culture"—there is transmittal from one generation to another. In any true subculture within the larger culture, a particular group with its special ways of doing things has *two or more generations*, of course overlapping but nevertheless reasonably distinct, and the group's specially valued ways of perceiving, behaving, thinking, and feeling, including their embodiments in material objects (artifacts), are transmitted from one generation to the next. Without such transmittal you have not a genuine subculture but merely group fad and fashion.

Again analogously to a society's culture, that transmittal from one subcultural generation to another is never perfect, and over time there is obsolescence. There is also, of course, innovation. Thus, just as one speaks of culture change, one can speak of subculture change.[19]

The death in 1997 of Allen Ginsberg underscores the fact that the counterculture had three generations, for he, like William Burroughs (dead later in 1997) and a very few others, in his career spanned all three of those generations: hipsters, beats, and hippies. Over the years of the counterculture's existence there were a good many subcultural changes that I cannot deal with here—to note only one, blacks (or African-Americans if you prefer) originally dominated the subculture and ultimately came to be a small minority swamped by the whites—but those three generations did constitute a particular subculture of antibourgeois and otherwise disaffected Americans.[20]

[19] I am aware that the concept of "culture" is dismissed by some epigoni of the Parisian Follies. But as Geertz notes in *After the Fact* (1995), that concept just won't go away.

Although Geertz appears not to recognize this, his particular view of "culture" is epistemologically and in other ways analogous to Ernst Cassirer's "philosophy of symbolic forms."

[20] The term *counterculture* has occasionally been applied to later bohemians—along with other terms, such as *Generation X*—but that is neither here nor there. The true "counterculture" died in the 1970s.

That subculture began to take shape in a small way just before and during World War II, with the advent of the hipsters. They were mostly those people in the jazz world, black and white, who used drugs. A population explosion took place with the succeeding generation, the beats of the 1950s, and an even bigger one took place with the arrival of their descendants, the hippies of the 1960s. For a combination of demographic and political reasons—the baby boom following World War II, the unpopularity of the Vietnam War (especially of course among youths of draft age)—the counterculture reached its peak size toward the end of the 1960s; and then it collapsed virtually overnight with the end of America's undeclared war in Vietnam.

For example, by the late 1960s the counterculture had developed a flourishing "underground press" or "alternative press" as its members variously called it: well over two dozen beat and hippie newspapers, ranging from the *Berkeley Barb* to the *L.A. Free Press* to the *Chicago Seed* to the *Georgia Peach* to the *NOLA Express* (in New Orleans) to the *East Village Other*. It had also developed its own little mags, of which the most important were *Beatitude*, *Floating Bear*, *Fuck You: A Magazine of the Arts*, *Kulchur*, *Semina*, and *Yugen*. By about the end of 1972, almost all of the counterculture's newspapers and magazines had folded.

Allen Ginsberg, and the publicity given to him, more than anything else instigated the explosive growth of the counterculture from its hipster to its beat generation. There were of course other vital figures influencing that growth. Chief among them, I think, was the relatively unpublicized Ed Sanders, proprietor of the Peace Eye Bookstore (a key gathering place for beats), editor-publisher of the clandestinely distributed magazine *Fuck You*, co-founder and leader of the singing group The Fugs, disrupter of a nuclear submarine launching, and so forth (lots of "and so forth"). But Ginsberg was the main formative influence on the beats (far more than Kerouac or Burroughs), and he remained a very active patriarch of their hippie successors. One of his obituarists remarked, with pardonable exaggeration, that without Allen Ginsberg's energy there would have been no beat generation.

However one may judge Ginsberg's strictly literary achievement, he was unquestionably the great *moral force* in his generation, whose huge influence on that generation derived from his absolute moral integrity. And he was nothing if not *engagé*, endlessly involved in trying to right social wrongs even when this meant not just inconvenience but real danger to himself. Above all, and again regardless of personal danger, he was concerned always to speak out the truth publicly as he saw it. (Among those commenting on his death, William Burroughs got that point exactly right.) Moreover, he was extraordinarily generous. Those and other aspects of his personality, which together account for the influence he exerted on all who met him, despite the recent encomia have, I think, not been given their full due. So I shall try to illustrate some of them via personal recollections.

Allen and I had only a half dozen or so meetings, the first in 1957 or 1958 and the last sometime in the mid-1970s, and in only three of those meetings (two are noted below) did we spend something like an entire day together. Even before our first meeting he knew, via mutual friends and things that I had written or said publicly, that I thought his poetry was poor, and also that we disagreed on some other matters of importance to him, e.g., that I rejected Eastern empty-your-mindism as a way to wisdom. Nevertheless, in all of our meetings he was very kind to me and without a trace of rancor. If you are acquainted with the egos typical of either artists or ideologues, that fact in itself tells you something of importance about the man.

A couple of obituarists noted his financial generosity, which was indeed remarkable. When money began to roll in from the sales of *Howl* and *Kaddish* and the reprinting of parts of them in anthologies for the college textbook market, he set up a foundation to get most of the money and dispense it to starving beats and junkies, and he continued to "live poor." Around 1965 a mutual friend, working with Allen on his files and on a bibliography of him, told me that his true income was over twenty-five thousand dollars a year but that he took only six thousand for himself. But there was more to his generosity than money, much more, which the obituaries that I have seen did not mention. He was always among the first to volunteer his services for benefit readings, to spend time in helping to get people out of jail, and so on. He allowed both his New York City apartment and his farm upstate in Cherry Valley to be used as crash pads, refuges for psychic casualties of the counterculture such as people trying to kick a heroin habit or recover from a bad LSD trip.

In January 1968 the State University of New York at Stony Brook, where I was a professor of sociology, made international headlines because of a then-record campus drug bust: After months of undercover work the county police arrested thirty-eight students and hangers-on, and then fourteen more in a followup raid. Politicians began howling for scalps, the administration ran scared and instituted a stupid crash anti-drug program, and campus morale was completely shattered. Allen offered to give a speech on campus, and I drove him out there from New York and then back to his apartment afterward. His speech was an appropriately fiery one, denouncing the drug laws, the police, and the administration's craven responses, and urging the students not to take the actions against them lying down and to fight back for their rights. It was the first thing to begin restoring morale. As I told Allen on the way home, when I looked around the room I could see, both among students and faculty, gloom being lifted and spines being stiffened. As a result of that speech the Faculty Senate was able to pass two anti-administration resolutions (one of them introduced by myself) and after a while the anti-drug program was quietly dropped.

In December 1969 a friend of mine and Allen's, Bob Ockene, died young of leukemia. He had been, among other things, a co-founder of the counterculture's guerilla group of provocateurs calling themselves the Youth International Party or "Yippies," which group played the key role in disrupting the 1968 Democratic National Convention in Chicago. At our memorial meeting in Brooklyn his widow, Ann, holding an urn with Bob's ashes, forlornly remarked that he had hoped his ashes might one day be scattered on "free soil," but she couldn't think of any such place. Allen immediately lifted her up by getting her to agree that Bob might have regarded Allen's farm as "free soil." Whereupon Allen got busy arranging a caravan of cars to leave for Cherry Valley the next day (it was about a six-hour trip) and arranging a myriad other details that made it a perfect Yippie funeral.

As I hope the above paragraphs indicate, even more extraordinary than Allen's financial altruism was the amount of time and effort that he devoted to helping others. The only person I have ever known who came even close to him in that respect was the art historian Meyer Schapiro. (The painter Wolf Kahn once said to me, "If you have Meyer Schapiro there are two other things that you don't need—a reference library and an employment agency.") Allen, like Schapiro, eventually had to retreat and shield himself because too many people took advantage of that generosity, but he held out as long as he could. For years after he became famous he kept his name in the telephone directory, because he wanted to be sure that people who needed his help could reach him.

The counterculture received much publicity in its day because the deliberately challenging activities of Allen Ginsberg and many others made it good copy for journalists. But despite all the publicity, it never enlisted more than a minuscule fraction (certainly under one percent) of American adolescents and youths, to say nothing of the rest of the population. And the views of Allen Ginsberg and his comrades on what constitutes a just society have had little impact on their society. For example, back in 1960 I noted (p. 155) that the beats were engaged in a "Permanent Strike" against, among other things, our society's "Permanent War Economy." The latter, despite the ending of the Cold War, has not been abandoned, although its nature and direction have changed: As of 1997 the United States is, by a wide and increasing margin, the world's leading exporter of military arms.

The one truly major and enduring imprint of the counterculture on American society, as already noted in my 1969 revision (see pp. 167–71), is that its proselytizing for marihuana spread the use of it to a very large minority of middle-class and upper-class Americans, where it has remained firmly established.[21] Below I note three additional lasting, but

[21] I should note that the counterculture had nothing to do with the great revival, beginning in the 1960s, of cocaine use. That complicated story cannot be dealt with here.

much lesser, imprints of the counterculture that seem not to
have been previously observed.

In his excellent *Fashion, Culture, and Identity* (1992), Fred
Davis points out that under modern conditions of mass-commu-
nications technology and mass travel, fashions not only "trickle
down" but increasingly trickle up or sideways; he also notes
that ethnic and other groups often adopt certain costumes to
identify themselves and then have those fashions taken up by
outsiders. An example frequently pointed out is that blue jeans,
originally worn as work pants by cowboys and farmers and
miners, ended up in the hands of fashion designers, and also
spread globally. Omitted, in every discussion of that example I
have seen, is the major role of the beats in this process. Until
they came along, the only wearers of jeans who were not lower
class were in rural areas and small towns; in cities, only some
people toward the very bottom of the economic ladder wore
jeans outside of the workplace. The beats were the first urban
people of middle-class origin to adopt jeans; from there—aided
by much publicity about the beats—began the further trickling
upward and sideward across the planet.

A second enduring contribution started among the hippie
descendants of the beats in the Haight-Ashbury district of
San Francisco. There, about 1965 (give or take a year), penny
capitalists on the sidewalks, selling such things as bead neck-
laces and rolling paper for marihuana, began to bid farewell
to customers with a smile and the phrase "Have a nice day."
Then the phrase had the charm of both novelty and sincerity;
today it is an empty ritualistic phrase used by almost every
cashier in the land.

A third lasting imprint of the counterculture is, alas, one in
which I played a decisive role.The alert reader of the first five
chapters will have noticed the frequent use of the word
lifestyle. When I wrote those chapters in the mid-1960s, that
usage was a conscious and deliberate attempt on my part to
revive a useful term, originating in Adlerian psychology, that
had become obsolete except for an occasional rare appearance in academic psychology journals; the last use of it elsewhere that I knew of was from the early 1940s. When this
book was originally published in June 1967, it was reviewed
or quoted in several of the counterculture's "alternative"

newspapers and magazines and excerpted in one of them. After that, such periodicals first began to use *lifestyle*, and from there it spread to larger circles. As the term has become a cliché of the adman, it should now be avoided by any serious writer. *Mea culpa*.[22]

One instance of subculture change is that the hippie generation of the counterculture largely turned away from the writing of fiction and poetry. Its expressive talents were devoted rather to such things as rock music, journalism, psychedelic light shows, cartooning, and the use of exotic materials in the crafting of hash pipes. The hippie generation's chief artistic figures were the cartoonist and musician Robert Crumb and the musician Frank Zappa.

The hipster and beat generations, especially the latter, produced the writings that, for a variety of mostly nonliterary reasons, now receive much attention in academe. There are symposia and conferences on the beats, as well as a number of regular courses devoted to them. As one would expect, attention is paid mainly to the famous trio of Jack Kerouac, Allen Ginsberg, and William Burroughs, but there also are side glances at John Clellon Holmes, Diane di Prima, Gregory Corso, and others. Of all the beat literary products, it is some of Allen Ginsberg's poems that are most firmly canonized in academe; they turn up everywhere in textbook anthologies, not least in those designed for Freshman English. They have even received America's ultimate academic accolade of the moment, praise from Helen Vendler.

Unhappily—truly so—I remain unconvinced by Allen's mishmash of Blake-Whitman-Pound-Williams. His talents did not include precision of language, metrical sophistication, imaginative play with the sounds of words in combination (Auden's criterion), or structural subtlety, and rarely is there an unusual simile or metaphor. And despite his demotic predilections, Allen had no ear or inclination for representing

[22] Whether a linguistic innovation or attempted revival will take hold is unpredictable. As a young editor adapting a British dictionary for an American publisher, I inserted a word of my own invention—*callimastian*, adj.—but it never caught on.

human speech other than his own; he always did the anti-police in the same voice. His chanting poems often do acutely itemize the things about his world that he hates or loves, and artistically that's about it. The fearless content of his work greatly encouraged in other writers emotional honesty and candor and unstuffiness, for which we should all be grateful as those are no small things, but he left no truly literary legacy; in a formal sense there is nothing much to inherit.

Richard Howard went a bit too far when, unconsciously echoing F. R. Leavis's remark on the Sitwells, he wrote that Allen Ginsberg belongs to the history of publicity rather than poetry. However, it does seem to me that Allen will ultimately be regarded as a literary analogue of what the music critic Donald Tovey called "IHFs"—Interesting Historical Figures, whose importance in music history was more substantial than the merit of their compositions—the way that we now regard, say, "proletarian novelists" of the 1930s such as Jack Conroy or Lewis Grassic Gibbon. Which is not to deny that I generally agree with the sentiments expressed in Allen Ginsberg's poems; nor is it to deny the propagandistic appeal of his rhetoric to idealists everywhere, especially to young ones grappling with the world of adult hypocrisies and evasions; nor is it to deny that if you write thousands of lines of poetry, you will come up with an arresting phrase or a striking image now and again (although in Allen's work they tend to be the early ones, such as "angelheaded hipsters").

I do wish that I could like the poems more than I do. Doubtless some readers will feel that, given my admiration for the man, my negative view of his poems should have been withheld. Allen Ginsberg would have been the first to disagree and to insist that you should tell the truth publicly as you see it. That's one of the things that made him a moral exemplar and a marvelous human being.

The beat literary heritage has a double aspect or meaning (like any other "literary heritage"). On the one hand, as indicated above, it refers to beat writers who are read today. But it also refers to the question of their possible influence on today's writers. I turn now to consider two contemporary writers, in some ways at opposite extremes, in that latter context.

Over the past couple of decades, the writer most visibly descended from the beats has been the novelist Kathy Acker. She imitates William Burroughs's intercutting of realistic descriptions with fantasies, and also his techniques of literary appropriation. The main thematic difference is that his focus on drugs is replaced by her focus on sex. She is the literary darling of New Age dropouts, youths who missed out on the old counterculture and hope to revive it, and she has been interviewed in their periodicals.

Her sexually frank novels—*Kathy Goes to Haiti* is probably the best known—are cast as memoirs, but one cannot tell the extent to which they record her own experiences because her interview statements about this are inconsistent. They also belie the novels in other ways; for example, she says that she majored in classics and still keeps up her Latin, yet this Latinist has published a novel entitled *In Memoriam to [sic] Identity*. (The title of course also reflects the declining competence of publishers' personnel in America's new era of computer-literate semiliterates.)

In any case, the novelized reports of her sexual fantasies or realities are in a different artistic universe from something like *Histoire d'O*. There is absolutely nothing that is distinguished about her diction or syntax or imagery or sentence rhythms or eye for visual detail or ear for human speech. And creation of character is beyond her solipsistic ken. (Hence the memoir form, and her appropriations of characters from other works of fiction.) Moreover, her psychological insights are negligible and her social observations are more banal than those of the stereotypical sociologist. Ms. Acker's work appeals to readers whose only test of literary merit is "letting it all hang out," people who mistake for art what is merely case history.

Going from Kathy Acker's work to that of the considerably older Gilbert Sorrentino is like exchanging a sleeping pill for LSD. He also descends from the beats, but in a peculiar and perhaps unique way—the way of a renegade rather than a disciple.

At the beginning of his career, Sorrentino, whose first book is from 1960, was directly and heavily involved in the beat literary scene. He participated in the beats' literary readings, contributed to beat little mags (*Floating Bear*, *Fuck You*,

Kulchur, Yugen) and helped to edit one of them. But his position among the beats, though not marginal, was certainly anomalous. Most obviously and valuably, he turned his back on their sappy literary aesthetic (Kerouac's "spontaneity," Ginsberg's "first thought, best thought," etc.) and instead applied himself to learning the technical skills involved in his art.

Eventually his deepest literary kinship—whether consciously chosen or even recognized by him I know not—came to be with the high modernism of James Joyce's last two novels, which feature among other things the characteristics that our dimmer literary theorists claim to be "postmodernism," such as intertextuality, polysemy, self-referentiality, and all that jazz. (Years ago both Irving Howe and Frank Kermode noted that the modernist/postmodernist distinction is one without much difference.)

Among the Joycean talents that Sorrentino has going for him is the satiric gift of the master (who expressed surprise that so few people had commented on the comic spirit in his work). Additionally and more remarkably, Sorrentino has the finest ear of any novelist since Joyce—yes, even better than that of Anthony Burgess or William Gaddis. (I think Joyce's edge on all three derives from the fact, which Joyce scholars seem to have missed, that he had not only a great ear but extensive technical knowledge of phonetics. *Finnegans Wake* refers to such arcana as the observations by the ancient Sanskrit and Prakrit phoneticians on *svarabhakti* vowels— "epenthetic" vowels in our terms—and the experiments of R. H. Stetson on "arresting" and "releasing" consonants.)

Sorrentino is also the finest adept since Joyce at the comedic use of manic breathless listmaking, part of the grand tradition that includes the Aristophanic *pnigos*, medieval *occupatio*, Rabelais' riffs, Shandy's gaff, operatic catalogue arias, Shem's shenanigans, and the early routines that Sylvia Fine wrote for Danny Kaye. One example is the long and ingeniously punning list of drummers in jazz history that Sorrentino works into page 87 of *Mulligan's Stew*. (But it's partial. *Ubi sunt* Baby Dodds, Vic Berton, Kaiser Marshall?)

There are other Joycean influences, such as his parodic use of the Roman Catholic catechism, but, above all, Sorrentino is Joycean in this: Whatever his ostensible subject, his over-

riding concern is with language and the different ways that it
can be made to dance.

The strangest aspect of Sorrentino's development since he
turned away from the beats is how underrated his achievement is. In books on modern American literature he is never
discussed as a "major" novelist but is either placed among
the also-rans or neglected entirely. And this despite the fact
that his many books include at least three masterpieces
(very different from one another): *Mulligan's Stew*,
Aberration of Starlight, and *Crystal Vision*. My hunch is
that the problem stems from the fact that he is not self-criti-
cal enough (unlike Joyce, who refrained from publishing
Stephen Hero). In most of Sorrentino's fictions he has nothing much to say. They seem intended merely to demonstrate
his great technical facility—to show us that he has picked
up on Pinget and Perec, that he can do the one-end-of-a-
conversation routine as well as Gaddis, and so forth. Such
things may be fine to distribute to a class as examples of
technique (Sorrentino teaches creative writing) but not to
offer the public; they are not Debussy études but Czerny
exercises. Nevertheless, it needs to be emphasized, and
needs to be recognized, that Sorrentino at his best is one of
the most important American novelists to have emerged
since World War II.

On the Sociology of Pornography

As noted at the beginning of the fifth chapter, that text
was the first work on the sociology of pornography.
Additionally, as that chapter suggests, there was hardly any
research on pornography from other academic disciplines.
Now, of course, there is a ton of it from academics in the
social sciences, natural sciences, and humanities. Here I can
but touch on only a few of its main conclusions.

Before doing so I remind readers of something discussed
early on in this new chapter, the radically lessened importance of America's "Puritan heritage" over the past three
decades or more. What was banned as "hard-core" pornography at the time this book was originally written, and
brought heavy prison sentences to producers and sellers of

it, can now be sold quite openly to adults. Thus the pornography industry's growth rate has been even more enormous than I originally suggested. And of course the industry keeps on the cutting edge of communications technology—progressing from 8 mm movies to videos to CD-ROMs to on-line computer services to Nietzsche knows what next. Just think of what may happen when most people have attached to their telephones a screen on which they can see the caller.

But one must, as always, be cautious about prediction. One reason is that the existence of a technology is no guarantee that it will be used, nor of the way in which it will be used. Another, as pointed out earlier, is that social trends often cease to be, and in fact may reverse themselves; it is conceivable, if unlikely, that with respect to pornography, America might one day become "puritanical" again. Sociologists always must hedge their predictions with some such phrase as "if present trends continue," in the knowledge that trends rarely continue exactly as they are at the moment because of unforeseeable factors such as new inventions, laws, wars, and so on. (Sometimes of course social trends accelerate, as in the case of the explosive growth of the "counterculture" because of the Vietnam War.) To the old saw about nothing being certain except death and taxes, most social scientists would perhaps add only one more item: population growth.

A principal claim of "On the Sociology of Pornography" was that art and pornography are not mutually exclusive, and that, contrary to both popular and "expert" opinion, art can also be pornography. That point is now widely accepted, not because of my influence but that of Susan Sontag. She independently reached the same conclusion as mine by coming to it from the opposite direction; that is, she argued that pornography can also be art.[23]

A vividly detailed sexual narrative that is also art does not thereby lose its capacity to sexually arouse the beholder. But

[23] Susan Sontag, "The Pornographic Imagination," *Partisan Review*, vol. 34, no. 2 (Spring 1967), pp. 181–212.

an exception to the rule, which both Ms. Sontag and I failed to note, concerns satire or high comedy—from, say, Aristophanes' *Lysistrata* to Terry Southern and Mason Hoffenberg's *Candy*—for the comedic effect usually obliterates the sexual one. It is hard to stay hard if you're laughing too hard. That is why the chief pornography publisher of the mid-twentieth century, Maurice Girodias of the Olympia Press in Paris, allowed his stable of pornography writers to use humor "only so long as the result did not turn into parody that would have a detumescent effect on the expectant one-handed reader."[24] (Girodias wisely permitted an exception for *Candy*.)

In addition to hedging predictions about pornography (or any other aspect of social life), we have to hedge, and try to quantify when feasible, our generalizations about the existing state of affairs, such as America's current "permissiveness" with respect to pornography. Obviously, norms and values and attitudes and behaviors are never uniformly distributed even among members of a small and "pre-industrial" society, much less a society such as ours, so we must try to specify the limits of our generalizations. Statisticians are right about that.

Some of those limits to our generalizations can be got at by survey research, and some can be got at only by a slow cumulation of field studies (see p. 133). I received a field-research lesson about careless overgeneralizing when, in trying to bring the original final chapter up to date, I spent several days and nights hanging around a very large pornography store—talking with the proprietor and employees, estimating the proportions of the total space devoted to various types of pornography, observing the customers, and so

---

[24] John De St Jorre, *The Good Ship Venus: The Erotic Voyage of the Olympia Press* (1994), p. 70. Unlike other such publishers, Girodias openly admitted that he published pornography and, more interestingly, claimed that pornography was socially valuable (*ibid.*, p. 298). After the 1966 public symposium in New York on pornography (see p. 183 of this book), Girodias, who was in the audience, came up to thank me for being the only symposiast to take a position similar to his.

on. (Once I also helped out, at an employee's request, by keeping an eye on a customer whom he said was a booster.) The store had, among many other things, a video monitor on which customers were permitted to preview their prospective purchases—with freeloaders being avoided by the store's requirement of a nonrefundable deposit for such viewing. One night when I walked in, there were two police officers, in uniform, intently watching for something on the monitor. Knowing that what used to be banned as "hard-core" pornography was now permitted, I went up to them and asked, "What are you looking for? I thought anything goes now." One of them turned to me, smiled, and said, "Not kiddie porn." From other dealers I learned later that at that time (at least in that city), there were also two other kinds of videos that had to be sold strictly under the counter: those showing (1) intercourse with animals, or (2) fist-fucking.

Although reviewers commented favorably about "On the Sociology of Pornography" and it was reprinted in anthologies, the reception of one aspect of it was disappointing—not because that aspect was criticized but because it was ignored. As noted in the first paragraph of this book's Preface, the chapter was "an exercise in theory." More precisely, it was an exercise in functionalist theory, which at the time was being denounced especially by "conflict" theorists (Marxist and otherwise) because it had, in their view, an inherently conservative bias. The original chapter was, among other things, an attempt to defend functionalism against its critics, but apparently I buried that subtext too deeply to be noticed.

Functionalism, as originally formulated and used by the British social anthropologists Bronislaw Malinowski and A. R. Radcliffe-Brown, and by many later practitioners as well, was unquestionably biased against social change. The "function" of something was the way it helped a society to keep on going just the way it was; anything that worked to upset the apple cart was "dysfunctional." But the theory was recast in 1948 in Robert K. Merton's magnificent essay, "Manifest and Latent Functions"; in ways that I cannot rehearse here (read Merton!), functionalism was converted into a value-neutral theory.[25]

Part of what I take to be Merton's view is indicated, much too briefly and oversimply, on page 193, where I state that we should define pornography functionally, "in terms of what it actually does to or for society—what are its particular uses and effects on people, intended or otherwise." The functions of something are simply the ways that it in fact "works" in a society, whether those ways are intended and largely recognized (manifest) or unintended and largely, though not always, unrecognized (latent), and *whether they promote social stasis or social change or do neither.* That kind of functional analysis by no means always supports political conservatism (my "pro-pornography" conclusion, at least at the time I offered it, hardly did that). Sometimes its conclusions can support political radicalism, as when we apply Mertonian functional analysis to functionalism itself: The manifest function of the original British variety was to advance social science, but its latent function was to buttress British imperialism by teaching colonial officials how to manipulate the natives and keep them from getting too restless.

Latent functions, it should be added, are not always negative. The manifest functions of laws requiring a deposit on soda bottles and cans are to promote recycling and reduce littering; their latent function is to give a bit more cash to people who live off other people's garbage.

However, the functional view of pornography that I originally offered, which might be summed up as a "safety-valve" theory, needs more careful delimiting than I gave it. True enough, there is more than "something to it"; too many different kinds of data, from too many different societies, in

---

[25] Merton's essay is most readily available in his *Social Theory and Social Structure* (1949 and later editions). His value-neutral type of functionalism is ignored both by practitioners of the early British version and by critics who hold that functionalism is inherently conservative. Among such critics, the most notable is the philosopher Bernard Williams writing in *Common Knowledge*, vol. 1 (1992).

too many different historical periods, cohere and make sense if we view pornography as a safety valve that makes tolerable the institutionalizing of legitimate sex within the family. To the data of that sort earlier cited one could add myriads more. But as I did not spell out fully enough on p. 187, it is only part of the story when it comes to the functions of pornography at the individual-psychological level (as distinguished from the societal level).

You can especially be misled if you accept, as I did at the time, a "vulgar Freudian" model of sexuality; it holds that people have a strong inborn sexual drive that has to find expression somehow, if not in real sex with a partner then in fantasy and masturbation, often facilitated by pornography. Much of the newer sex research indicates that the level of one's sexual interest is itself socially induced or "scripted," and, moreover, that people with high levels of sexual interest often use all available outlets; they engage in lots of "real" sex *and also* lots of masturbation, the latter often accompanying perusal of pornography. So the notion that pornography use is a substitute for "real" sex is too simple; it is true for some people but not others. Furthermore, the evidence seems to be mounting that in societies that have made pornography easily available, such as present-day America, those other people constitute the good majority of pornography consumers.[26]

For most of the public and perhaps also most of my readers, the key question about pornography is the sociologically less interesting one of pornography as a possible cause of rape and other sex crimes. Government funding being what it is, that is where the great bulk of the scientific research has been concentrated. Abundant results are in, and they abundantly contradict the views expressed by such anti-pornography ideologues as Catherine Mackinnon, Andrea Dworkin, Susan Griffin, and Robin Morgan. Pornography is not a significant cause of rape or any other sex crime. In

[26] On the newer findings, see especially Edward Laumann, John Gagnon, Robert Michael, and Stuart Michaels, *The Social Organization of Sexuality* (1994).

fact, some research finds that it actually reduces two sex crimes: Peeping Tom episodes and child molestation.[27] To be sure, given the wide publicity that contrary assumptions have had, one can occasionally find a rapist who will claim in his defense that "Pornography made me do it."

Absurdity about pornography's crime-causing effect on "the susceptible," however, is sometimes expressed even by people with no obvious axe to grind, such as Roger Shattuck in his *Forbidden Knowledge: From Prometheus to Pornography* (1996). The root of the trouble there is that linguists and social scientists have a special problem in common (one that is not shared with, say, molecular geneticists): Just as people often believe that they are experts on the nature of language simply because they speak it, they often believe that they are experts on the nature of society simply because they live in it. In consequence, like Mr. Shattuck, they can't be bothered to consult the serious empirical research. It would be very hard, in such consulting, to find a scientific investigator of pornography's effects (one observing such usual canons as adequate sampling technique, control groups, etc.) who concludes that pornography causes sex crimes.[28]

Why do myths about the alleged harm done by pornography continue to be widely proclaimed in the face of much empirical evidence contradicting them? The major part of the answer has to do with the psychology of "true believers"

[27] Berl Kutchinsky, *Pornography and Sex Crimes in Denmark* (1975). For an overview of other research, see for example Richard Posner, *Sex and Reason* (1995). Among works not cited by Posner, quite typical is the study by Dwayne Smith and Carl Hand, "The Pornography/Aggression Linkage," *Deviant Behavior*, vol. 8, no. 4 (1987), pp. 389–99. It concludes: "There was, in short, no evidence to support any hypothesized connection between pornography and aggression."

[28] The exception is Heinrich Schmutz, "Die Pornographie als Grund der Vergewaltigung in den ostfriesischen Inseln," *Zeitschrift für allgemeine Sexualwissenschaft*, Band 69. With equal sense Lorena Bobbitt, who in 1993 cut off her husband's penis, could have claimed in defense that "Andrea Dworkin made me do it."

and their attempts to reduce "cognitive dissonance," the scientific studies of which I cannot review here. (Consult your nearest psychology professor.) Suffice it to note that true believers do not merely proclaim some mythology justifying their belief and often suppress the evidence against it; more interestingly, when you force that evidence upon them, rub their noses in it, they do not abandon their belief but instead invent yet another myth justifying it. For example, when anti-marihuana ideologues (such as Gabriel Nahas, M.D.) finally had to give up their favorite myths (that marihuana caused crime or insanity or heroin addiction), they did not abandon their anti-marihuana stance but invented new mythology justifying it, e.g., that marihuana atrophied the brain or that it caused a pathological condition that had somehow gone undetected in the entire previous history of medical psychology, "the amotivational syndrome."[29] And so it goes with the anti-pornography ideologues. They deliberately ignore or suppress, as much as they can, the evidence that pornography does not cause sex crimes; and when forced to confront such evidence, instead of abandoning their position they invent new mythology justifying it, e.g., that pornography must harm women by "degrading" them.[30]

[29] Of all the myth-making by such antiscientific ideologues, the most amusing has been their drive to replace the term "drug abuse" with "substance abuse." The latter term allows them to make a scientifically baseless distinction between "drugs," which they oppose, and alcohol, which they enjoy. Similarly, the Rastamen on the block where I live make a scientifically baseless distinction between "drugs," which they oppose, and *ganja* (marihuana), which they sell.

Other varieties of nonscientific and antiscientific nonsense about marihuana are well surveyed in John Morgan and Lynn Zimmer, *Marijuana Myths, Marijuana Facts* (1997).

[30] The activities of anti-pornography ideologues have created a small but significant backlash among feminists whose only complaint about pornography is that it is by and for men, and such women have begun to produce their own pornography. The backlash has been led by lesbians—see for example the magazines *Bad Attitude* and *On Our Backs*—but is by no means composed exclusively of them. My statements on p. 195 about female lack of interest in pornography now need some modification, but I have not had time to do research on this.

Another part of the answer has recently been given by a philosopher, Alan Soble, whose *Sexual Investigations* (1996) offers sharp analyses of some major writings on sexuality, including pornography. Soble profitably examines something about sex that is so very obvious that it is usually ignored in discussions of pornography: Sex is highly pleasurable, and indeed many people name it as the most pleasurable activity that there is. More important, sex is pleasurable in and by and for itself, quite apart from any social function it may have in ensuring reproduction or in promoting emotional intimacy between people (as Kingsley Davis pointed out). Pornography emphasizes that basic fact. However, for a variety of reasons, such as the teachings of Pauline Christianity, some people either take little pleasure in sex or, more commonly, feel very guilty about the pleasure that they do take in it, and as a result they sometimes become "anti-sex." Soble points out, and I agree, that an anti-sex message is the real text of writings by the anti-pornography ideologues. They can't abide the fact that for most people, including most women, fucking is fun.

NAME INDEX

SUBJECT INDEX